Germany and the Origins of the Second World War

The Making of the 20th Century

Germany and the Origins of the Second World War

Jonathan Wright

palgrave
macmillan

First published 2007 by
PALGRAVE MACMILLAN
Houndmills, Basingstoke, Hampshire RG21 6XS and
175 Fifth Avenue, New York, N.Y. 10010
Companies and representatives throughout the world

PALGRAVE MACMILLAN is the global academic imprint of the Palgrave Macmillan division of St. Martin's Press, LLC and of Palgrave Macmillan Ltd. Macmillan® is a registered trademark in the United States, United Kingdom and other countries. Palgrave is a registered trademark in the European Union and other countries.

ISBN-13: 978–0–333–49555–1 hardback
ISBN-10: 0–333–49555–1 hardback
ISBN-13: 978–0–333–49556–8 paperback
ISBN-10: 0–333–49556–X paperback

This book is printed on paper suitable for recycling and made from fully managed and sustained forest sources. Logging, pulping and manufacturing processes are expected to conform to the environmental regulations of the country of origin.

A catalogue record for this book is available from the British Library.

A catalog record for this book is available from the Library of Congress.

10   9   8   7   6   5   4   3   2   1
16   15   14   13   12   11   10   09   08   07

Printed and bound in China

To the memory of Markus Huttner (1961–2006)

Contents

Acknowledgements

I am most grateful to Jeremy Noakes and Klaus-Jürgen Müller for reading and commenting on the text. They have made many helpful suggestions and saved me from committing many errors. Those that remain are, of course, mine alone. I am also grateful to Geoffrey Warner for suggesting, longer ago than I care to remember, that I write this book; to successive editors at Palgrave Macmillan, most recently Sonya Barker, for their patience; to the anonymous reviewers of the text for their comments and to Jürgen Förster for his help and advice.

I would also like, together with the publishers, to thank holders of copyright material for giving permission for its use: (C) Crown copyright material from the series *Documents on German Foreign Policy*, Series C, vols. I–VI (Foreign Office, HMSO, London: 1957–83) and Series D, vols. I–XIII (Foreign Office, HMSO, London: 1949–64) is reproduced with the permission of the Controller of HMSO and Queen's Printer for Scotland; extracts from *Die Tagebücher von Joseph Goebbels*, ed. Elke Fröhlich and the Institut für Zeitgeschichte, Teil I *Aufzeichnungen*, vols. 2–9 (2nd edn, K. G. Saur Verlag, Munich: 1998–2006) and Teil II *Diktate*, vols. 1–2 (K. G. Saur Verlag, Munich: 1996) are reproduced with the permission of the copyright holders. Every effort has been made to trace copyright holders. If any have been inadvertently overlooked the publishers will be pleased to make the necessary arrangement at the first opportunity.

The book is dedicated to the memory of Markus Huttner, historian and friend, who in a tragically short life achieved so much.

Jonathan Wright

List of Abbreviations

DDP	Deutsche Demokratische Partei (German Democratic Party)
DGFP	*Documents on German Foreign Policy*
DNVP	Deutschnationale Volkspartei (German National People's Party)
DVP	Deutsche Volkspartei (German People's Party)
KPD	Kommunistische Partei Deutschlands (German Communist Party)
NSDAP	Nationalsozialistische Deutsche Arbeiterpartei (National Socialist Party)
SA	Sturmabteilung (Nazi paramilitary organization)
SD	Sicherheitsdienst (Nazi intelligence and security organization)
SPD	Sozialdemokratische Partei Deutschlands (German Social Democratic Party)
SS	Schutzstaffel (Originally Hitler's personal bodyguard, later developed by Himmler into a Nazi elite, taking over police and intelligence functions and with its own military formations)

Glossary

Anschluss	German union with Austria
Anti-Comintern Pact	Literally pact against the Communist International Movement, i.e. anti-Soviet pact
Auslandsorganisation	Nazi party organization for relations with ethnic Germans abroad
Aussenpolitisches Amt	Nazi party office for foreign affairs
Auswärtiges Amt	German Foreign Ministry
Barbarossa	German campaign against the Soviet Union 1941
Blitzkrieg	Literally 'lightning war'. Defined as a campaign intended to destroy the enemy in a single operation often wrongly applied to the German offensive in the west in 1940, but correctly applied to Barbarossa
Commissars	Communist party officials attached to the Soviet armed forces. But Reich Commissars, the name given to Nazi governors of parts of the Soviet Union intended for eventual integration into Germany
Concordat	Treaty between the state and the Catholic church
Confessing Church	Part of the Protestant church which was driven into conflict with the state in defence of its independence
Einsatzgruppen	Special task forces of the SS employed to murder Jews and other groups in Poland, the Balkans and the Soviet Union
Gauleiter	Nazi party administrator of a region (Gau)

General Government	The remainder of Polish territory under German occupation that was not annexed to the Reich
German Christians	Pro-Nazi organization of the Protestant church
Gleichschaltung	Process of co-ordination of all aspects of life under Nazi control
Heimwehr	Austrian, pro-Fascist 'home defence' organization
Labour Front	Nazi Labour union organization
Lebensraum	Literally, 'living space' i.e. empire
Luftwaffe	German air force
Maginot line	French fortifications on the German frontier
Mefo bills	Credit bills nominally of the 'Metallurgische Forschung' but in fact accepted by German banks as a covert way of financing rearmament
Mein Kampf	Hitler's main treatise, literally *My Struggle*
Mitteleuropa	Literally Central Europe, but also carrying the sense of a natural region of German economic and political influence
Obersalzberg	Hitler's alpine retreat
Polish corridor	Territory giving Poland access to the sea and separating East Prussia from the rest of Germany – established by the Treaty of Versailles
Reich Chancellery	Reich Chancellor's office
Reichsbank	German central bank
Sportpalast	Palace of sport (Berlin)
State Secretary	Senior official in a government department
Sudetenland	Frontier area of Czechoslovakia containing most of the large German minority of some 3 million people
völkisch	racist
Volksgemeinschaft	Community of the whole nation
Warthegau	Province of German occupied Poland

Introduction

The origins of the Second World War lay in and with Germany. This book has therefore in one sense a simple task: to explain German policies which led to war. But a moment's thought shows that is far from simple. Hitler and the origins of the Second World War or the Third Reich and the origins of the Second World War could be dealt with as an essay in policy making.[1] But Germany and the origins of the Second World War introduces another, much larger and more obscure picture. Why were the German people prepared to follow Hitler and the Nazis into war, and not just the European War which broke out in 1939 but the world war which followed after 1941? For if Hitler had not been able to secure the support or at least the consent of civil servants, the military, industry, the judiciary, the universities, the churches and the great mass of ordinary people who fought and died, there would have been no war.

The need to explain public support is all the more pressing because the kind of movement that Hitler represented, though present in German politics from the 1890s, had never before the 1930s been capable of moving from the fringe to the mainstream. To take one example, the forced expulsion or elimination of German Jews, ideas which were commonly expressed in racist circles after the First World War, would not have been considered by any German Chancellor before Hitler and that Germany might soon carry out a programme of genocide as part of European conquest would not have entered their imagination.

What changed? In the immense literature on the Third Reich, a range of explanations for public support or submission may be found, some competing, some complementary: the coercive apparatus of a totalitarian dictatorship, the attraction of a secular religion, the competition of different elites loosely held together by the charismatic authority of Hitler, to name but the most prominent.[2]

This book concentrates on how Hitler took Germany to war. In doing so, it revisits some well-established debates about Hitler's aims and the nature of government and society in the Third Reich. It also aims to contribute to those debates by linking the different explanations which have been developed for the Third Reich as a whole, specifically to the area of foreign policy and war. Indeed there is a strong argument for saying that the distinction between domestic and foreign policy in the Third Reich is a false one as all policy was in some way related to preparation for war. The debates that have raged about Hitler's aims and intentions and, whatever they may have been, his capacity to carry them out given the disorganized structure of decision making, the physical limits on the ability of the economy to satisfy the rapidly escalating demands of rearmament, and uncertainty about public support – these debates are all central to understanding why and how Germany went to war. And the preparations for war also raise important questions for the debates about the nature of government in the Third Reich. Did Hitler take the key decisions over foreign policy himself, unlike other areas where he allowed his subordinates to fight among themselves? Did foreign policy as a result follow a more consistent course than other policies? Indeed, were the confusions in other areas in part a result of their subordination to foreign policy? If preparation for war was the be-all and end-all of the Third Reich and Hitler took all the major decisions connected with that preparation, then his influence must clearly come first in any explanation.

Most authorities agree that, whatever happened in other areas, Hitler was central to the making of foreign policy. This raises an immediate question about the extent of public support. How far did the elites, on whose expertise Hitler depended, and the wider public that saw the rearmament boom and the expansion of the armed forces, understand that Hitler was in charge and that he was pursuing a policy of expansion and war? Did they support that policy or were they misled?

There are different possible answers to these questions. Hitler was not specific about all his goals at once, enabling German conservatives to deceive themselves that he would be content with their aims: rearmament, frontier revision, union (*Anschluss*) with Austria, restoration of Germany's place as a great power in the centre of Europe. Perhaps at first Hitler had only vague ideas himself for a more radical programme for domination of the European continent and even beyond Europe. His philosophy, sometimes called Social Darwinism, was built around such a radical vision. He saw the whole of history as a ceaseless struggle between races for domination and the purpose of international relations as the conquest of living space (*Lebensraum*) to sustain the expanding population of the race. But a radical vision is not the same as a programme. Until conquest was under way, no studies were made of which territories were to be exploited or how. The radical vision remained at the ideological level and could be ignored by those who did not believe it would ever be put into practice. They excused or turned a blind eye to warning signs such as the concentration camps and persecution of Jews and other minorities. As the vision became policy – in some ways all the more arbitrary and terrifying for its lack of preparation – it was too late to stop it by argument. And war made resistance more difficult both in terms of what was feasible and because it took a special kind of courage to commit treason in war.

In leading Germany to war Hitler operated consciously on two levels. As a revolutionary leader, he laid out in general terms the case for conquest, living space and a racial reconstruction of Europe. These ideas may be found scattered throughout his writings from the 1920s to the 1940s. But Hitler was also a highly astute politician. He knew the dangers of acting prematurely – the failure of the Munich putsch in 1923 had taught him that revolutionary action by itself did not guarantee success. By building up the Nazi party, taking advantage of the great depression to become a mass movement, refusing to join a coalition unless it was led by him, he played for the highest stakes and won. His appointment as Chancellor in January 1933 was testimony to his political gifts.

But he was still a long way from being able to realize his ambitions for Germany. That depended on rearmament, public support, and the reaction of external powers. To manage each of these he needed to employ all his political gifts, in particular to know how far and how fast he could go without provoking the kind of opposition that would bring down his regime. That does not mean that he lost sight of the radical vision or that he ceased to take risks. On the contrary, Hitler was committed to taking risks because he believed that the alternative was stagnation and decline. Nations either expanded or contracted, rose or fell: there was no stability. But although risks were unavoidable to conquer new living space, not all risks were equal. Political leadership consisted in deciding where the greatest gain could be made with the least risk and manoeuvring to bring about the most favourable conditions for victory.

That applied both externally and internally. Enemies had to be divided, isolated and picked off singly until Germany had enlarged its resources sufficiently to face a major European war. At home similarly, he had constantly to judge how far he could carry both the elites, on whom he depended to prepare for war, and the wider public with him. Hitler did not forget that – as he saw it – the home front had collapsed in Germany in 1918, 'stabbing' the undefeated German army 'in the back'. If his revolution was to succeed, he had to negotiate both the external and internal constraints. Until 1939, and even arguably until 1941, he was remarkably successful at managing both.

Hitler's political skills are certainly an important part of the explanation of how he took Germany to war. But he could not have succeeded if the German people had not been willing to follow him step by step. They accepted the direction towards making Germany once again a great power, even if they did not know the destination, the supremacy of the German race in Europe at which he aimed. There was a fatal overlap between Hitler's views and those of a wider public, based on a shared experience of war, defeat and revolution. The mindset established before the First World War that Germany's destiny was to become a great imperial power, that the other powers had encircled it to keep it down and then overwhelmed it after four years of war during which German armies fought the world virtually alone, that Germans were a 'people without space' – all these ideas made people vulnerable to Nazism.

The Weimar Republic, established after the First World War, brought first an intensification of the sense of bitterness and isolation in a mood where nationalist sentiments were in any case inflamed by war and defeat: the apparent hypocrisy of an imposed peace settlement – the Treaty of Versailles – supposedly based on liberal principles of self-determination and equality but offering the new German democracy neither, the humiliation of territorial losses, disarmament, occupation of the Rhineland, reparations and the allegation of war guilt. That was followed by the Franco-Belgian occupation of the Ruhr in 1923 when the German response of 'passive resistance' throughout the occupied territories – a general strike by all public employees including civil servants and railwaymen – led to an almost total collapse of the economy and political authority. The cost to the government of supporting the strike led to hyperinflation and the ruin of the currency as it lost all value. There were food shortages as farmers were unwilling to exchange produce for worthless money. Shops were looted and armed gangs raided the countryside. A new government under Gustav Stresemann was forced to abandon passive resistance in order to introduce a new currency and keep it stable. Giving up passive resistance, however, was seen by the nationalist Right as a second surrender, like accepting Versailles. Disaffected ex-soldiers, those who had been unable to readjust to civilian life after the war, the rootless, the unemployed, sometimes roving bands of thugs, gravitated towards those German states which were thought to be most patriotic, hostile to the Republican government in Berlin and willing to maintain the resistance against the French. In Bavaria Hitler acquired a reputation as a leader of one of these 'patriotic leagues', the SA, and tried to persuade the Bavarian authorities to march on Berlin – in imitation of Mussolini's march on Rome in 1922. In opposition to this trend to the Right, in the left wing states of Saxony and Thuringia in central Germany Socialist–Communist coalition governments were formed and proletariat 'hundreds' were organized to resist any attempt to suppress them whether by the 'patriotic leagues' or the regular army. In Berlin the army chief, General von Seeckt, tried to force Stresemann to resign and planned to put in place an authoritarian government dependent on himself instead. As the tension built up to Hitler's Munich putsch in November 1923, it looked as though Bismarck's Germany might break up into different states: a Rhineland under French and Belgian control, right-wing regimes in Bavaria and the eastern provinces of Prussia, socialist–communist republics in Saxony and Thuringia and a right-wing 'directorate' effectively under army control in Berlin.

The brief interval which followed the failure of the putsch and the restoration of the authority of the civilian government from 1924 to 1930 suggested that there could be an alternative: revision of the peace settlement by agreement with the Western powers, a period marked by the Dawes loan under which mainly American capital financed German reconstruction, the Locarno treaties giving guarantees of the Rhineland frontiers against attempts from either side to change them by force, and Germany's entry into the League of Nations with a seat on the Council with the other great power members.

But that brief interval was not enough to redraw the German mind map. There remained a large gap between German expectations, revision of the frontiers with Poland – which cut off East Prussia from the rest of Germany – and union with Austria, and on the other side the unwillingness of the Western powers, particularly France, to make further concessions. It was unclear how this gap could be bridged peacefully. That created a climate favourable to rearmament and the use of force or at least the threat of force. The depression and mass unemployment (40 per cent of the labour force was unemployed in

1932), following as it did almost immediately after the Young Plan of 1929 had set a schedule for reparations lasting until 1988, was a perfect gift to Nazi propaganda. The pre-war belief in Germany's economic and political vulnerability and the need for living space to make it secure and independent was reinforced. Reparations became a symbol for the way in which Germany was being exploited by the other powers as a kind of European colony. The depression was blamed not so much on the capitalist system, as the Communists argued, but on the Treaty of Versailles and Germany's enemies, though the two could also be combined in the mythical hate-figure of international Jewry capable of manipulating the markets for its own profit while the rest suffered.

Hitler as Chancellor was able therefore to exploit the opportunities of a public which was willing to be led in the direction he wanted to go. Between him and the elites, there was agreement on the need for rearmament and expansion of some kind. A wider public too welcomed a strong leader, able to stand up to outside powers. The League of Nations and all it represented had no great following in Germany. Despite German membership of the organization since 1926, it was still seen by many Germans in subsequent years as the instrument of the victors – providing a fig leaf of respectability for French exploitation of the Saar coalmines or Polish access to the ethnically German port of Danzig, failing to prevent Lithuanian annexation of another German Baltic enclave at Memel while, on the other hand, ruling illegal an attempted Austro-German customs union in 1931. Little wonder that when Germany left the League in 1933, the decision was approved by 95 per cent of the population in a plebiscite.

But, if Hitler started in a strong position, he also faced potential limits to his public support. It was far from clear that either elites or the public as a whole were willing to accept a major war, especially a war on two fronts, with the lessons of the First World War less than a generation old. He had to persuade them that expansion was not only necessary and desirable but also feasible. In this he was helped crucially by the weakness of his enemies and, to some extent, by alignment with other states that wanted to revise the peace settlement, most importantly Italy and Japan. Fortunately for Hitler, the overriding aim of his enemies was to avoid war. And so long as he played on their fears to extract concessions without war, he could be assured of popularity at home.

Even when German forces were finally committed to a European war in 1939 he was able for a time to win easy victories over weaker opponents. Each victory added to his reputation. In 1940 after the fall of France, he seemed invincible having triumphed against the enemy who had remained undefeated in 1914–18. In June 1941 he launched the war against the Soviet Union to implement fully the radical vision for a racial reconstruction of Europe, a vision whose outlines had already become apparent in occupied Poland. In December his Japanese ally launched an attack on the American base at Pearl Harbor in Hawaii, bringing the United States into the war in the Pacific. Hitler responded by declaring war on the United States, as he regarded an American declaration of war on Germany as inevitable and he wanted to give the impression that he had plans to cope with it. That was already an admission that he knew his standing with the German public would be at risk. As the German armies became bogged down in the Russian land mass first in the winter of 1941 and then, decisively, in the winter of 1942–43 and suffered their first major defeat at Stalingrad, the time of cheap victories and easy popularity was over. Hitler had let loose the racial war for mastery of the European continent in which he had always believed. The German people, having been his willing instrument thus far, now found there was no way back.

In writing a book of this kind, different approaches are possible and I should explain mine. As I have suggested, the explanation for German attitudes to war in the 1940s may be traced back at least to the 1890s. But to try to give equal weight to each part of that story would require either a much longer book or a reduction of each phase of the development to a mere summary. I have chosen therefore to set the scene with two short chapters on Hitler's view of the world and, secondly, the way in which the Great Depression made his ideas common currency, in order then to concentrate the main part of the book on the Third Reich itself. I have divided that part into four sections – dismantling Versailles, preparing for war, the European war and world war. The reason for this division is that each of these phases confronted the Nazi leadership and the German public with specific challenges. Each phase had its own character. It would be possible to divide the story differently, to take certain themes like Hitler's policy making, the attitudes of the armed forces, industry, or the wider public as separate chapters across the whole period. That, however, would either have obscured what is distinctive about each phase or involved tedious repetition. I have therefore preferred to treat each of these themes as part of each phase and identify them by the chapter sub-headings.

A further choice has been how much space to devote to the historiographical debate, which has turned essentially on Hitler's intentions and the degree of his control. Since that debate is now 30–40 years old, I have not thought it necessary to rehearse it in detail. Instead I have included a brief summary of the different approaches and the main themes of this book in the chapter which follows this introduction. In the main part of the book, tracing developments during the Third Reich, I have then tried to strike a balance between the different interpretations by considering them in the light of specific instances of Nazi foreign policy. These can be understood in different ways but there is also, I believe, room for substantial agreement. Put very baldly Hitler had goals and he also developed plans but he was not in control of everything either at home or abroad. In particular, he could not make the German economy produce more than it was capable of and ultimately he could not bend foreign powers to his will. Neither of these, however, made him desist, showing the irrational element in his leadership which ensured eventual destruction. In order to illustrate the complexity of the processes involved I have also given space to primary sources, for instance the Goebbels' diaries for Hitler's decision making and the reports of agents of the Social Democratic Party in exile for German public opinion. Primary sources offer both an immediacy and a sense of the complexity of the evidence that confronts historians, which is too easily simplified in the clash of debate between them. I hope in this way to have provided at least some of the evidence for the reader to make up his or her own mind about how best to explain these extraordinary events.

1 Debates and Themes

A history of nineteenth-century Germany opens with the words 'In the beginning was Napoleon'.[1] The same could be said in relation to the writing of the history of the Third Reich about Hitler. Particularly as regards foreign policy, interpretations were and remain Hitler-centric.[2] But that is not the whole story. In 1961 A. J. P. Taylor stirred up a hornets' nest by arguing that while Hitler may have had some vague notions of expansion to the East he had no clear plans.[3] In Taylor's view he simply seized the opportunities presented to him as any German statesman would have done. That challenged the general consensus among historians that Hitler's aims were both radical and implemented in a logical order. Those who subscribed to that view included Hitler's then leading English biographer, Alan Bullock, and Hugh Trevor Roper and German scholars like Klaus Hildebrand and Andreas Hillgruber.[4] With varying emphases they maintained that Hitler imposed on German foreign policy the specific goals, timing and methods of expansion. He followed, they suggested, a clear programme, from removing the sanctions clauses of Versailles, to expansion in Europe, to living space in the Soviet Union and from there to an – albeit less well-defined – final conflict for world mastery. These historians became loosely lumped together in the discussion as the 'intentionalists' because they stressed Hitler's intentions as the primary part of any explanation. Taylor too was an intentionalist – he simply did not believe that Hitler had any real intentions.

A new challenge of a different kind to the Hitler-centric view arose from historians who worked on particular policy areas in the Third Reich. Some of them came to the conclusion that basic problems of the economy and of the way government was organized, or disorganized, in the Third Reich mattered more than Hitler's intentions. In explaining rearmament, for instance, it was not enough to say what Hitler wanted. It was also necessary to understand what the economy could produce and how rearmament was managed. If Hitler

9

demanded the impossible and, in addition, responsibility for rearmament was divided between competing authorities, then the outcome would not be what Hitler intended. His intentions therefore would not provide a reliable guide to what happened. Rather one needed to look at how the gap between what he intended and what was possible was filled, a process some suggested of constant ad hoc improvisation or crisis management. Again there were many variants of this approach, grouped together in the discussion under a generic label as the 'structuralists' to contrast with the 'intentionalists'. One of the most distinguished, and the most provocative, was Hans Mommsen with his eye-catching description of Hitler as a 'weak dictator'.[5] Other examples included Tim Mason who from his study of labour problems suggested that Hitler was forced into early expansion by shortages of raw materials, labour and foreign currency which were themselves a result of the initial rearmament programme.[6] The precise way in which economic problems like these are linked to a specific decision for war is difficult to establish and, in addition, another economic historian, Richard Overy, has argued that the economic difficulties in 1939 were not as critical as Mason suggested.[7] The way rearmament was organized has also been the subject of intense research with studies of the competing programmes of the armed forces, the accumulation of power by Göring which Hitler tolerated, the sometimes hesitant co-operation of industry and, on the other side, the real constraints of the economy which despite the huge resources transferred to military expenditure could never satisfy the ever escalating demands placed on it.[8]

From the work of these historians and others a new view of the Third Reich began to take hold. Instead of a monolithic dictatorship ruled by Hitler's will, it began to be seen as an arena where different powerful groups competed for influence, the state bureaucracy, the party and its various agencies, the military, the police and the SS to name only the most obvious. In the area of foreign policy in the period 1933–38 there was competition between (among others) the official Foreign Ministry (the *Auswärtiges Amt*), the party foreign office (*Aussenpolitisches Amt*) under Alfred Rosenberg, a separate party unit (the *Auslandsorganisation*) to stir up unrest among German ethnic minorities abroad (for instance in Poland and Czechoslovakia), and lastly Hitler's personal representative, Joachim von Ribbentrop.[9] The Third Reich was, in a somewhat pretentious word to convey the many elements involved in its government, a 'polycratic' regime. Hitler presided over its unstable structure but because he disliked administration, he did not give it order – though he sometimes issued orders. He intervened when he had to or in policies (notably foreign policy) that mattered most to him. Otherwise he was content to allow the law of the jungle, the survival of the fittest, to prevail. That suited both his political instinct – to allow powerful underlings to compete among themselves without himself getting involved in their conflicts – and his bohemian lifestyle.

Despite this major shift in interpretation from the 'intentionalists' to the 'structuralists', Hitler did not disappear entirely from the picture. The Third Reich was not shaped simply by warring power groups. It also had a direction – it moved over time towards more radical policies. It moved, in particular, towards war, expansion and racial annihilation. In foreign policy, for instance, as part of a major reorganization in February 1938, Ribbentrop became Foreign Minister and the organization concerned with ethnic Germans abroad was taken over by the SS leaders, Himmler and Heydrich. Was this direction of the regime towards more radical policies simply the result of economic limitations or competition between its leaders? Did it not also reflect a particular ideology and one whose focus was the führer himself? And was not his authority – if one could get it – the ultimate currency of power in the Third Reich? And so explanations turned back to Hitler and, in particular, to the insight that what made sense of the Third Reich was the idea of all these powerful groups trying to anticipate the führer's will in everything they did – 'working towards the führer' as the charismatic leader who inspired and empowered them.[10] That approach offered a resolution of the problem of how to explain both the confusion and the overall direction of the regime. It was in many ways a jungle but with its own particular law of the jungle and Hitler as lawgiver.

The controversies about what kind of state the Third Reich was were mainly concerned with the power structure and how policy was made. They left to one side the question of how much support the regime enjoyed, the degree of consent for its foreign and racial policies. Nevertheless there were clear implications of the different theories. Was it a dictatorship that relied on coercion? Was it an arena in which powerful groups were able to push their own agendas? Did it have the support of a wider public which was indeed won over to the regime by rearmament and success in foreign policy following the humiliations of the previous years? Was the German public cowed and oppressed, making the best of things, or also working enthusiastically towards the führer?

Recent work suggests, unsurprisingly, that each of these was true to some extent and the difficulty is to draw the balance between them.[11] There was terror and coercion and in this, at least, the state was efficient. There were also ways of adapting, accepting the order the regime provided and living for private goods – work, money, leisure and holidays. There were areas of life that retained some autonomy. Local loyalties in the countryside could afford some protection against harassment by the party. Religious life continued, though the Protestant church was divided with a pro-Nazi wing. In the universities it was possible to deflect the more rabid Nazis into specialist institutes and continue with something approaching the normal routines of academic life. There were also ways of escaping the monotony of the party's control over more and more areas of daily life – the American romance about the Civil War, *Gone with the Wind*, sold well. But there was also genuine enthusiasm and admiration for the regime, particularly for its foreign policy achievements and particularly among the younger generation. Hitler occupied a special place in public esteem. He was seen by many as standing above and separate from the party, as the man who had saved Germany from civil war and was successfully restoring Germany as a great power. It was possible therefore to celebrate 'his' triumphs while criticizing the corruption of party bosses and the shortages of food and consumer goods. The myth that, 'if only the führer knew' he would put things right, helped to maintain support.[12]

Even that support, however, was shaky.[13] There is much evidence that in the summer of 1938 as war loomed over Czechoslovakia, the mood was anxious and sceptical. Provoking a crisis over Czechoslovakia, unlike previous actions such as the reoccupation of the Rhineland and union with Austria – both of which could be justified by the principle of national self-determination – seemed very likely to lead to a European war with France and Britain and possibly the Soviet Union. Apart from convinced Nazis and some young people, there was little appetite for such a war. And though by September 1939, war against Poland was accepted more readily and with a sense of fulfilling a patriotic duty, there was not the enthusiasm that had been part of the experience of July 1914. From then on, morale varied with the fortunes of war, with the Polish campaign and even more the stunning defeat of France in 1940 raising support to new heights, but thereafter a gradual decline as victory over Britain proved elusive and as the campaign against the Soviet Union ground to a halt outside Moscow in December 1941. Goebbels sensed the changed mood and put a stop to repeated claims of imminent victory, which only increased disillusionment when they proved false. Instead, he shifted the emphasis to the final result saying that was all that mattered and warning of the catastrophe that would result from a victory of Bolshevism. Fear of defeat began to supplant hope of victory as the reason to keep fighting.

The ups and downs in public support for the regime show that the Nazi ideal of a warrior race had not been achieved. This raises an important question. How far did public support extend beyond the traditional goals of restoring Germany as a great power, reversing the defeat of 1918? Did German elites and the wider public also come to accept the more specifically Nazi goals of a racial reconstruction of Europe, involving genocide against Jews, Poles, Russians and others?

Again there is no single or simple answer. The co-operation of elites and the support of a wider public for the traditional goals is clear. There was an almost universal consensus that Versailles should be dismantled as a matter of right. Hitler was assured of popularity when he demanded equality for Germany and played on the differences between the 'have' and 'have not' nations in terms of economic resources – after the experience of the depression that was bound to echo with Germans of all classes. His successful and theatrical coups – leaving the League of Nations, rearmament, the reoccupation of the Rhineland and union with Austria – all helped to establish his reputation as a national statesman who had made Germany count again. He had exposed the weakness of the French and British who reacted only with protests and his success contrasted with the humiliation suffered by the governments of the Weimar Republic.

Conservative elites co-operated enthusiastically in the achievement of these initial goals. The officials of the Foreign Ministry resented the influence of the party, and particularly of Ribbentrop, whom they regarded rightly as an amateur, but with hardly an exception, they put their expertise at the service of the regime. The armed forces were delighted to be given the opportunity to rearm and made the most of it at breakneck speed and with total disregard for the consequences in terms of forcing other nations to rearm. Industrialists, though they had concerns about their growing dependence on government contracts, also co-operated willingly and earned huge profits. Not everyone benefited in the same way. Manufacturers of consumer goods and those involved in agriculture suffered from shortages of materials and labour which were increasingly directed to armaments industries. The consequences for industrial labour were also mixed. Although economic recovery produced an acute labour shortage by 1938, real wages had only just reached their 1928 level again and the German standard of living remained significantly lower than that of the United States or Britain. In these circumstances, foreign policy success and the way it reflected on Hitler's leadership was arguably the most important common factor in cementing support for the regime across different groups. Crises such as food shortages in 1935–36 or the major changes in the military power structure in February 1938 were overcome partly by the distraction of foreign policy success – the reoccupation of the Rhineland in 1936 and union with Austria in March 1938. Other aspects of foreign policy also found support among important elites – for instance the churches, despite their own conflicts with the regime, nevertheless fully endorsed its anti-Communism, particularly during the Spanish Civil War as stories spread of atrocities committed against the church by Spanish Republican forces.

Despite the success of Hitler's foreign policy, fear that it would result in a new European war grew from 1936 and, as we have seen, became widespread in the summer of 1938. The German public did not share the pacifism that was strongly represented in the democracies, nor did they have confidence in the League of Nations as a forum for settling disputes peacefully. Rearmament seems to have been regarded as necessary and right, if only to re-establish German power on the basis of equality with other nations. But there was unsurprisingly also fear, particularly among those who had experienced the world war, of a new European war. So long as Hitler got away with his foreign policy coups peacefully, he was admired. But when the German public sensed that he was taking one risk too many, concern grew. That concern could be found during the Czech crisis at all levels – among the senior officials of the Foreign Ministry, in the highest ranks of the army, even within the Nazi leadership, where Göring did not share Ribbentrop's enthusiasm for war.

How then does one explain the willingness of Germans to fight when the European war finally broke out in September 1939 over Poland, and spread in 1940 to Denmark and Norway, the Low Countries and France, to the air and sea war with Britain, to the invasion in 1941 of Yugoslavia and Greece and to the campaign in North Africa and finally to the invasion of the Soviet Union? How, more particularly, does one explain the fact that Hitler was able in the East, in Poland and the Soviet Union, to put into practice the racial wars which lay at the heart of his ideology? These involved, as is now well-established, not simply the trained task forces of the SS but regular army units and their officers and thousands of Germans involved in the administration of the occupied areas. In planning the campaign against the Soviet Union, the military's economic staff accepted that to obtain food for the German army and the home front, millions of Russian civilians and prisoners of war would be forced to starve. The military leadership also accepted without demur Hitler's order that Communist Party officials should be shot out of hand. Should one then conclude that the public had come to support not only the traditional goals of restoring Germany as a great power but also the specifically Nazi goals of genocide against races which were seen as inferior?

These questions remain the most difficult to answer and are still the subject of differing interpretations.[14] War had its own imperatives and led to a heightened sense of national solidarity, as well as intensified coercion against dissenters. The war against Poland could be presented as putting right a legitimate grievance from the Versailles Treaty and the intervention of France and Britain as a repeat of their attempt in the First World War to cheat Germany of its rightful place in Europe. The victories of 1939 and 1940 extinguishing the trauma of defeat in 1918 seemed to require no further justification. And once the campaign against the Soviet Union foundered, it became a life and death struggle for survival in which any means was seen as legitimate by both sides.

But what of the racial policies in the east? Put simply, two processes reinforced each other. There was first the influence of inherited attitudes of superiority towards Poles and other Slav peoples and also towards Jews, particularly towards the unassimilated (i.e. retaining their traditional dress and religious customs) Jewish populations of eastern Europe and, among army officers, against 'Jewish-Bolshevik' commissars (Communist party officials) in the Soviet forces. Second, the ideology of race had found receptive minds after the First World War in a generation which all too easily saw history in Social Darwinian terms as the conflict of nations for survival. Such attitudes took hold not only among the crude ideologues who found their natural home in the Nazi party but also among highly educated university students who later made careers in the SS. The power of

racial ideology in this period is difficult to recapture. Yet it alone ultimately explains how otherwise rational people could willingly plan the
murder of millions of innocent civilians.

This does not mean that all or even most Germans now supported
genocide. But the dividing lines between Nazism and other German
traditions had become blurred. There was a spectrum of opinion where
inherited attitudes of cultural and political superiority overlapped with
beliefs that the future of the German race depended on the deportation
and murder of 'inferior' races. There remained some important differences between Hitler's view of the future and that of most Germans.
Hitler believed, for instance, that war should be renewed indefinitely
to maintain the fighting quality of the race. Most Germans longed
for peace. As Goebbels knew by December 1941 morale was starting
to flag. Nevertheless, the narrow gap between inherited attitudes of
superiority and the Nazi goal of racial reconstruction of the continent
was all too easily crossed under wartime conditions. As a result, Hitler
was able to find the support he needed not only for a war for German
domination of the continent but also for the specific Nazi war for racial
mastery.

2 Hitler's World

To understand how far Hitler's foreign policy represented the wishes of most Germans we have first to consider where he came from and how his politics related to other German political traditions. Hitler was born in 1889 in the Austrian part of the then Austro-Hungarian empire. This was a multinational state that had survived into the age of European nation states. Its constitution was that of a dual monarchy from 1867, representing its Austrian and Hungarian halves and presided over by the Habsburg dynasty in the person of the Emperor Francis Joseph from 1848 to 1916. But in addition to the Austrian and Hungarian ruling groups, the empire also contained populations of Poles, Czechs, Slovaks, Serbs and Croats.

In the atmosphere of intensified nationalism at the end of the century, it was easy for the German Austrians to feel that their position was at risk from the demands of these subject nationalities for equality or independence. Against the 'Slav tide' and attempts by the Habsburg authorities to accommodate it, a form of hyper-German nationalism found expression in the pan-German movement of Georg von Schönerer. Together with the less extreme, more populist Christian Social movement of the mayor of Vienna, Karl Lueger, these anticipated most of Nazism's later attitudes, anti-Slav, anti-Semitic, anti-Catholic, anti-socialist, anti-democratic, and in favour of a state uniting all those of German race.

As a young, shy, down and out, reject from the academy of fine arts and would-be architect, Hitler read avidly and identified with the politics of radical German nationalism, though it is uncertain how far at this stage he was personally affected by anti-Semitism.[1] His later account of these years in *Mein Kampf*, though in some respects misleading to cover up his dosser's existence, singled out Schönerer and Lueger for praise.[2] He belonged to the underclass of a ruling ethnic group, whose future was uncertain and whose leaders seemed willing to allow the further dilution of German influence in a chaotic parliamentary system. He reacted with the intensity of those whose

17

group identity is their most important possession and who fear being 'swamped' by other cultures and betrayed by their own leaders.

It was only after the experience of war and the turmoil of the immediate post-war period, however, that he developed the dogmatic ideology from which he never again deviated. At the same time, he experienced success as a public speaker and turned his ambitions from architecture to politics. In 1913, he moved from Vienna to Munich, partly to dodge military service in the army of the Austro-Hungarian empire which he despised. On the outbreak of war in 1914, he succeeded in enlisting in a Bavarian regiment and served as a runner taking messages from the command headquarters to the front, was wounded and towards the end of the war temporarily blinded by mustard gas, and received the iron cross for bravery.

In *Mein Kampf* Hitler described how he welcomed the outbreak of war as a release from the 'lingering disease' of peace. 'I fell down on my knees and thanked Heaven from an overflowing heart for granting me the good fortune of being permitted to live at this time.' In the army he found for the first time in his adult life a regular occupation, emotional fulfilment and purpose. Defeat was correspondingly bitter, especially as it was associated with the collapse of the home front and revolution. In a famous passage in *Mein Kampf* he described his reaction when the local pastor gave the news to the patients at the hospital where he was recovering from the mustard gas:

Again everything went black before my eyes; I tottered and groped my way back to the dormitory, threw myself on my bunk, and dug my burning head into my blanket and pillow...And so it had all been in vain. In vain all the sacrifices and privations; in vain the hunger and thirst of months which were often endless; in vain the hours in which, with mortal fear clutching at our hearts, we nevertheless did our duty; and in vain the death of two millions who died. Would not the graves of all the hundreds of thousands open, the graves of those who with faith in the fatherland had marched forth never to return? Would they not open and send the silent mud- and blood-covered heroes back as spirits of vengeance to the homeland which had cheated them with such mockery of the highest sacrifice which a man can make to his people in this world? There followed terrible days and even worse nights – I knew that all was lost. Only fools, liars and criminals could hope in the mercy of the enemy. In these nights hatred grew in me, hatred for those responsible for this deed.[3]

Whatever the exact truth of these passages, there is nothing improbable about the sentiments which were – as Hitler knew in writing – common to millions of Germans. The trauma of defeat, and the need to be able to explain that defeat, became one of the mainsprings of Nazism's later success. None of the explanations was reassuring. On the Left, socialism taught that the war was the result of the system of capitalism and imperialism – in which case it had been fought in vain. Another option was to recognize that Germany had simply not been strong enough to prevail over its enemies. That was the truth acknowledged by the more intelligent and honest politicians and military leaders who came, as a result, to accept the Republic and work for peaceful revision of the peace settlement. But it was much easier and more satisfying emotionally to conclude that Germany had been defeated because of an enemy within, Socialist, Jew or both, and that only an intensified form of nationalism and the eradication of these enemies could atone for the immense suffering they had brought and make national renewal and revenge possible. And so Hitler knew what he was doing when he concluded his chapter of *Mein Kampf* on the war with an attack on Marxism, the Jew and the inability of the bourgeois parties to stand up to them and his chapter on the revolution with 'In the days that followed, my own fate became known to me...There is no making pacts with Jews; there can only be the hard: either–or. I, for my part, decided to go into politics.'[4] By the time he dictated these words in prison in 1924, if not earlier, the association of war, defeat, and the Jew with his own mission in life had taken root.[5]

Little is known about Hitler's attitudes during the war. However, after the war he was first employed by the army to give political education to disaffected troops and subsequently moved into politics and gained a reputation as a public speaker. His speeches from this period, reported in the press or by police monitoring the activities of anti-Republican agitators, and his own writings provide the main evidence for his attitudes. They reveal a number of influences on him – the German (as against Austrian) pan-German leader Heinrich Class, the circle of racist agitators he joined in Munich like Gottfried Feder with his theory of Jewish 'interest slavery' and Alfred Rosenberg who as a Baltic German was inspired by hatred of the Russian revolution which he saw as 'Jewish Bolshevism', General Ludendorff who together with Field Marshal von Hindenburg had been responsible for the defeat and break-up of the Russian empire by the Treaty of Brest-Litovsk, and Karl Haushofer, a Professor of Geography at Munich University who gave the idea of Germany's need for greater 'living space' academic respectability in the 'science' of geopolitics, and whose favourite pupil was Rudolf Hess.[6]

Whatever the relative importance of the various influences on him, Hitler developed from 1919 to 1923 a view of the world and of the way Germany could change it that became the fixed point of his politics thereafter. In this period his ideas adapted readily to new insights and events. At first he espoused the racial anti-Semitism nourished by tales of war-profiteering that found a ready audience after the war. In foreign policy he adopted Class's idea that if Russia threw off Bolshevism it could be persuaded to allow German expansion east which would in turn make it possible for Germany to attack France and Britain, the powers that enforced the Versailles Treaty. During 1920 a vital shift took place in his thinking (perhaps following the Russian invasion of Poland that summer) to identifying Russian Bolshevism with Jewish rule as the primary enemy and the Soviet Union as the primary object of living space. Thereafter the images of Bolshevism, the Jew and Russia as the source of living space fused into a single prophetic vision. As he put it in the second volume of *Mein Kampf* written in 1925: 'The giant Empire in the East is ripe for collapse. And the end of Jewish rule in Russia will also be the end of Russia as a state. We have been chosen by Fate as witness of a catastrophe which will be the mightiest confirmation of the soundness of the *völkisch* theory of race.'[7]

Hitler's concept of the future war underwent a corresponding shift. He had already identified Italy as a potential ally in 1920, given Italy's dissatisfaction with the peace settlement. In 1923, during the crisis caused by the French and Belgian occupation of the Ruhr, he saw a more important opportunity in British opposition to that extension of French power and he projected a future Anglo-German alliance which would keep France in check. If Germany concentrated on a war for living space on the European continent, Hitler reasoned, it would not cut across either Italian interests in the Mediterranean or Britain's overseas empire. They would have no grounds for hostility towards Germany. That would alter the balance of forces as compared to the war. Hitler came to the conclusion that the German empire had been wrong to try to fight a war for both continental and overseas expansion. By giving up the aim of overseas expansion, which he in any case thought less desirable than continental empire, he believed he had found a viable strategy.[8]

These ideas are an interesting mixture of theory and practice, and of adapting his experience to the circumstances of the post-war world.

Hitler showed confidence in his own judgement and a willingness to learn from others. As his success as a politician grew, he also began to see himself not only as a propagandist, or 'drummer', but also as a leader or 'führer'. That process was accelerated by the Munich putsch in 1923 when let down by the Bavarian authorities, who toyed with separatism but had no stomach for a march on Berlin, he emerged as the only genuinely revolutionary leader. At his subsequent trial, he lived up to this reputation and gained a national audience by attacking the legitimacy of the Republic, itself a result of the revolution of November 1918, the work of the 'November criminals' he despised.[9] His attitudes were in many ways characteristic of his time and place. The hugely dramatic events of total war, defeat and revolutions spreading across Europe, the collapse of the Russian, Austro-Hungarian, German and Ottoman empires, the creation of a whole new state system, all this fed the need for explanation. Hitler belonged to a generation which had seen its leaders fail, their policies lead to defeat and collapse. He felt justified in arguing that he had seen through their errors and weakness, particularly in relation to the Austro-Hungarian empire which could not survive because it did not have a secure racial basis, and therefore also the error of German policy in allying with Austria–Hungary. That was compounded by their weakness in being unable to subdue the ideology of Marxist socialism and the 'parasite' Jew, the twin enemies of a racial state.[10]

Hitler saw himself as both a revolutionary theorist and a practical politician. As the first, he propounded the racial theory of history. There was a hierarchy of races with the Aryan race, to which the German people belonged, at the top. It was the only race which was truly creative – a founder of culture, as against a bearer or destroyer of culture.[11] All history was a struggle between the different races for mastery. That struggle took the form of competition for living space. If living space was insufficient for the race – as for Germany with, he claimed, before the war an annual increase in population of nearly 900 000 – it was its duty to expand. That was both a law of nature and part of the divine plan for the world, a scientific truth and a religious duty. Nothing could change it. Alternatives such as birth control and increased production were rejected, the first interfered with the natural process of survival of the fittest and the second could be at best only a temporary expedient.[12] Hitler echoed a common sentiment from the 1890s: 'Germany will either be a world power or there will be no Germany.'[13] In his unpublished 'Second Book', written in 1928, he argued that Germany needed another 500 000 square kilometers of land – roughly the area of France – and that only Russia and the lands between Germany and Russia could provide such an opportunity.[14] In other passages of the same book he made it clear that Germany must not allow its own racial basis to be diluted by incorporating other peoples in the process of expansion. Foreign elements were to be isolated or removed – Czechs or Poles, for instance, were not to be annexed in the hope that one day they would turn into Germans.[15]

On a practical level there were two main alternative areas for expansion, either on the continent or overseas. The latter was rejected as unrealistic given that the British empire was already in possession. In any case Hitler thought Europe more suitable for settlement by German farmers – who would produce the food for the rising population and maintain a healthy balance to the evils of industrial society – and he also saw the obvious strategic advantages for a continental state, like Germany, in dominating its continent.[16] At a practical level he was also quite prepared to make the necessary concessions for an alliance policy. So where Italy was concerned, he expressly renounced the goal of recovering South Tyrol, a region which had been ceded by Austria to Italy at the peace settlement despite its large German-speaking population.[17] Between his pan-German loyalties to all Germans and the goal of living space, the clear priority was living space. Hitler had no compunction about making a necessary sacrifice of principle to achieve the greater goal.

Once committed to the view that Germany's future lay in the conquest of Russian territory, Hitler held to it unerringly. He was not moved by the strength of the alternative strategy – alliance with Russia against the western powers – which remained popular in nationalist circles and had its own advocates in the Nazi party. Indeed, after his release from prison following the putsch, he insisted on the submission of the party to his view of the future course of expansion and devoted a chapter of the second volume of *Mein Kampf* to the subject.[18]

The strongest point he made was that Russia was in no position to help Germany even if it so wished. As the Ruhr crisis had demonstrated Germany could not defend its western frontiers from attack by France, and Russia would also have to march through France's ally, Poland, before it could come to Germany's assistance. In any case, Hitler added, the aim of the Jewish masters of Russia was to spread Bolshevism to Germany: it was not for the National Socialists to aid them in that task.

Hitler was on less strong ground in arguing that Britain would be available as an ally. He had himself noted in *Mein Kampf* that for 300 years British policy had been to maintain a balance of power in Europe to protect her rear while she expanded overseas.[19] Since France was now asserting its power over the continent – and could also threaten Britain directly – Hitler expected British policy to switch to support of Germany. But, if Britain objected to France in the Ruhr, why should one believe that it would submit to Germany conquering a vast empire in the east and in turn becoming the dominant continental power? Hitler was conscious of this objection and in his unpublished 'Second Book', written in 1928, he argued that contrary to 'a very erroneous idea' Britain would not 'immediately fight any dominant European power'. Britain became involved only when such powers threatened its empire: it had not come into conflict with Prussia in the eighteenth century or Germany in the nineteenth until Germany embarked on naval and colonial expansion. Hitler added a brief reference to Russia as, with France, the 'natural enemies' of the British empire – the Conservative government had indeed broken off diplomatic relations with the Soviet Union in 1927 – another reason for thinking that Britain would be a natural ally against Russia. Hitler also thought that in the future Britain would come into competition with the United States which was increasingly asserting its economic power. Despite these arguments for thinking that Britain would be willing to ally with Germany, Hitler cautioned that there was still a danger that Jewish influence in Britain might succeed in turning British policy against Germany, whereas for his other ally, Italy, he thought that Mussolini's Fascist rule made Jewish influence less of a danger there.[20]

There has been considerable discussion about whether Hitler had further plans beyond continental expansion for a truly global empire.[21] Right at the end of the 'Second Book' he suggested that 'in the distant future' one could imagine an association of nations 'of superior national quality' challenging 'the imminent overpowering of the world by the American union'. This reference to further conflicts was in keeping with Hitler's belief in the endless, inevitable struggle of races for mastery. The strong would always expand at the expense of the weak. Hitler had no time for democratic movements for European union, themselves prompted by the economic competition of the United States, because such movements lacked a racial core. But his vague speculation about a future global war did not have the same status as the definite goal of continental expansion against Russia. The power of the United States also provided a further argument for alliance with Britain for, as he said in the same passage, Britain's 'world domination' was preferable to the emergence of an American one.[22]

In the period when Hitler's views were taking shape, the Nazi party was a small, extreme group on the fringe of serious politics. As the Republic consolidated between 1924 and 1928, the Nazi share of the vote fell from 6.5 to 2.6 per cent. Hitler had no serious chance of power. His programme was that of a politician, dedicated to the overthrow of the existing regime, not an immediate agenda for government. He was concerned to demonstrate the futility of existing policy, the absence of alternatives to his solution – the conquest of living space in the east sufficient for a hundred years – and at least a plausible strategy for how it could be brought about. That does not mean that he invented a programme for the sake of opposition. He was committed to it. He also thought it essential to win over public opinion to his view of future alliances, so that Britain and Italy would have confidence in Germany.[23] For that reason it was vital that the Nazi party should itself be united behind him. But unless the Republic were to be undermined by some catastrophe, he knew that in all probability his would remain a voice crying in the wilderness.

He predicted that the foreign policy of the Republic would end in failure. If Germany continued, as in the past, to muddle along with no particular goal it would inevitably become the victim of those with clear aims, just as Poland had in the eighteenth century: 'Anyone who does not wish to be the hammer will be the anvil in history.'[24] It had no power to recover the frontiers of 1914 again, which were in any case wholly inadequate. And if it returned to the policies of foreign trade, colonies and a navy, it would again meet the enmity of Britain.[25] Hitler was contemptuous of the efforts, such as those made by the Republic's foreign minister Gustav Stresemann, to reach agreement with France. France would never abandon its goal of keeping Germany weak and it had the military power and an alliance system with Poland and Czechoslovakia to maintain that position. Together they were capable of attacking almost all the major German industrial regions from the air within an hour, and Germany would be helpless.[26] Hitler therefore dismissed all the policies he attributed to Republican governments as wrong-headed and unrealistic. Their attempt at peaceful revision by accommodation with the western powers, the policies of acquiring American loans through the Dawes plan and securing the Rhineland

frontiers by the Locarno treaties would lead only to economic suffoc-
ation, political decay and racial weakness, until Germany was finally
reduced to the level of a second Holland or Switzerland.[27] This might
indeed be the future under bourgeois governments. But, in another
passage, he argued that Germany could be saved from that fate, as at
other times in her history by a sudden reversal of fortune, 'by an iron
fist'.[28]

In July 1928, when Hitler wrote these words, the Weimar Republic
seemed more stable than at any previous time in its troubled history.
In the elections to the Reichstag in May the Social Democrats (SPD)
had won the largest share of the vote (nearly 30 per cent) and formed
a coalition with the Catholic Centre Party and its Bavarian sister party
(with together 15 per cent) and the two liberal parties (with together
13.6 per cent). The main opposition consisted of the German National
People's Party (DNVP) on the right (14 per cent) and the Communists
on the left (10.6 per cent). There were also a number of small protest
parties representing regional and sectional groups (together nearly 14
per cent) and the Nazis (2.6 per cent). The SPD had 153 seats in
the Reichstag to the Nazis 12. The government's programme was
approved by a vote of 261 to 134 against.

These figures are not, of course, the whole story. It was difficult
to hold together a coalition stretching from the SPD to the middle-
class liberals as the depression divided labour and business over public
spending. Stresemann's foreign policy had achieved significant results
in dismantling the penal clauses of the Versailles Treaty but it was
not clear that the further goal of frontier revision could be achieved
peacefully. And a financial crisis already loomed should the flow of
foreign loans into the German economy, which enabled it to pay
reparations, be cut off. The Nazi vote also understated the support
for its views which extended to the more radical elements of the
nationalist DNVP and the protest parties. The DNVP indeed reacted
to the election by choosing a new leader of extreme views, Alfred
Hugenberg, an arch-nationalist and anti-Republican, a natural ally in
due course for Hitler.

In addition, what the Nazis lacked in voting power they made
up for in the dedication and discipline of their activists. With about
100 000 members in 1928, they were a force to be reckoned with
wherever anti-Republican sentiment was strong, increasingly finding
a ready reception among peasant farmers in north and east Germany
suffering from a fall in prices, or among the young unemployed in

cities, or upper-middle class groups who reacted against coalition with the SPD. One particularly fertile recruiting ground for a new élite was among the upper-middle class students in universities, those born before the war but too young to take part in it. Here the racist version of history found open minds. The idea that the pressure of population on resources required a racial reconstruction of Europe and the linked belief that Jews were a threat to the race acquired the status of sober scientific facts for some of that generation. They became the brains behind Himmler's apparatus in the 1940s, dispassionately planning the elimination of whole peoples in the interests of German settlement of the conquered lands and racial purity.[29]

Nevertheless, the election results in 1928 and the formation of a majority coalition under an SPD chancellor serve to put Hitler's views in perspective. They were not the views of the majority of the German people. No-one, except a fanatical adherent, could have imagined that he would become chancellor in five years time and lead Germany into a new war to fulfil the terrible vision he had conjured up in *Mein Kampf*.

3 From the Margin to the Mainstream

The crisis that brought Nazism to power was the great depression. Yet this was not a simple matter of cause and effect. The unemployed did not vote overwhelmingly for the Nazi party. On the contrary the working class in the main continued to vote for the Social Democrats and, in increasing numbers, for the Communists (KPD). The Catholic Centre Party also held its ground though its policies shifted to the right. The main effect of the great depression was to drive the Protestant middle classes into the right-radical camp.[1] The liberal parties virtually disappeared and the Conservative DNVP suffered heavy losses. As the crisis deepened, the various middle-class protest parties – regional parties, a 'business' party, a savers' party, farmers' parties – also went under. In addition, turn-out rose from 75.6 per cent in 1928 to 84.1 per cent in July 1932. The Nazi party was the single beneficiary of this volcanic eruption within the middle-class camp, though the KPD also made gains among the working class. The Nazi share of the vote rose from 2.6 per cent in 1928 to 18.3 per cent in 1930 and peaked at 37.4 per cent in July 1932 (the KPD rose from 10.6 per cent in 1928 to 16.9 per cent in November 1932). The Nazi party became a genuine mass party of the Protestant middle classes, the first one in German history, and it succeeded in attracting a significant minority of the working-class vote as well. It was this extraordinary achievement which gave it its claim to power and its hold on its followers. If we are to understand why the German people followed Hitler into war, we have therefore first to understand why nearly 14 million voted Nazi in July 1932.

The simplest answer is that the depression demonstrated the inability of the Weimar Republic to govern effectively. Republican government provided neither security nor hope. The Protestant middle classes had never been much attracted to the Republic although there was initial enthusiasm for a new start among Protestant liberals in 1919.

27

During the Republic's best years there was some progress towards a pragmatic acceptance of the regime. Stresemann led the German People's Party (DVP) – the successor of the old National Liberal Party which had supported Bismarck's wars of unification – into government. Together with the left-liberal Democrats (DDP), who had identified with the Republic from the beginning, they held around 14 per cent of the total vote. Even the Conservative DNVP joined the government briefly on two occasions. Nevertheless deep resentments remained. Traditional loyalties within these groups had been to the German empire. The effects of war and revolution had increased their political awareness, as it did for all sections of German society. But they were politically homeless and volatile after defeat and revolution in 1918 and tended all too easily to see the Republic as an alien imposition, a regime of Socialists, Catholics and Jews. In the eyes of Protestant farmers, traders, businessmen, civil servants and professional people, it never functioned well. It produced weak governments, coalitions either in a minority in the Reichstag or so broad – stretching from the bourgeois DVP to the SPD – that they were incapable of consistent policy.

The last three years of the Republic seemed to prove its incapacity to govern effectively.[2] The depression brought down the last majority coalition in March 1930 because it was unable to reach agreement on how to finance the ballooning costs of unemployment insurance. In addition, army leaders wanted to see a government less dependent on the Reichstag and the SPD and, under their influence, President Hindenburg was prepared to make use of the Presidential decree powers to keep the SPD out of office. The new Chancellor from the Centre Party, Heinrich Brüning, led a minority bourgeois coalition which depended on toleration by the SPD to pass its legislation in the Reichstag. He was, however, unable to find a formula for the budget which would satisfy both the business groups represented by the DVP in his coalition and the SPD. The rejection of the budget by the Reichstag in July 1930 was followed by the use of Presidential emergency decree powers to impose it. The decree was in turn annulled by an alliance of the left and the radical right in the Reichstag leading Hindenburg to authorize new elections in September. These events seemed to demonstrate the deadlock of Weimar's political institutions and produced the first Nazi breakthrough in the elections to 18.3 per cent of the vote and 107 seats in the Reichstag.

During the following two years the political crisis intensified as the electorate polarized between Republican and anti-Republican camps. Brüning governed by emergency decree powers which were tolerated by the SPD, now alarmed by Nazi success and fearful that if they created a parliamentary impasse democracy would not survive. But by 1932 Hindenburg and those around him tired of even this degree of dependence on the SPD and Brüning was summarily dismissed. There followed the elections of July 1932 when the Nazis gained 230 seats (the next largest party was the SPD with 133). Hitler's refusal to join a coalition except as Chancellor led to an attempt at presidential rule without the Reichstag under von Papen and von Schleicher, but this could not be maintained without breaking the constitution. The only alternative was military dictatorship but the army leaders drew back at the prospect of becoming involved in a civil war with both the Nazis and the combined left of Socialists and Communists. In these circumstances Hindenburg's advisers decided to risk the appointment of Hitler as Chancellor but to contain him in a coalition with a majority of conservative ministers like Hindenburg's favourite, von Papen, who became Vice Chancellor. In January 1933 Hitler formed what was still a minority government. In March, in elections where terror was already used freely against the SPD and the Communists, the Nazis achieved 43.9 per cent and together with the DNVP were able to form a majority government. On 23 March, Hitler having satisfied the Centre Party with assurances of autonomy for the churches, the Reichstag passed an Enabling Law by the required two-thirds majority which provided the legal basis for dispensing with the Weimar Constitution for good.

Behind political failure lay economic failure. The middle classes suffered in various ways and blamed the Republic for their misfortunes. Savings were lost in the hyperinflation of 1923. There were winners as well as losers since debts were also written off. But this lottery created a deep sense of injustice: the Republic was seen to have failed to act fairly. Farmers had to borrow in the new re-valued currency and faced difficulties paying off the debt in a period of falling agricultural prices. Civil servants had suffered cuts in their numbers and salaries and were cut again in the depression. Big business felt that the social welfare and industrial wage bargaining systems introduced after 1919 were too generous to the workers and insupportable. Bankers knew that the economy could not survive the withdrawal of foreign loans on which German business had come to depend after 1924. Small businesses feared the impact of depression on their customers. By 1932 industrial production had lost 40 per cent of its value in 1929 (compared to 11 per cent in Britain) and there were six million unemployed or nearly half the industrial workforce (compared to 22 per cent in Britain). The cumulative effect of political weakness and economic crisis drove significant numbers of the Protestant middle classes first into protest parties in 1924 and 1928 and then from 1930 to a wholesale rejection of the regime and of all those parties that had tried to make it work. They turned instead to the most anti-Republican party available to them, the Nazis.

The effect of the depression was therefore to divide Germany more acutely than it had ever been divided before. In the July 1932 Reichstag elections the Nazi 37 per cent was matched by the SPD–KPD 36 per cent with the only other group to reach double figures being the Catholic Centre party (together with its Bavarian sister party) with 16 per cent. The polarization had another effect on the frightened Protestant electorate. It mobilized not just against the Republic but against Socialism and Communism. Memories of the revolutionary movements of 1917–19 were still alive. The fear that Bolshevism would emerge triumphant after all from the depression was fuelled by the political violence of the early 1930s. The Nazis gloried in their reputation as the only party that would take on the Communists on the streets. The street brawls, which were often provoked by the SA, became an essential part of their claim to legitimacy. In Nazi propaganda, their heroism had saved Germany from Communist revolution. The fear of the enemy within, the psychology of civil war, provided the Nazis with an invaluable reservoir of support, one on which they continued to draw throughout the Third Reich.

While playing on middle-class fears of civil war, the Nazis also claimed to be the party of national unity. They appropriated the concept of the 'community of the whole nation' – the *Volksgemeinschaft* – and appealed to the idealism as well as the fears of the electorate. Since the First World War the concept of national unity had been used in contrary ways – first in the immediate sense of burying party divisions in wartime, but second from 1917 as a way of uniting the right in the so-called Patriotic Party (*Vaterlandspartei*) against the left. In the Weimar Republic, it was again used by Stresemann as chancellor in 1923 in its first sense as a rallying cry for unity against both the French occupation of the Ruhr and the extremes of Communism and Fascism at home. Stresemann hoped to make his party (the DVP) the natural party for the Protestant middle classes to support and lead such a party into acceptance of the Republic. He saw that this would stabilize the Republic by giving the Protestant middle classes a recognized place in the system, in a way similar to that of the Conservative party in Britain.[3] Under the impact of the depression Protestant voters turned instead to the alternative concept, however paradoxical it might sound, of national unity against the Republic. The Nazis successfully portrayed the Republic as an alien, divisive, sectional and corrupt regime against which the nation should revolt. The idealism of a movement of national unity thus ran together with the fear, brutality and terror of civil war.

Further, for the Nazis and their movement, the enemies were not simply at home. The Republic was despised as a craven regime, created by foreign pressure. They saw it as the regime of losers, of those whose strikes and revolution had stabbed the German army in the back, who had agreed to the Treaty of Versailles with loss of territory, colonies, the capacity for self-defence and honour (the war guilt clause) and the imposition of enormous reparations, who had then attempted revision by reconciliation with former enemies and membership of the League of Nations, and who had in 1929, the year before the great depression set in, signed the Young Plan – a final reparations settlement with German payments stretching out to 1988. The Republican parties represented those who believed in Germany's place in the world as a peaceful democracy, part of a growing international economy where tariffs would be lowered and exports would grow. Trade not empire would solve Germany's economic problems. The depression delivered a fatal blow to that view of the world. Instead the ideology of empire, race, living space and economic autarky seemed to provide the answer to many people's everyday experience of an increasingly desperate struggle for survival. Other major powers, the United States, France and Japan turned increasingly towards protection of their home or imperial markets by tariffs and in 1932 the British Government, as one of the last, introduced measures of 'Imperial preference'. Nazism was a call to believe that there was an alternative for German policy as well, to the peaceful vision of Republican leaders which was seen to have failed. In this the Nazis were able to build on ideas of empire from the 1890s and of a 'natural' economic region for Germany in central Europe (*Mitteleuropa*) which had enjoyed wide currency before and during the First World War.

The mood infected even those parties that had previously supported the Republic's foreign policy. When the French Foreign Minister, Aristide Briand, put forward a plan for a united Europe on the basis of existing frontiers, Chancellor Brüning rejected it telling the cabinet that Germany required 'a sufficient natural living space' in any European new order.[4] When his government took the first step in this direction in 1931 by creating a customs union with Austria, however, it was immediately frustrated. The proposal was ruled incompatible with Austria's obligations under the peace treaties by a majority of one at the international court at the Hague and Austria was in any case forced to withdraw by French financial pressure, a fiasco which seemed to confirm the bankruptcy of Republican foreign policy. The alternative to peaceful revision of Versailles could only mean rearmament and ultimately war or at least the threat of war. An important part of the attraction of Nazism, popular beyond its core voters, was the promise of a strong foreign policy. The negotiations and compromises of the Republic would be replaced at home and abroad by national unity and the 'iron fist'.

To understand the nature and appeal of Nazism, one must understand that what it offered from the beginning was a radical alternative. It was a revolutionary movement. It needed enemies at home and abroad to justify its view of the world. In 1930–32 it stamped a mass party mainly, not only, of the Protestant middle classes out of the ground. People driven by resentment, exasperation and despair but also in some cases by hope and idealism turned to it for salvation. But the groups involved had very different interests, rural and urban, large and small businesses, state employees and those in private enterprise. In opposition, the Nazis had organized special campaigns and party formations to appeal to as many different sections of the community as possible. But to keep that support once in government, let alone to reach out to other groups – the Catholics and the bulk of the working class – Nazism had to maintain the sense of crisis which had first made it a mass movement. Hitler firmly believed that politics was essentially about conflict, against the enemies of the race at home and ultimately for mastery over other races. The great depression provided a kind of plausibility for that view. At its height it was easy to blame the collapse on enemies at home and abroad. Hitler's success in power depended on his ability to project that experience forward and outward so that the German people would continue to follow him, ultimately into war not just for a revision of frontiers but for a racial reconstruction of Europe.

On 30 January 1933, when he was appointed Chancellor as head of a coalition government, it was far from clear that he would succeed. His cabinet was composed mainly of conservatives, including von Papen as Vice Chancellor, Alfred Hugenberg, the leader of the DNVP, and 'experts' like Constantin von Neurath, a professional diplomat who remained in post as Foreign Minister from the Papen Government and, on the insistence of Hindenburg a general, Werner von Blomberg, as Minister of Defence (though in fact unknown to Hindenburg he was a Nazi sympathizer). There were only two other Nazi Ministers, apart from Hitler himself, – though they held the key posts in terms of control of the police through the Reich Ministry of the Interior (Wilhelm Frick) and Prussian Minister of the Interior (Hermann Göring). In addition, Hitler still faced the authority of Hindenburg as head of state as a restraining influence.

More important than these formal limitations on his power, Hitler also faced the obvious problem that something like half the nation, Socialists, Communists and Catholics in the main, was hostile or at least sceptical toward what he offered. Some of those who had voted Nazi were also already worried about its violent methods against opponents and its claim to total control. In the last free elections in November 1932, the Nazi share of the vote had fallen to 33.1 per cent and the Conservative DNVP had recovered somewhat to 8.9 per cent. It was possible that the electoral fever that had brought the Nazis success would subside again, proving to be just another example of the volatility of the Protestant electorate. In addition, elite groups in the army, in government administration and in business hoped to be able to use the Nazis to further their own aims – rearmament, a strong foreign policy, redressing the balance between business and labour – without losing control to the radical elements in Nazism. And Hitler needed the co-operation of these elites if he was to achieve his policy goals.

But Hitler also had certain advantages. He had refused to allow the Nazi party to be incorporated into a coalition led by others. He had insisted on the Chancellorship and got it. He was prepared to employ the most ruthless terror against his enemies, breaking their resistance and frightening the doubtful into conformity or silence. His enemies were demoralized and had no convincing alternative to offer. Neither Communist revolution nor a return to the Weimar Republic was attractive. And the ideas of Conservatives, like von Papen, for some sort of authoritarian Christian state would never have mass appeal. As in 1919, there was also in 1933 a rush to identify with what appeared to be a successful revolution. This seemed to critics to show a lack of character and a betrayal of principle. But it was more than that. The way in which the middle-class parties and so many of their social institutions voluntarily agreed to go into liquidation and become co-ordinated (the process of *Gleichschaltung*) showed, like the electoral landslide of 1930–32, the degree to which they had been politically homeless since 1918. For those of a Conservative or National Liberal tradition, the Nazis seemed to offer once again strong government and clear leadership around the values of family, nation and race. They had never expected such values to be capable of inspiring a mass movement. Some ideologues were also attracted to the more radical theories of racial science. The doubters soon found themselves on the defensive. They agreed with the broad aims of Nazism, the restoration of traditional values and the recovery of Germany's leading role in Europe. As the regime enjoyed success both in restoring employment at home and dismantling the Versailles Treaty, opposition seemed increasingly futile. By July 1933, the government commanded all the resources of single party control through terror and propaganda over every dimension of politics, society, culture, education and leisure.[5] The constant mobilization continued after 1933 through organizations like the Hitler youth, the Nazi women's section, the Labour front, special collections, harvest festivals, party rallies with the high point of the führer's speeches: a seemingly endless theatre on film and radio for popular consumption.[6] Total control was never achieved – the churches retained a limited autonomy – and different branches of the state and party often pursued contradictory policies. But the Third Reich did succeed in eliminating any realistic threat to its survival, at least until the last years of the war.

In all this activity, foreign policy played a central role. It provided indeed the fundamental rationale of the whole system. So long as it was successful it bound regime and people together in a process of overcoming the national humiliations of the past. The successes of Nazi foreign policy reinforced those views which had first taken root in the 1890s that Germany had been cheated of its destiny to be a world power, that it had been encircled and that only by domination over others could it be free. The novelist W. G. Sebald later wrote that 'the combination of fantastic delusions on the one hand and an upright way of life on the other is typical of the particular fault line that ran through the German mind during the first half of the 20th century'.[7] The sense of encirclement by foreign powers became a form of mental imprisonment, an inability to perceive the outside world except through the lens of being the victim. In this respect above all, Hitler's view of the world was widely shared among the German people.

4 Dismantling Versailles, 1933–36

THE NEW COURSE AND THE PROFESSIONAL ELITES

Hitler wasted no time in setting the new course and winning over the military leadership. On 3 February 1933, only four days after his appointment as Chancellor, he addressed a group of senior officers at the home of the commander-in-chief of the army, Kurt von Hammerstein-Equord, together with the Foreign Minister, Neurath.[1] The notes of the discussion by one of the generals present, Curt von Liebmann, have recently been confirmed by a second account from an unlikely source. It seems that one of General Hammerstein-Equord's daughters, who was a Communist, passed on a record of what Hitler said to a KPD contact and from there it went to the offices of the Communist International in Moscow.[2]

Hitler started by referring to the causes of the depression which he attributed to the decline of the previous system of exchange of industrialized goods from Europe with raw materials from the colonies as colonies developed their own industries. Additional factors were the effects of the war, the disruption of reparations and the poison of Bolshevism. He claimed that for 14 years he had seen that the only cures for unemployment were either an all-out export programme or

> a settlement policy conceived on a large scale, whose precondition is an extension of the living space of the German people. This last way would be my proposal. In a period of 50–60 years one would have a state which was completely new and healthy.

However, that task could begin only once the present form of state had been consolidated. That meant eliminating democracy and pacifism. The German people, he declared, were divided fifty-fifty for and against National Socialism. That meant that political power had first to be conquered, treason punished with the death penalty and Marxism suppressed. There was no point in expanding the army until Marxist influence on recruits had been eliminated. That was why he was striving for 'total political power'. He gave himself six to eight years to destroy Marxism.

> Then the armed forces will be able to carry out an active foreign policy and the goal of expansion of the living space of the German people will be achieved by armed force – that goal would probably be in the east. But Germanization of the population of the annexed or conquered lands is not possible. One can only Germanize soil. One must ruthlessly expel a few million people as Poland and France did after the war.[3]

The most dangerous time, Hitler warned, was the period before rearmament had been achieved. If French statesmen were clever, they would attack perhaps in alliance with Russia.[4] Germany had to act with the utmost speed. The political transformation would be carried out by the party – the armed forces were asked to provide only moral support. Hitler and his movement would stand by them. Their task was to solve foreign conflicts not domestic ones. Hitler closed with an appeal for support, saying 'you will never again find a man who dedicates himself as I do with all his strength for Germany's salvation.'

Hitler was obviously concerned to win the support of the service chiefs who might still obstruct the revolution at home and on whom, in any case, he would in time depend to carry out his foreign policy. His remarks were therefore pitched to persuade them that the terror which was about to be unleashed against domestic enemies was necessary although he would not require the armed forces to be involved in it. That would be the task of the Nazi party. Further Hitler offered an assurance that the army's autonomy would be respected, effectively ruling out the threat of takeover by the SA with its four and a half million members under its unruly leader, Ernst Röhm. Hitler also emphasized that rearmament would have immediate priority because he understood that in delay lay the danger of foreign intervention. And he made it clear that in the future the armed forces would play a vital role in the expansion of German territory. This combination of reassurance and flattery was effective. The generals were relieved to be excluded from the domestic revolution and, with only one resignation, they stood aside and in effect gave Hitler their moral support. The priority given to rearmament, to which Hitler was genuinely committed, was also naturally welcome to them. It is interesting how open Hitler was about the goal of living space in the east and 'its ruthless Germanization'.[5] It is not clear how far the generals understood what this meant. They may have discounted it as an ideological aspiration which would be unlikely to be carried out in practice.[6]

The lack of opposition from the army was crucial to Hitler's success at this stage. With the nation split in his own words, fifty-fifty, he needed the generals' acquiescence. The army for its part needed Hitler. Ever since the First World War, it had been obvious that modern warfare required total mobilization: mass armies, a war economy, the use of new technologies and maintaining public morale through effective propaganda. The army required the support of a mass movement and the resources of the whole of society. Nazism offered it just that. In addition the values of Nazism seemed to be consistent with the values of the armed forces, unlike the Republic which had always symbolized – however unfairly – defeat, Marxism and pacifism. It was not surprising, therefore, that the military leadership rallied to Hitler. Hitler clinched their support by making a key concession, assuring them that their autonomy would be preserved and referring to the army and the party as 'the twin pillars' of the state.[7] This revived memories of the special status of the Prussian army before 1914 when it had enjoyed direct access to the Kaiser on an equal basis with the civilian government. The more traditional officers still saw their responsibility not simply in military terms but as extending to the political sphere, making judgements for instance as to when war was justified and could be successful. That led to clashes between some of the military leaders and Hitler later. For the time being, however, they were impressed by the similarity of their aims and Hitler's.

There were still significant differences, however, among the military leaders. Their attitudes towards the regime varied from the enthusiasm of the Defence Minister, Blomberg, to the cautious conservatism of General Werner von Fritsch, who became commander-in-chief of the army in February 1934. But recognition that they had no realistic alternative to co-operation with Hitler was common to them all. The situation was well-described by the head of Blomberg's ministerial office, General Walther von Reichenau, speaking to a colleague in the summer of 1933,

All power is now concentrated in one person and he will know how to underpin it still further. The masses applaud him like no one else. What was left of the parties has melted away like snow in the sun. The trade unions have been smashed, the Communists driven into a corner and provisionally neutralized, the Reichstag has surrendered its rights with the Enabling Law. The workers are keeping their heads down and, after the previous slump, their wage packets will be more important to them than any politics. The whole state apparatus with the police, the civil service concerned about their due rights, the communications media...press, radio, in short, everything through which the public can be kept on a lead is under firm control and is doing what it is told. And then we are supposed to come along with our seven decrepit divisions scattered over the whole of the Reich and be the only ones to dance out of line. Only fools can imagine that....

I regard it all the more as my task to keep in close personal contact which in a dictatorship is more vital than all the work of the ministries. And I am certain that this remarkable man [Hitler], despite all the blemishes which his movement understandably still has, is following a clear path towards the goal of creating a state which can once more respect itself and also be respected by its neighbours, who have caused enough trouble for us in recent years. One must not forget that among all the negative impressions which go against the grain.[8]

This is a perfect statement of the attitude of many intelligent conservatives, a mixture of realism about their inability to offer an alternative to the Nazi revolution, hope that it would turn out for the best and determination to remain at their posts to achieve influence. The same attitudes can be found throughout government. At senior levels in the Foreign Ministry there were serious doubts about the competence of the new regime. These doubts were made worse by the actions of Nazi figures, like the party ideologue, Alfred Rosenberg, author of '*The Myth of the 20th Century*', who in April 1933 established a separate party office for foreign policy. In most cases, however, Foreign Ministry officials overcame their doubts and decided to stay in post to limit the damage. Some saw a parallel in the way officials had continued to serve the Republic in 1919, despite the overthrow of the monarchy. Neurath had been the ambassador in Rome from 1921 to 1930 and had come to the conclusion that Fascism became more moderate once in power – he seems to have expected the same to happen with Hitler.[9] Only one senior figure, Friedrich von Prittwitz, who had been ambassador to the United States since 1927 resigned on principle because of the violation of democratic principles by the new regime. The others had little or no objection to an authoritarian state and were concerned only about how effective it would be. The top official, the Secretary of State, Bernhard Wilhelm von Bülow drafted a letter of resignation in the early summer of 1933 because of the damage caused by the new political leadership to Germany's reputation. He instanced the discrimination against the Jews which had alienated Britain and the United States, the militarist ambitions of the SA that worried the French, and mistakes in policies towards the Soviet Union and Poland – in the latter case carrying the risk of provoking a war which Germany would lose. In the first draft, Bülow associated three senior colleagues with his resignation – the ambassadors in London, Paris and Moscow – though he subsequently cancelled the reference to them. For whatever reason the letter was never sent. Presumably Bülow recovered his confidence that the situation could be managed. Like the others, he instead put his expertise to use to defend what was happening to other governments.[10]

Another key professional was the banker, Hjalmar Schacht. Schacht had been president of the German Central Bank – the *Reichsbank* – from 1923 to 1930. He had overseen the stabilization of the mark and with good contacts abroad, especially in the City of London, he had been able to manage the return of Germany to the gold standard. An ambitious and volatile man he turned against the Republican governments for making, as he saw it, excessive concessions to achieve a settlement on reparations through the Young Plan in 1929. He resigned from the *Reichsbank* and soon threw in his lot with Hitler. He returned as President of the Bank in 1933 and was appointed Economics Minister in 1934. He took charge of the repudiation of Germany's crippling foreign debt, successfully dividing Britain from the United States in the process.[11] His ingenuity also created the special credit mechanism – the so-called Mefo bills – through which the first phase of rearmament was financed and kept secret. In fact these were simply a form of credit accepted by an arms company which existed only on paper and was in fact a front for the *Reichsbank*.[12] Schacht's policies soon ran into difficulties as inflationary pressures built up in the economy again and by 1936 he lost influence with Hitler as he recommended slowing the pace of rearmament. He later had loose contact with opposition circles and was arrested after the July 1944 plot. But he is a striking example of the way in which Hitler was served by the ambition and opportunism of outstanding people at the top of their professions, as well as by those who acted from more honourable motives.[13]

HITLER'S ROLE

The central question, as Hitler admitted in his address to the generals, was how could Germany rearm without provoking foreign intervention. Hitler was determined on rearmament and he was prepared to make whatever concessions were necessary to achieve that goal. This was the context for his initial moves in foreign policy. But Hitler was not entirely free. Each of the choices he made had consequences. Those consequences produced constraints on his further choices. A complex process resulted which is at the centre of understanding the Third Reich and its foreign policy. Hitler started a revolution by dictatorship and rearmament to prepare Germany for war. Those processes acquired a momentum of their own which Hitler had to manage as well as to lead. The degree to which he remained in control or was swept along by events has divided historians. On the one side, as we have seen in an earlier chapter, are the so-called 'intentionalists' who see Hitler's intentions as the key to any explanation and on the other the 'structuralists' who see the constraints on his freedom, whether political, administrative, economic, or international as essential.[14] Both factors, as is now generally recognized, are important and striking the balance between the two is the most interesting part of the story. It is complicated not least by the fact that Hitler was at some level content to be swept along, provided the general direction was the one in which he wanted to go. Indeed he often disliked taking clear decisions between alternative policies, preferring to let crises develop until the crisis itself forced a solution to be found. Perhaps he felt that he was being carried along by the mysterious forces of history, those laws of nature, racial laws – which he sometimes called 'providence' – to fulfil his destiny. After all, a force greater than himself, the collapse of the international economy, had swept him into power. Might it not be that a parallel collapse of the international order – the order of the Paris peace settlement of 1919 – might open the way to power on the European continent, provided only he kept his nerve and maintained his faith in the triumph of the Aryan race?

Although the choices and constraints became ever more stark as the regime progressed, one can see the process starting in the first few months. The imposition of dictatorship, persecution of political opponents and Jews, and the violence which accompanied it, were a necessary basis for Hitler's future goal of racial expansion and he could not avoid the hostile reaction these initial measures provoked in democracies abroad – France, Britain and the United States. Equally, giving rearmament priority had implications for the rest of the economy, as it came up against constraints like lack of foreign currency and shortage of raw materials. Choices had to be made between capital goods and consumer goods. If resources were held back from consumers for the sake of rearmament, public support might be lost. Yet preparation for total war required not only the material resources but also the moral resources of public opinion. Hitler knew that foreign and domestic policy had to be a single process. He always believed that it was the collapse of the home front that had led to defeat in 1918. Yet he also understood that starting with a divided and effectively disarmed nation, the process of preparing for war in his lifetime would involve living with risk. In his view just as it was his task as führer to set the goal of acquiring living space, so it was his task as a politician to maintain morale at home and to seek out those situations abroad which enabled greatest gain at least risk. If that necessitated both tactical concessions and deceit, so be it. The prizes in statesmanship went not to the nice but the ruthless.

In one way foreign policy stands out from other areas of policy making in the Third Reich. The confusion of decision making with overlapping competences of different government and party authorities, and the competition of powerful individuals to win Hitler's favour and extend their own empires, has been rightly identified as a key feature of the Third Reich. It limits the usefulness of the older concept of a monolithic totalitarian dictatorship: a 'polycratic' regime with many competing centres of power seems a better way of understanding it. Administrative efficiency was hampered by confusion. Decisions which only Hitler could take were left in abeyance because he was either not interested or not willing to commit himself. His preference for a bohemian lifestyle and his contempt for bureaucrats and dislike of the grind of administration were a source of weakness. At the same time, his reliance on his personal authority or charisma meant that there was a continuing push by party leaders to earn his favour by anticipating what he wanted and this created an impetus to ever more radical policies. That maintained the revolutionary momentum of the regime which was itself willed by Hitler. So the price of administrative confusion was one he was willing to pay to achieve ideological goals.[15]

In foreign policy as well there were different groups competing for influence.[16] Apart from the Foreign Ministry and the Defence Ministry, there was the party office of Rosenberg, though he soon lost influence, other party organizations to cultivate contacts with German minorities abroad, and from 1934 and increasingly important, Hitler's so-called personal representative for special missions, Joachim von Ribbentrop who eventually became Foreign Minister in 1938. Others played specific roles like Hermann Göring, especially in the economic aspects of foreign policy and in wartime Heinrich Himmler and the SS. But in one way foreign policy was different. Hitler never neglected it. It was his overriding interest. He was well-briefed for meetings and able to conduct negotiations without notes. According to his press aide, Otto Dietrich, Hitler read a hundred pages of foreign news reports every day.[17] Whatever may have been the case in other areas, Hitler quickly took command of foreign policy. That was not surprising. It was what mattered most to him. This is an important limitation on the picture of Hitler, the amateur bohemian. In foreign policy his direct influence was decisive when he wanted.

REARMAMENT AND THE LEAGUE OF NATIONS

The diplomacy of the first months in power which culminated in Germany leaving the League of Nations on 14 October 1933 provides a good example of the interaction of foreign and domestic politics. The issue was German rearmament. First, there was its impact on other powers. As we have seen, Hitler was worried about the danger that it would provoke foreign intervention. Second, how would it be seen at home? If the nation could be united behind the demand for rearmament that would not only strengthen the regime but also make foreign intervention less likely.

The diplomatic context was set by the Treaty of Versailles. Under its terms Germany was limited to a volunteer army of seven divisions (100 000 men) with comprehensive restrictions on its weapons, a tiny navy and no air force. German disarmament was however, under the terms of the League of Nations Covenant, to be but the first step to general disarmament. That gave Germany an obvious diplomatic pretext to argue that either the other powers should also disarm or that Germany should be allowed to rearm. For most of the Weimar Republic other issues, like the occupation of the Rhineland by Allied forces, had been more pressing. But in 1928 a rearmament plan was agreed by the cabinet to raise a 16 division 'field' army by 1932 – field refers to actual mobile combat units in war in addition to the reserve army at home – and in 1932 that was replaced by a second plan for a 21 division field army (300 000 men) to be achieved by 1938. In 1932 a disarmament conference met under the auspices of the League of Nations at Geneva. Germany demanded 'equal rights' with other powers and backed up this demand by walking out of the conference in July. The other powers gave way and after agreement was reached in December that Germany should have 'equality of rights in a system which would provide security for all nations', the conference reconvened at the end of January 1933.[18]

The first question for Hitler and his ministers was therefore what position Germany should take. Foreign Minister Neurath and Defence Minister Blomberg did not believe that it would be possible to reach an acceptable agreement. They feared being offered an interim solution which would have the effect of postponing German rearmament to a remote future. Hitler had made it clear that he intended to rearm as quickly as possible and a programme of that kind could not be hidden indefinitely. Neurath and Blomberg therefore decided to work for the failure of the conference but to try to make the blame fall on France for refusing in practice to allow Germany 'equal rights'.[19] Hitler however, being more fearful of foreign reaction, was prepared to temporize and instructed the German delegation to work for a 'positive conclusion' which would be better than 'rearmament without a treaty'.[20] Interestingly, Neurath felt strong enough to override these instructions a few days later and he and Blomberg continued to blame the French and pour cold water on the possibility of agreement.[21] At this early stage they felt they could ignore Hitler's judgement and follow their own line.

The subject was discussed in cabinet on 12 May and Hitler held to his position that in view of the tense international situation Germany should show the 'greatest restraint'.[22] Two developments influenced him. There had been rumours of a possible attack by France and Poland. At the same time, Mussolini had proposed a four-power pact which would enable Britain, France, Germany and Italy to decide about revision of the peace treaties through the League. Hitler did not want to risk foreign intervention and he also wanted to conciliate Mussolini and see what benefits might be derived from the four-power pact. He therefore took up a suggestion from Neurath that he should make a formal declaration of German policy to the Reichstag. Seeing the way in which public opinion could be exploited, he declared 'The German people were united on the disarmament question. This unity must be demonstrated to the world.'

Hitler's speech to the Reichstag on 17 May was a tactical masterpiece.[23] He claimed the moral high ground, playing on the themes of Germany as the injured innocent of the Versailles system, on the responsibility of reparations for the depression and of the war guilt clause for making Germany a pariah and preventing a truly peaceful international system emerging. At the same time he committed himself to peace – a new European war could not improve matters but would, on the contrary, create the conditions for Europe to sink into Communist chaos.[24] He presented Germany as wanting only its due as a nation among other nations, recognizing the rights of the new nations and explicitly renouncing any intention at renewed attempts at Germanization of other peoples like the Poles (an ironic twist since, as we have seen, he did not believe in Germanizing other peoples but eliminating them). He added, however, that Germany's inequality had to be addressed, both as a matter of right and – more threateningly – because it was impossible to keep a nation of 65 million people down for ever. He poured scorn on the idea that Germany in its disarmed state could be a threat to other nations and declared himself willing to consider fresh proposals for security, provided Germany's equal rights were respected. He ended, however, with a warning that if Germany continued to be discriminated against, it would have no option but to withdraw from the disarmament conference.

The speech was addressed to two audiences. Abroad it aimed to underline German claims to revision of the treaty and also Germany's commitment to peace. That established continuity with the foreign policy of the Weimar Republic. However, there was also a subtle new tone. If Germany was not given its due, it would be forced to take what was its by right anyway. The problem for other nations on the continent, as Hitler well knew, was that equality for Germany – given the size of its population and economic resources – could all too easily turn into superiority. The only way that German power on the continent could be contained was if it remained committed to international organizations like the League or all the other powers combined to form a common front against it. But once Germany had recovered its power, who could guarantee either? Hitler's speech seemed reasonable and peaceful but it posed a dilemma for other powers. Whether they allowed Germany military equality or Germany took it anyway, the result would be the same. Germany would again have the potential to dominate. That divided the democracies. It helped to create a willingness for unilateral concessions in Britain – the policy of 'appeasement'. And with appeasement went a tendency to blame France for obstruction. France, as the power most directly threatened, naturally wanted to postpone German rearmament as long as possible. But it could not afford to alienate Britain whose support would be essential in any future war. French policy was therefore half-hearted and inconsistent, which was just what Hitler needed.[25]

However, it was with his audience at home that Hitler's speech had its most obvious and immediate success. The Reichstag voted unanimously for the policy he set out. When the SPD members declared their support, Hitler in a theatrical gesture rose and applauded them. This was the first and a perfect illustration of Hitler's ability to manipulate foreign policy to create a sense of national unity. His demand for equality for Germany and his commitment to peace echoed the policies of previous governments. That made the SPD's support possible. At the same time the threat that Germany could also act alone was popular with a public which felt that Germany was still being treated unfairly by the League. The demonstration of national unity was, in turn, impressive abroad. Foreign policy served domestic politics which in turn served foreign policy – a perfect sequence from Hitler's point of view. The difficulty would come when he was ready to use force and needed to persuade the German people that war might after all be necessary, but that lay some years ahead.

Hitler continued the policy of co-operation at the disarmament conference during the summer and he also accepted Mussolini's four-power pact. However, in October he reversed his position. The latest British proposals, which had been modified to meet French objections, were seen by German officials as simply a device to freeze German armaments at their existing level for four years with ample safeguards to maintain French superiority indefinitely. Hitler reacted by declaring Germany's withdrawal from the conference and from the League of Nations on 14 October, the first of the coups that were to become his trademark in the years that followed. At the same time, he announced that a plebiscite would be held to confirm the decision together with new elections to the Reichstag on 12 November. Hitler told the cabinet that the plebiscite would be used to 'ask the German people to identify themselves...with the peace policy of the Reich Government' which in turn would make it 'impossible for the world to accuse Germany of an aggressive policy'.[26] The plebiscite was approved by 95 per cent and the single remaining party, the NSDAP, duly won all the seats in the Reichstag.

These demonstrations of support were contrived in conditions that were neither free nor fair, with Goebbels' propaganda machine controlling the news and fear that a negative vote would be observed and reported. Nevertheless, there is reason to believe that Hitler's decision to leave the League had general support. The main campaign theme was that a vote for leaving the League was a vote for peace because peace could come only when Germany's rights were accepted.[27] The success of this tactic can be seen from the description of the events by a sworn opponent of the regime, the Jewish intellectual, Victor Klemperer, who had the courage to vote 'No' both in the plebiscite and on the ballot paper for the Reichstag election. In his diary for 11 November he noted:

> The extravagant propaganda for a 'Yes' vote. On every commercial vehicle, post office van, postman's bicycle, on every house and shop window, on broad banners, which are stretched across the street – quotations from Hitler are everywhere and always 'Yes' for peace! It is the most monstrous of hypocrisies.

And on 14 November after the results were declared:

> I must also acknowledge that millions were made drunk by the weeks of boundless and boundlessly mendacious 'propaganda for peace', which was countered by not a single printed or spoken word. – For all that: When the triumph was published yesterday...I was laid low, I almost believed the figures and held them to be the truth. And since then we have been told in every possible key: this 'election' is recognised abroad, 'all of Germany' is seen to be behind Hitler, [the foreign powers] admire Germany's unity, will be conciliatory towards it, etc. etc. Now all of it makes me drunk, I too am beginning to believe in the power and the permanency of Hitler.[28]

THE NON-AGGRESSION PACT WITH POLAND

On 25 January 1934 Germany and Poland signed a 'Declaration of Non-Aggression and Understanding', which committed them to settle their disputes exclusively by peaceful means, and was to last for a minimum of 10 years.[29] This agreement caused surprise both within Germany and abroad. The German–Polish frontier established by the Versailles Treaty was bitterly resented by Germans. It separated East Prussia from the rest of Germany by giving Poland a 'corridor' to the sea at Danzig, which – though ethnically German – had been made a Free City under the League of Nations. No German government under the Weimar Republic was prepared to recognize the frontier and the German minority in Poland was secretly subsidized so as to keep it there and maintain Germany's claim to revision. Intermittently, Weimar governments also conducted a trade war with Poland.

The change of policy towards Poland which started in 1933 was made on Hitler's initiative, imposed by him on the Foreign Ministry and carried out regardless of dissent within the Nazi party or among a wider public. It showed his control on an issue where he had clear views. It also showed that his priorities were not those of Weimar governments. Hitler shared their aim of revising the Versailles Treaty but for a different purpose. Where they had been keen to maintain relations with the Soviet Union in order to put pressure on Poland, Hitler was prepared to seek an accommodation with Poland at the expense of relations with the Soviet Union. In a report to cabinet on 7 April 1933, Neurath presented the traditional view: 'We cannot do without Russia's cover for our rear with respect to Poland...An understanding with Poland is neither possible nor desirable.'[30] Hitler made no comment but a few weeks later he started to talk of a settlement with Poland and ordered the Nazi party in Danzig to show restraint.

What were the reasons for this dramatic shift? It can be seen first as a defensive move, prompted by fear of a possible preventive war by France and Poland, alarmed at the prospect of German rearmament. There had been plausible rumours that Poland and France were considering taking action. In fact France had rejected the idea, making the Poles interested in the alternative of an accommodation with Germany. Coming as it did soon after Germany left the League of Nations, the agreement with Poland helped to defuse the danger of a new Franco-Polish combination.

This interpretation has much to be said for it. Hitler was perfectly prepared to make concessions to save what mattered most to him. Since coming to power, he had made frequent adjustments of this kind both in foreign and domestic policy. In July 1933, for instance, he approved a Concordat with the Vatican, negotiated by Vice-Chancellor von Papen. The Concordat was the first international agreement concluded with the Nazi regime, helping it to overcome the isolation caused by its violence and anti-Semitic measures. Hitler told the cabinet that the Concordat was a 'great success...particularly significant in the urgent fight against international Jews'. It also offered substantial advantages in limiting the political activity of clergy and confirming the dissolution of the Catholic Centre Party and the Christian unions. He made no reference, however, to the guarantees that had been given of religious freedom, the legal rights of the church, and the important role of the church in education. He noted only that 'Possible shortcomings...could be rectified later when the foreign policy situation was better.'[31] In fact within two months the Vatican was already protesting that the terms of the Concordat were being broken.

Hitler no doubt had the same tactics in mind towards Poland. The agreement could be disregarded if necessary later when Germany was stronger, as indeed happened in September 1939. According to Hermann Rauschning, who became the president of the Danzig senate in 1933 but soon broke with the Nazis, Hitler said as much to him at the time.[32] However, there are more interesting possibilities. By diluting the Franco-Polish alliance of 1921, Hitler may already have been thinking not only of defence but of offence. Might Poland be persuaded to remain neutral in a future war between Germany and France? Hitler knew that the western powers would oppose the conquest of living space and spoke of the necessity of Germany delivering 'short, decisive blows to the west and then to the east'.[33] Might Poland, which had a territorial dispute with the Soviet Union going back to its annexation of Soviet territory in 1921, be prepared to play a subordinate role in a future German–Soviet war? It is noticeable that Goebbels, recording a conversation with Hitler on 18 August 1935 about foreign policy noted: '...with England eternal alliance. Good relations with Poland. Colonies to a limited extent. On the other hand expansion East. The Baltic belongs to us.'[34] Göring too was told to cultivate close relations with Poland and is alleged on a visit to Warsaw in January 1935 to have proposed almost an anti-Russian alliance and a joint march on Moscow.[35]

Whatever Hitler's precise calculations, his attitude to Poland was simply instrumental. As Goebbels noted Hitler telling the cabinet at the end of 1936: 'With Poland a marriage not of love but of convenience.'[36] Hitler saw Poland in terms of his much larger goal of living space in the east at the expense of the Soviet Union. In this instance, racial considerations – the Poles as part of the inferior Slav species – were subordinate to geopolitical ones. It was the same kind of reasoning that led him to sacrifice the Germans of South Tyrol for alliance with Italy. In the long run, if his plans for a continental empire succeeded, Poland would become at best a German satellite.

Unlike Weimar governments and the diplomats of the foreign ministry, Hitler was not interested in mere frontier revision. So in signing a declaration of non-aggression with Poland, the protests of traditional Prussian conservatives or of the German minority in Poland were a matter of indifference to him. The officials of the Foreign Ministry were unhappy with a non-aggression pact since that implied recognition of the frontier, something which they took seriously and had always studiously avoided. They therefore suggested instead the unusual form of a 'Declaration'. Hitler was not bothered about such niceties. Rosenberg, the Nazi party's expert on foreign policy, was also unhappy with the agreement as it conflicted with his own pet scheme for recreating an independent Ukraine from both Soviet and Polish territory but he was ignored.[37] Prussian conservatives protested to Hindenburg that Poland would not respond with concessions (as Hitler claimed), but Hindenburg did not react.[38] Nevertheless, when Hitler defended the agreement to the now all-Nazi Reichstag, the Polish envoy to Berlin, Jósef Lipski, recorded it was at first greeted with 'deep silence'.[39]

Despite the reservations in some quarters, Hitler's policy was not seriously challenged. It showed his control once he had made up his mind. Whatever their doubts, foreign ministry officials and service chiefs could see the tactical advantages of the pact in loosening the Franco-Polish alliance. For the rest Goebbels was justified in claiming to Lipski:

When the Chancellor says something, whether for the moment it is popular or not, public opinion accepts it. Everyone believes him, and everyone obeys him.[40]

As Victor Klemperer noted bitterly:

> My belief in an alteration in the political situation is increasingly
> faint. Today the peace agreement with Poland. If a Socialist or 'liber-
> alistic' government had done that! High treason, Jewish defeatism
> and the mind of the shopkeeper! Now: 'Adolf Hitler's magnificent
> new achievement.'[41]

FAILED PUTSCH IN VIENNA

Hitler's control of foreign policy in the first two years was not always
complete nor was he always successful. The most glaring failure was
his attempt to export the Nazi revolution to his Austrian homeland.[42]
He felt confident that the Nazi party in Austria could succeed in the
same way as it had in Germany. He compared the way in which
National Socialist ideas would cross the frontier to the way in which
the French revolution had spread to the whole of Europe.[43] On the
other hand, he told the cabinet in May, if they were not supported from
Germany there was a danger that six million Austrian Germans would
be lost to the nation, becoming more like the Swiss. He recognized
that formal union (*Anschluss*) with Austria would be unacceptable to
other powers, especially Italy which would oppose the expansion of
German influence south to the Alps. Hitler thought, however, that
elections in Austria would make the Nazis the largest single party,
bringing about 'Austria's internal *Gleichschaltung*, which will obviate the
need for actual Anschluss.'[44] A cheap victory in Austria would also
balance the unpopular accommodation with Poland.[45]

The Austrian Chancellor Dollfuss had already established an
authoritarian regime in March 1933 to preserve the rule of his Christian Social party and other right-wing organizations against the threat
from the Social Democrats on the left and the Nazis on the radical right.
Dollfuss proved more determined to maintain Austrian independence
than Hitler had calculated. Austrian independence was also supported
by Mussolini and, at greater distance, by France and Britain.

Hitler at first believed that Dollfuss could be brought down by
economic pressure and in May 1933 the German tourist trade to
Austria was throttled by the imposition of a prohibitive charge of 1000
marks for a visa. Hitler also encouraged the Austrian Nazis through
his appointed leader, Theodor Habicht, to destabilize the regime by
a campaign of protest and terror. Dollfuss responded by banning the
Nazi party in June, expelling Habicht (who had been appointed to the

German embassy's staff in Vienna) and appealing to Mussolini for support.

There followed months of complicated manoeuvring.[46] Mussolini wanted Dollfuss to suppress the Social Democrats and rely on the pro-Fascist *Heimwehr* (Home Defence) organization. Hitler moderated his position somewhat for fear of foreign reaction and supported negotiations for the Austrian Nazis to join Dollfuss's government. Dollfuss balanced precariously between the demands of his two powerful neighbours. On 12 February 1934 he came down on Mussolini's side and allowed the *Heimwehr* to crush the Social Democrats. Mussolini meanwhile warned Germany that he would permit neither Anschluss nor Gleichschaltung. On 17 February Italy, Britain and France issued a joint declaration in favour of the maintenance of Austrian independence and on 17 March Italy, Austria and Hungary agreed to measures of political and economic co-operation, emphasizing Italian leadership in the region.

In view of these unfavourable developments Hitler made some concessions. In an apparent volte-face, he told his senior officials that 'he was entirely disinterested in Austria, politically and economically'. He added in a revealing aside that 'politically the significance of a country was expressed exclusively by its armed forces'. Money spent rearming Austria, he went on, would be better spent in Germany, and the economic links were also not important. 'He was quite ready to write Austria off for years to come.'[47] The Austrian Nazis were told to adopt a 'new course', to stop all propaganda against the Austrian government and instead to build up their strength over the long term. Habicht complained that with these restrictions their movement might gradually disintegrate.[48]

Hitler may have been exaggerating his lack of interest in Austria to reassure his officials. In fact he maintained the economic pressure, refusing to rescind the tourist visa charge. He also allowed the 'Austrian legion' – several thousand paramilitaries – to continue to train in camps on the German side of the border. At the same time he sought a meeting with Mussolini to end Germany's isolation. When they met on 14 June 1934 in Venice without officials present and with Mussolini insisting on speaking German, they failed to understand each other. Hitler thought he had gained Mussolini's consent to the formation of a new government in Austria in which the Nazis would be included, though without bringing about *Anschluss* or even *Gleichschaltung*. Mussolini, however, thought he had made it clear that such changes must wait and that for the present he would continue to support the Dollfuss government.

The situation was transformed by the Nazis in Vienna. Intending to create a *fait accompli* which Hitler could then endorse, they launched a coup on 25 July. Austrian SS troops killed Dollfuss but failed to overthrow the regime. The Austrian army remained loyal, as did the *Heimwehr*, and the Austrian SA – which had seen its German parent butchered in the Röhm purge only weeks before on 30 June – stood aside. Hitler knew that a putsch was intended, but he may have been misled by Habicht into thinking that the Nazis would simply support an overthrow of the regime by the Austrian army.[49] In any case he did nothing to stop the plot and was caught unprepared by its failure. He had to face the humiliation of his policy ending in fiasco and the fact that German complicity in the murder of a fellow head of government was generally assumed abroad. Following the recent events of the Röhm purge, for which Hitler had taken full responsibility in the Reichstag, his regime was revealed in its true colours as a terrorist organization. Mussolini, who had to break the news of his death to Dollfuss's widow who was staying with him at the time, was furious. He let loose an Italian press campaign blaming Germany for the atrocity and local troop units were moved to the Austrian frontier as a political gesture though in military terms this was no more than a bluff.[50] Although no stranger to terrorist tactics himself, he later described Hitler as 'Dollfuss's murderer' and in a public speech in September poured scorn on 'certain doctrines taught beyond the Alps by the descendants of people who were wholly illiterate in the days when Caesar, Virgil and Augustus flourished in Rome'.[51]

Hitler was forced to accept defeat. Official denials of involvement lacked credibility. He therefore took measures to dissociate Germany from the Austrian Nazis. Habicht was dismissed, the Munich headquarters of the Austrian Nazis closed and the Austrian legion moved away from the border. Papen was sent as the German envoy to Vienna to calm the storm, a convenient way for Hitler to get rid of him.[52] The attempt to export revolution through a brother party had failed. Hitler had to accept that Austrian resistance with international backing was too strong. He had overestimated the power of the movement and had also failed to keep control over it at the vital moment. As a result he had been left at the mercy of events, isolated and discredited. Expansion, even in Austria, would have to wait for rearmament.

The damage to Germany's reputation of the Röhm purge followed by the abortive Vienna putsch was enormous. Bülow confided to the chief of the general staff, Ludwig Beck, that Germany's foreign policy position was 'hopeless'.[53] But the effects on public opinion within Germany are less clear. There seems to have been widespread support for the purge of the SA because people believed Hitler's explanation that they were planning a revolt and because of the unpopularity they had caused by their bullying, violence and general nuisance.[54] The regime's accusations against the SA leadership for debauchery and pederasty also struck home.

The army might have been expected to react, particularly since among the victims of the purge were General Schleicher and his assistant, von Bredow. However, the army was complicit in the purge, having assisted in the elimination of its rival the SA, and was therefore in no position to protest.[55] Hitler was soon able to consolidate his hold over the armed forces further. When President Hindenburg died on 2 August, the President's powers were combined with the Chancellor's. In that way Hitler became the supreme commander of the armed forces and, in addition, Blomberg ordered all service personnel to take an oath of unconditional loyalty to the führer.

Similarly in the case of the Dollfuss murder, while senior officials like Bülow knew that it was a blunder, the wider public was less affected. The Sopade, the organization of the SPD in exile in Prague, reported unrest in Catholic circles in the Rhineland. There the murder of the leader of the lay organization Catholic Action, Erich Klausener, who was killed under the cover of the Röhm purge although he had no connexion with the SA, followed by the murder of Dollfuss, had spurred underground agitation against the regime. On the other hand, it noted that many of the Catholic middle class did not want to believe that Hitler had anything to do with the events in Austria.[56] The tendency to turn a blind eye to the crimes of the Nazis and to see Hitler as standing above such 'mistakes' remained strong and enabled him to ride out his first significant foreign policy failure.

SUCCESSFUL BRINKMANSHIP

Conscription

Hitler's defeat in Austria did not make him more cautious in other areas. On the contrary, the hostile reaction abroad made him all the more determined to press on with the most important task, rearmament. He had predicted that the first few years would be the most dangerous before Germany could defend itself. Foreign reaction simply convinced him that he had been right. At first the rearmament programme remained secret but it became an open secret when Germany's budget for 1934 revealed an increase in arms spending of 90 per cent and funds for an air force which was still prohibited under the terms of the Versailles Treaty.[57] In 1935, Hitler's tactics changed. Instead of playing down German rearmament, he not only made it public but boldly exaggerated it as a deterrent to any possible intervention. He also showed considerable skill in playing the diplomatic game, exploiting the differences between Britain, France and Italy. At the same time he saw and seized the domestic political advantages of taking a strong stand in foreign policy. While the regime was losing support because of rising food prices, stagnant wages and continuing unemployment, he was able to reap the kudos of shaking off the last shackles of Versailles. That involved risk and trusting his own judgement over that of his advisers. But in each case it paid off. Hitler became increasingly confident and impatient of warnings. Perhaps he was a genius, chosen by providence to carry into effect the racial laws which, he believed, determined all history. He told a crowd in Munich after successfully reoccupying the Rhineland in March 1936: 'Neither threats nor warnings will divert me from my path. I tread with the certainty of a sleepwalker the path which providence bids me take' though he was careful to add the usual reassuring mantra: 'My goal is peace founded on the equality of nations. We are a European great power and we want to be acknowledged as a great power.'[58]

After Germany had withdrawn from the disarmament conference, the rearmament plans were revised sharply upwards in December 1933 to a peacetime army by 1938 of 21 divisions or 300 000 men, a field army of 33 divisions and a full mobilized wartime strength of 63 divisions. The intention was to create an army which could fight 'a defensive war on several fronts'. These numbers required conscription. Further, a defensive war against France could be fought only once the demilitarized Rhineland had been reoccupied by German troops. Hitler had therefore to take the risk of both measures if he was to stick to the rearmament programme.[59] His diplomacy in these years was about finding the right opportunity.

German rearmament and Hitler's plans as laid out in *Mein Kampf* were seen as a serious threat abroad and nowhere more so than in the Soviet Union and France.[60] Hitler, as we have seen, reversed the policy of the Weimar Republic – which went back to the 1922 Rapallo Treaty – of co-operation with the Soviet Union. Although initially in May 1933 he renewed the Soviet treaty, he then moved to the opposite policy of accommodation with Poland. After Hugenberg (the DNVP leader and Minister of Economics) made a crass speech at the world economic conference in London in June 1933 asserting Germany's need for living space, the Soviet Union cancelled the programme of co-operation with the German army which had grown up in the 1920s and which made it possible for Germany to experiment with new weapons and train pilots out of reach of Allied controls. Hitler was adamantly opposed to reviving relations with the Soviet Union and, supported by Neurath, rejected the pleas of the German ambassador to Moscow for a different policy.[61] Germany also refused to be drawn either into a Soviet-sponsored multilateral pact guaranteeing the Baltic states or a wider pact for Eastern Europe. Hitler disliked multilateral pacts which would commit Germany for the future and might involve new restrictions on armaments. His preferred instrument was the bilateral pact, like the non-aggression treaty with Poland, which instead created division among potential adversaries and could be revoked when it no longer served his purpose.[62]

Like the Soviet Union, French governments were increasingly concerned at developments in Germany. In April 1934 France rejected further negotiations for a disarmament agreement, because German rearmament violated the Versailles Treaty. This cut through Hitler's attempt, addressed mainly to Britain, to keep the negotiations going while Germany rearmed. The French foreign minister, Louis Barthou, worked energetically to put new life into France's alliance system with the so-called 'little entente' countries of Czechoslovakia, Romania and Yugoslavia. He also joined with the Soviet Union in proposing the multilateral pact for the Baltic states and Eastern Europe.

The combined opposition of Germany and Poland was sufficient to thwart that proposal. However, it did not stop the reorientation of Soviet policy under its Foreign Minister, Maxim Litvinov, away from Germany towards the West. In September 1934 the Soviet Union joined the League of Nations and in May 1935 it concluded mutual assistance pacts with France and Czechoslovakia. The Franco-Russian 'encirclement' of Germany, which was widely believed in Germany to have been a prime cause of the First World War, seemed to be taking shape again.

Hitler as we have seen was not surprised by these developments. Indeed he had been responsible for provoking them. He told his immediate supporters that Germany needed until 1936 to be in a position to defend itself and until then should 'keep its nerve'.[63] He was also untroubled by mutual assistance pacts that had no provision for economic sanctions or military clauses. He was essentially daring the other powers to risk intervention. After the failure of the last French attempt to coerce Germany – the occupation of the Ruhr in 1923 – that seemed unlikely. It was especially unlikely if he could continue to demonstrate overwhelming support for his actions. Foreign intervention could be effective in the long run only if it was able to bring about an alternative German government which would return to the League of Nations. But of that there was no sign.

Hitler benefited in January 1935 from a lucky legacy. Under the Treaty of Versailles the coal mines of the German Saar territory (just to the north of Alsace-Lorraine) were transferred to France as reparation for the destruction of French mines by the German armies. Political control of the province was put in the hands of a commission appointed by the League of Nations. However, that arrangement was made subject to a plebiscite after 15 years when the population would be given the choice between continuing on the same basis, union with France or union with Germany. The plebiscite, held on 13 January 1935, produced an overwhelming vote for Germany – 90.67 per cent, with 8.8 per cent voting for continuing with the commission, and 0.4 per cent for union with France. The result can be explained in terms of the unpopularity of the commission, a high rate of unemployment, a general surge of nationalism, and a degree of intimidation. Nevertheless, the elections were held outside Germany under League of Nations supervision in an area which was both overwhelmingly Catholic and with a large working class, the two main groups that had resisted the Nazis in Germany until 1933. The Catholic authorities supported the return to Germany (as a defence against 'Bolshevism') but the SPD leadership did not, using the slogan 'Beat Hitler in the Saar'. But at least two-thirds of the former SPD and KPD voters chose union with the Third Reich.[64]

So long as the Saar remained under League control, Hitler had been content to maintain a discreet silence on German rearmament. The disarmament conference in Geneva had also decided in November 1934 to await the decision over the Saar before resuming its attempts to reach an international agreement. With the Saar's safe return which occurred formally at the beginning of March 1935 – and buoyed up by public enthusiasm at the event – Hitler moved rapidly to pre-empt any new attempt to impose limits on Germany by boldly declaring Germany's military strength to the world. On 10 March, Göring made public the existence of the German air force, of which he was commander-in-chief, claiming for good measure that they had 1500 planes whereas in fact there were only 800.[65] Hitler followed on 16 March by announcing the introduction of conscription and setting the size of the peacetime army at 36 divisions (550 000 men).

The way he took the decision showed his increasing self-confidence. The army chiefs had been considering what strength they should demand in the event of new attempts to reach an international agreement. Before Hitler's announcement, the chief of the general staff Beck and the commander-in-chief of the army Fritsch concluded that the previous plan for a 21 division peacetime army was not adequate. Fritsch stipulated 'thirty to thirty-six divisions' as the goal – a goal which later, in July 1935, they planned to achieve by 1 October 1939.[66] Hitler having decided to make a public announcement on the pretext of a decision by the French National Assembly to increase military service from one to two years, intended to go ahead without even consulting Blomberg, Fritsch or Neurath for fear of a leak. He summoned the military representative on his personal staff Colonel Hossbach to Munich, took the figure of 36 divisions from him and proposed to make the announcement without further ado.[67] Hossbach, who did not want to take the responsibility himself, managed to persuade Hitler to consult Blomberg, Fritsch and others, and he returned to Berlin for a meeting with them on 15 March. Blomberg was appalled at the risk of foreign intervention and made no secret of his feelings, telling Ribbentrop – who simply echoed Hitler's views – that he was talking 'foolish nonsense'. However, by the following day both Blomberg and Fritsch were prepared to go along with the decision, leaving the foreign policy consequences to Hitler's judgement. Neurath seems to have been less concerned, though he was critical of Hitler's liking for the sudden surprise.[68]

Not for the last time, the tactic of taking the initiative and creating a *fait accompli* worked for Hitler. Britain, France and Italy lodged protests but the British government immediately showed signs of weakening. Hitler had himself called off a visit by the British Foreign Minister, Sir John Simon, and Anthony Eden (then Lord Privy Seal but in practice a junior minister in the Foreign Office) on 7 March by pleading a cold, in reaction against a British Government 'White Paper' which was critical of German rearmament. On 18 March Britain protested at the announcement of conscription but went on to enquire whether the German government would still be interested in the visit. Hitler was only too delighted to encourage division among his opponents. Simon and Eden were received in Berlin on 25–26 March and shown every consideration. Hitler conducted the negotiations confidently. He impressed the veteran German interpreter Paul Schmidt, who was working with Hitler for the first time, with his 'skill and intelligence...as if for years he had done nothing else but conduct such negotiations'.[69] Eden did not care for Hitler's performance but he too recorded in his memoirs that the Chancellor conducted the discussions well 'without hesitation and without notes, as befitted the man who knew where he wanted to go'.[70]

Hitler's tactics were to convince his British visitors that he represented German public opinion, that he had no expansionist aims (including against Austria) and that he recognized that a war would be disastrous, but that as German Chancellor he could do no less than claim equality of rights with other nations.[71] 'If any doubts were to arise among the [German] people about his determination on this point it would be the end of him.' He argued that Germany could not join in international agreements which did not give equality because that would simply be storing up trouble for the future. Multilateral pacts like the proposed pact for Eastern Europe would involve Germany in unpredictable obligations and also overlooked the fact that Russia was the greatest danger to peace. He also hinted at the possibility of 'special relations of friendship between England and Germany' in the future, suggesting Britain might help to restore German colonies and that Britain might itself require help in defending its colonial possessions. He repeated an offer already made through the British ambassador to restrict the size of the German navy in future to 35 per cent of the British navy. More threateningly, when pressed on the size of the German air force, he claimed that it had already reached parity with Britain.

Hitler's arguments did not convince the British ministers. However, the interpreter Schmidt reflected on the fact that had any previous German Chancellor made the kind of demands which Hitler now presented as a matter of course, 'the heavens would have fallen'. He could not suppress the thought that Hitler had got further by creating a *fait accompli* than would have been possible by negotiations.[72]

Hitler's claim in his talks with Simon and Eden that he was 'only a representative of the will of the people' was overstated. Public reaction to the announcement of conscription was in fact divided. The reports of the SPD organization in exile from various parts of the Reich showed a mixture of elation and admiration for Hitler's audacity but also fear of foreign reaction and depression at the prospect of another war.[73] From southern Bavaria people were reported as saying that Hitler had already achieved what Weimar governments had failed to get in 14 years, while others feared that in the event of a new war Germany would be razed to the ground, though some young people assumed that Germany was invincible. A report from Munich also suggested mixed reactions. Hitler's announcement of conscription was given an enthusiastic reception in Munich on 17 March: 'One can force people to sing but one cannot force them to sing with such joy.' But eight days later the mood had changed and fear of war was common especially among older people. However, trust in Hitler's 'political talent and honest intentions is growing all the time…He is loved by many.' Reports from Berlin suggested mainly scepticism and concern among the working class, despite some enthusiasm among the young: 'The great mass of the population fears war.' Reports from Silesia and south-west Germany suggested similarly divided opinions. Even allowing for a bias towards Social Democratic opponents of the regime, these reports show that fear of war and of the consequences of Hitler's actions, if not his intentions, remained a limit on popular support for the regime.[74] However, so long as he continued to get away with it, he was able to rally opinion behind him. As Klemperer noted:

Hitler has proclaimed compulsory military service, the protests of the foreign powers are weak-kneed and they swallow the *fait accompli*. Result: Hitler's regime is more stable than ever.[75]

In fact the risks which Hitler took with the announcement of German rearmament were not negligible and the regime was not as certain of the outcome as it liked to pretend. Hitler admitted to Rosenberg that he had not slept for 10 days before taking the decision.[76] General Fritsch described the news as exploding 'like a bomb' and Germany's ambassadors in Italy and Britain warned of serious consequences.[77] The heads of government and foreign ministers of Italy, France and Britain, meeting in Stresa on Lake Maggiore from 11–14 April, agreed to oppose 'by all appropriate measures any unilateral cancellation of treaties' and reaffirmed their commitments to the independence of Austria and the Locarno treaties. Locarno was particularly important since under its terms Germany had accepted the demilitarized status of the Rhineland and Britain and Italy were guarantors of the settlement. It was now widely expected that the reoccupation of the Rhineland would be high on Hitler's agenda. The League of Nations council also condemned the German action unanimously in a special session and a committee was established to consider possible economic sanctions. France and Italy started staff talks for joint military action in the event of German intervention in Austria. And the change in Soviet foreign policy towards Germany, already mentioned, led to the conclusion of the Franco-Soviet mutual assistance pact on 2 May and the Soviet–Czech pact on 16 May.

The mood around Hitler can be sensed in Goebbels' diary.[78] On 22 March, he was scornful of the French and Italian protests: 'Let them protest, we know from experience what protests achieve....Let them grumble while we arm....He [Hitler who was expecting the visit from Simon and Eden] is quite calm.' On 15 April commenting on the declaration of the Stresa conference, the tone was less certain: 'The old story. Condemnation of Germany's breach of the treaty. That does not matter, so long as they don't attack us...Just keep our nerve!' On 17 April his concern is more evident:

In Geneva [the League of Nations council meeting] they have not yet been able to agree. But Paris is well on the way to getting its military alliances signed and sealed. One should not underestimate the dangers. But that means that our only salvation lies in power. So arm, and grin and bear it. O Lord let us survive this summer. The way to our freedom goes through crises and dangers. But it must be trodden courageously.[79]

On 19 April after the unanimous decision of the League council against Germany, he was again defiant: 'The world is against us. But we don't need to let grey hairs grow for that reason. We haven't yet seen the end of the matter.' But, after a telephone call from Hitler, he noted: 'He is still undecided.'

The apparently united front of the other powers against Germany did not last long.[80] Already before Stresa, Mussolini was preparing his expedition against Abyssinia which was to alienate Britain and divide

Britain from France. The British government did not believe that Germany could be prevented from rearming and wanted to influence that process by negotiation rather than to build up an alliance against Germany. Simon and Eden thought that the division of Europe into two camps had helped to cause the First World War and they hoped to avoid that happening by drawing Germany back into a system of 'collective security' under the League of Nations. For that reason Britain also had reservations about the Soviet pacts with France and Czechoslovakia which were seen as contributing to just such a division. These pacts were in any case weak instruments, making no provision for military preparations against Germany. Neither France nor the Soviet Union thought that they could depend on them and both kept open the door to negotiations with Germany. For its part, Czechoslovakia had limited its pact with the Soviet Union by the proviso that it would fight only if France did. So beneath the facade of unity against Germany there were multiple cracks.

Hitler did his best to encourage these divisions with a major speech to the Reichstag on 21 May 1935 in which he again claimed to be carrying out the mandate of the German people who, he asserted, had elected him by 38 million votes. He justified German rearmament by the failure of other powers to disarm and re-emphasized his commitment to peace. He repeated a declaration he had made after the return of the Saar that Germany would make no further territorial demands on France and reassured Italy that Germany would not interfere in the internal affairs of Austria. He also promised to fulfil the obligations of the Locarno treaty, including the demilitarized status of the Rhineland, so long as the other parties to that treaty also stood by it – a qualification which was given added point by a passage earlier in the speech where he questioned whether the Franco-Soviet pact was consistent with Locarno.[81]

Ribbentrop and the Anglo-German naval agreement

The first open break in the Stresa front came with the signing of the Anglo-German naval agreement on 18 June 1935. This was a triumph for Hitler. It weakened the Stresa front, causing bitterness in France and resentment in Italy, where Britain was seen to have put its national interest before the principle of collective security. It was also for Hitler the first step to the alliance with Britain on which his hopes for the future rested. He is reported to have called it 'the happiest day of his life'.[82] The agreement was further a triumph for Ribbentrop, who negotiated it on Hitler's authority, and a defeat for the Foreign Ministry which had assumed that the British government would reject German proposals.[83] It therefore had an importance much wider than its actual terms.

Hitler's attraction to Ribbentrop throws an interesting light on his foreign policy. Although Hitler knew he needed the expertise of the Foreign Ministry, he was not content with its traditional outlook and methods. He wanted an independent representative who would mirror his views and be directly under his control. Rosenberg, the party's expert on foreign affairs, was too dogmatic and lacked the social skills and knowledge of foreign languages to play this part.[84] Ribbentrop fitted the bill perfectly. He was extremely ambitious, had lived abroad – including four years in Canada – and spoke French and English fluently. He had married into a wealthy family – the Henkel champagne and wine firm – and he was used to the society of the rich and influential.[85] He had no standing in the Nazi party but he had made himself useful to Hitler during the political intrigues of 1932–3 which led to Hitler's appointment as chancellor, and Hitler had been a frequent guest at the Ribbentrops' villa in the fashionable Berlin suburb of Dahlem. He had three things Hitler needed in a personal representative for foreign policy: total dependence on the führer, the brash self-confidence of the arriviste, and the social contacts acquired through his business connections.

Ribbentrop was disappointed not to be given a major position in 1933.[86] Neurath contemptuously dismissed his request to be appointed State Secretary in the Foreign Ministry and Ribbentrop had to be content with cultivating contacts abroad on his own initiative. He met the French Premier, Edouard Daladier, and the British Prime Minister, Ramsay Macdonald, and other British ministers including Baldwin and Simon, with no result other than to boost his reputation with Hitler. In February 1934 Neurath consented to his having the support of German embassies abroad, partly to keep an eye on him, and in April after Ribbentrop had complained to Hitler about his lack of status he was appointed special commissioner for disarmament questions. Ribbentrop proceeded to conduct independent missions which angered Neurath and irritated foreign governments but maintained his standing with Hitler. In August 1934 with Hitler's approval Ribbentrop established his own office, the Büro Ribbentrop, opposite the

Foreign Ministry and later in the year acquired a party position under the führer's deputy, Rudolf Hess.[87] Further trips to England followed, as a result of which Neurath complained to Hitler that Ribbentrop had been 'a complete disaster' but Neurath's anger seems only to have confirmed Hitler in his high opinion of Ribbentrop.[88] Ribbentrop was present together with Neurath at Hitler's discussions with Simon and Eden in March 1935, rather than the State Secretary Bülow. Ribbentrop then again wanted to be made State Secretary himself and Neurath prevented it only by threatening Hitler with his resignation. Hitler, however, found other ways to get what he wanted. He decided to appoint Ribbentrop to lead the German delegation to London for the naval talks and on 1 June he appointed him to the post of Ambassador Extraordinary and Plenipotentiary on Special Mission.

The background to the naval talks was that the existing agreements between the major naval powers, established after the war at the Washington Conference of 1921–22 and renewed at the London conference of 1930, were due to expire in 1936.[89] Preparatory discussions had already revealed that new agreements would be difficult to reach. Japan had announced its decision to withdraw from the existing system and had doubled its naval expenditure between 1930 and 1935. That was naturally a matter of concern to the British admiralty which was correspondingly anxious to avoid a repeat of the naval race with Germany before the First World War. During his meeting with Hitler in March 1935 Simon suggested that Britain and Germany should hold preparatory discussions, as had already taken place with other powers prior to the holding of a general conference. Hitler showed no interest in a general conference but made the offer to restrict the German navy to 35 per cent of the British fleet.

When the talks began in London on 4 June Ribbentrop, with a disregard for normal diplomatic courtesy which was to become legendary, demanded the immediate acceptance of the 35 per cent figure as a condition of further negotiations.[90] Simon who had told Hitler at their meeting in March that the ratio was too high, and would set off another naval race as France and Italy reacted to the German programme, was understandably put out at these tactics. In effect, Britain was being asked to agree to a navy three times the size of that allowed Germany under the Versailles Treaty without the consent of the other powers affected. Schmidt, acting again as interpreter, thought that Ribbentrop had bungled and started to wonder what the weather would be like on their return flight to Berlin.[91] Under pressure from the Admiralty, however, to reach an agreement with Germany while it was still on offer, the ratio of 35 per cent was accepted by British ministers. In subsequent negotiations the Germans also won the right to build a higher ratio of submarines provided that the fleet as a whole remained within the 35 per cent limit.

The results were eminently satisfactory from the German point of view. Although the commander-in-chief of the navy, Admiral Erich Raeder, would have liked a 50 per cent ratio, in fact the limit imposed no restriction on German naval rearmament up to the outbreak of war since Germany would not have been able to build up its fleet more rapidly in any case.[92] In return Britain gained only a paper agreement for the longer term which itself depended on Hitler's good faith, a very shaky strategic gain. And, as we have seen, the cost in diplomatic terms was to weaken the front against Germany's unilateral rearmament which had been formed at Stresa. On his return, Ribbentrop was not only congratulated by Hitler but also recognized by other Nazi leaders for the first time as a significant force.[93] However, in one respect the success was misleading. No British government would agree to become Hitler's ally in a future sharing of the world. In his speech to the Reichstag on 21 May 1935 he had given a clear indication that he still thought in these terms, recognizing 'the overpowering vital importance, and therewith the justification, of a dominating protection for the British Empire on the sea, precisely as we are resolved to do all that is necessary for the protection of our continental existence and freedom.'[94] In so far as Hitler thought that the naval agreement was a first step towards persuading Britain to see its future in the same way, he deceived himself.

Reoccupation of the Rhineland

Having recovered the Saar and declared that it would no longer observe the Versailles restrictions on rearmament, it was only a matter of time before Germany would challenge the last great limitation on its power – the demilitarization of the Rhineland. The military leadership regarded the reoccupation of the Rhineland as necessary for defence against France, for the protection of the industrial basin of the Ruhr, including key arms factories, and because conscription would then also apply to the large population of the Rhineland.[95] Neurath also regarded the reoccupation as a legitimate and necessary goal.[96] The

Foreign Ministry started to prepare the way by questioning whether the Franco-Soviet pact was consistent with the Locarno treaty and, in his speech to the Reichstag on 21 May 1935, Hitler claimed that the pact had introduced 'an element of legal insecurity' into the Locarno treaty.[97] The issues here were both political and technical. The German government argued that by allying itself with the Soviet Union, France had changed the structure of European politics on which the Locarno treaty had been based. Secondly it argued that under the terms of the pact France would itself decide whether to go to war with Germany in the event of a Soviet-German war, whereas under Locarno its decision was subject to League procedures. Both these arguments were rejected by France and Britain, though the British government was careful to avoid committing itself any further than Locarno, as it did not want to be dragged into war by French commitments to the Soviet Union.[98]

Hitler probably never expected the reoccupation of the Rhineland to be achieved by negotiation but he also knew that another sudden coup would be risky, particularly as the German army was not yet strong enough to resist French attack. By his own account until February 1936 he had always considered 'the spring of 1937 as the right moment'.[99] Nevertheless he was watchful for any opportunity. In August 1935 he speculated to Goebbels on the likelihood of a coming war in a few years between Britain and Italy over Abyssinia and between Japan and the Soviet Union in the Far East providing Germany with 'its great historic hour' for continental expansion, while the other powers were committed elsewhere.[100]

The Italian invasion of Abyssinia in October 1935 did indeed bring a change in the international situation, destroying the Stresa front and making Italy turn to Germany for support against Britain and France. Despite his anger at Mussolini's behaviour over Austria in 1934, Hitler did not want to see Italy humiliated by the democracies. In the summer of 1935, when war was already threatening, he had authorized arms shipments to Abyssinia presumably hoping that by strengthening its resistance it would help to keep Italy engaged in Africa and divert it from Austria. After the Italian invasion, however, he adopted a policy of neutrality, refusing to take part in League sanctions and even considered mediating to save Italy from defeat.[101] After an Anglo-French attempt at a settlement at the expense of Abyssinia (the Hoare–Laval plan) had failed because of public reaction, Mussolini's need for German support became even greater. On 6 January 1936 he told the German ambassador, Ulrich von Hassell, that he would have no objection if Austria were to become a 'German satellite' and that he regarded Stresa as 'dead'.[102] Hitler was aware that Mussolini might simply be trying to draw Germany into conflict with Britain and France to take the pressure off Italy and he reacted cautiously. Nevertheless he told Hassell and Neurath that given Germany's own isolation it could not afford to see Fascist Italy collapse as that would enable the other powers to concentrate against Germany.[103] Hitler was already thinking of the Rhineland. On 20 January he told Goebbels that he was ready to settle the issue of the Rhineland zone 'suddenly all at once. But not yet so as not to give the other powers the opportunity to turn away from the Abyssinian conflict.'[104]

By 12 February, however, Hitler had changed his mind about timing and started to think of reoccupation in the immediate future. Unlike the decision to announce German rearmament he consulted his senior advisers first.[105] Blomberg and Fritsch warned that Germany must not become involved in a war with France as a result of the operation. Göring was reported to be very nervous of the consequences.[106] Neurath felt that Hitler was being impetuous but he kept his objections to himself, perhaps for fear of Ribbentrop gaining further favour with Hitler at his expense, and perhaps because he had information that France would not take military action.[107] Ribbentrop as before was anxious only to ingratiate himself by adopting Hitler's views as his own.

On 14 February Hitler explained some of his thinking to Hassell. He argued that reoccupation was in military terms 'an absolute necessity' and he wondered 'whether the psychological moment for it had not arrived *now*'.[108] The pretext would be the ratification of the Franco-Soviet pact which had been put to the French chamber of deputies. Hitler said he did not expect Russia which wanted peace in the west, Britain which was in a bad military state and had other problems, or France which was distracted by internal politics, to take military action. Economic sanctions might be applied but they were unpopular with lesser powers and therefore, he implied, also not to be feared. Postponement of the issue to 1937, as he had originally intended, had the disadvantage that increases in German military strength might be offset by rearmament by other powers. In a second meeting with Hassell, Neurath and Ribbentrop on 19 February, Hitler sounded more determined. He countered Hassell's view that there was no hurry, saying that there was a danger that the demilitarized zone 'would gradually become a sort of inviolable institution' and that given the fact that both Fascist Italy and Germany were 'surrounded by democracies tainted by Bolshevism, passivity was, in the long run, no policy. Attack in this case too was the better strategy (lively assent from Ribbentrop).'[109] Hassell then sounded out Mussolini as to how Italy would react and received the reply he hoped for, namely that Italy would not support France and Britain against Germany.[110] Hitler, however, still hesitated and his difficulty in taking the final decision can be followed in Goebbels' diary. On 27 February Hitler still thought it 'somewhat too early'. The following day he was 'wrestling' with the decision and Goebbels advised waiting until the Franco-Soviet pact had completed its passage through the French senate but then 'seizing the opportunity with both hands'. On 29 February there was still no decision but on 1 March Hitler is 'firmly decided. His face radiates calm and firmness.'[111]

Hitler's hesitation was about fear of the reaction by France and Britain. He had earlier decided to confuse the opposition by combining reoccupation with an offer to restore the demilitarized zone provided it also applied to the French side of the frontier (thus undermining the French fortifications of the Maginot line), and new pacts of non-aggression with France, Belgium and Holland, an air pact and the revival of the four power pact proposed by Mussolini in 1933. In the last few days before the decision he decided to add an eye-catching offer to return to the League of Nations which he obviously felt would serve to forestall any rapid decision to impose League sanctions and could then be forgotten. The only disadvantage was to annoy Mussolini who was at the same time threatening to leave the League if it imposed oil sanctions against Italy.[112]

On 2 March Hitler communicated his decision to Göring, Blomberg, Fritsch, Raeder and Ribbentrop setting the date as the following Saturday 7 March, which would have the advantage of making a reaction unlikely before the weekend was over. The reoccupation was to be accompanied by a meeting of the Reichstag and new elections to capitalize on the foreign policy success. Secrecy was to be maintained until the occupation happened 'with lightning speed'. The Reichstag was to be told only that it was being invited to a 'beer evening'. Even so the date was still not finally fixed on 3 March since Hitler feared that a solution to the Abyssinian problem might be reached at the League, leaving it free to turn on Germany. Goebbels noted that Hitler was 'very serious and on tenterhooks'.[113] On 4 March the decision was to go ahead despite continuing uncertainty about the League. Hitler worked on his speech to the Reichstag and Goebbels made preparations for the election campaign. The next day Hitler was still 'serious' and predicted that 'France will react in some way'. Goebbels complained that alarmists now appeared on all sides – particularly from the Foreign Ministry – warning about the consequences.[114] According to Hossbach, Hitler and Ribbentrop even temporarily considered halting the operation but then the anxiety passed.[115]

It was obviously a nail-biting ordeal for all involved and Hitler had certainly not felt 'the certainty of a sleepwalker' – in fact, he admitted later that the 48 hours after the reoccupation of the Rhineland had been 'the most exciting of his life'.[116] However, the risk was taken and it paid off. To minimize the danger of foreign reaction most of the occupying force of 30 000 men remained on the right bank of the Rhine with only three battalions (3000) going further to occupy cities on the French and Belgian frontier. In the event of a French military reaction these battalions were to withdraw but only to a defensive position which would protect the right bank of the Rhine. There the enemy was to be resisted even though it was known that the French could mobilize vastly superior forces and, had they done so, Hitler knew that the German army would have been driven out in shame and disgrace.[117]

Anxiety remained in the days that followed. Blomberg lost his nerve when the three military attachés in London sent a joint warning on 9 March and he pressed for the forward battalions to withdraw behind the Rhine.[118] Hitler and Neurath however remained firm and the crisis passed, with damage only to Blomberg's reputation with Hitler. There was in fact little or no danger of military intervention. British public opinion would not have accepted war to prevent Germany reoccupying the Rhineland and France would not act without Britain. The League council met to condemn the German action and Goebbels commented happily that he 'couldn't care less'.[119] Hitler was able to bask in his success.

Like the withdrawal from the League and the declaration of German rearmament, Hitler turned this success into a domestic political triumph. The regime badly needed a popular boost since it had been suffering in public esteem from the effects of both economic shortages and the activities of the more radical elements in the party. The economic problems were a result mainly of the priority given to rearmament which led to scarce foreign currency being allocated to imports of raw materials instead of food, driving up food prices and leading to shortages. On the other hand, cutting back on the rearmament programme threatened to lead to increases in unemployment. The more radical elements in the party had antagonized popular opinion by attacks on the churches in both devout Protestant and Catholic areas. By the winter of 1935–6 there was a real crisis building up and Hitler was forced to allow foreign currency to be diverted from rearmament to food imports to avoid having to introduce rationing.[120]

The desire to distract attention from domestic problems may have influenced Hitler's decision to launch the Rhineland coup. Certainly Neurath and Hassell thought this was the reason that he was not prepared to wait for a diplomatic solution.[121] Hitler mentioned his domestic political motives to Hassell saying he wanted to explain his action 'both to foreign countries and to his own nation'. But his main arguments, not only to the diplomats but also to Goebbels, were in terms of the international situation. He did not know how long the opportunity created by the Italian invasion of Abyssinia and the consequent rift in the Stresa front would continue. He was naturally impatient, not least of the caution of the Foreign Ministry and the military leadership. Hassell probably got closest to the truth when he referred to Hitler feeling 'an irresistible urge to stop being passive'.[122]

Nevertheless once the decision was taken, with his acute political antennae he exploited it for all it was worth. In his speech to the Reichstag on 7 March, which was broadcast simultaneously to the nation, Hitler as usual made Versailles and Bolshevism the enemies.[123] It is noticeable that he linked Versailles to the economic problems of Germany, complaining of Germany's land shortage compared to other countries especially Russia, and saying that Germany could not be held together if it was 'treated permanently as the world's slave'. The announcement of the reoccupation which followed in the closing stages of the speech was greeted with hysterical applause by the wholly Nazi audience. In the final paragraphs Hitler appealed for support, claiming that the successes of the last three years had been made possible by the strength he derived from being 'inseparably united with my people as man and führer', a peroration which Goebbels described as 'moving to tears'.[124] The Reichstag was dissolved and new elections, asking for approval for 'the policy of recovering national honour and sovereignty', set for 29 March.

The election campaign followed in a mood of euphoria with as Goebbels said 'an election theme no-one could have anticipated'.[125] There is no doubt that the reoccupation of the Rhineland appealed to the patriotic instincts of the great majority and acted to rally support for the regime.[126] Cheering crowds and telegrams of congratulation were the order of the day. The Catholic archbishop of Cologne welcomed the return of the army to the Rhineland and a leading Protestant churchman thanked Hitler specifically for 'acting with the firm decisiveness which came from his responsibility before God'.[127] Hitler's speeches were replete with quasi-religious phrases – urging people to believe in him and to be the source of 'my strength and my faith', reminding people that the 'Almighty' promised to help those who helped themselves and claiming that 'providence' had chosen him to carry out the reoccupation.[128] On hearing the results with a 98.9 per cent yes votes Goebbels wrote in his diary ecstatically

> The nation has arisen. The führer has united the nation. We did not hope for that in our wildest dreams. We are all dazed. The führer is quiet and silent. He just puts his hands on my shoulders. His eyes are moist.... The whole of Germany is a sea of joy.... Now the führer has a mandate towards the outside world.[129]

This entry conveys the curious atmosphere in Hitler's immediate circle where the sense of communion with the people was still seen as the ultimate source of authority despite the facts of dictatorship. The results were taken at face value even though Hitler and Goebbels knew perfectly well that the election had been subject to a monopoly of propaganda and to intimidation and actual manipulation to improve the statistics – there was no space to record a 'no' vote and spoilt ballots were counted as 'yes' votes.[130]

There was another side to the picture. The quite detailed reports of the SPD organization in exile from various parts of Germany, even allowing for some bias, show opinion was again divided.[131] Fear of war – in extreme cases even psychosis – was a recurrent theme, particularly given the preparations everywhere to be seen not simply in the build-up of the armed forces but in classes on air defence and gas warfare. However, young people and convinced Nazis and in some areas even sections of the working class were reported to be unworried. Some businessmen were concerned about the effects of possible economic sanctions but industrialists in the Ruhr were reported as realizing that the whole economy depended on preparations for war and many saw a victorious war as the only alternative to collapse. Another report, however, spoke of fear that the whole industrial district would be reduced to dust and ashes if war broke out. These fears vied with feelings of admiration for Hitler's daring and his ability to pull off yet another coup. In Catholic areas too there was still the feeling that Hitler was a lesser evil than the Communists. It was telling that opponents of the regime felt that change could now be brought about only if foreign countries stood up to Hitler – the system was obviously felt to be too well-established for change to come from within. Goebbels' propaganda (likened in one report to an enormous injection of opium) and a general willingness to support the government on the Rhineland issue were seen as having turned opinion in Hitler's favour. The election results on the other hand were widely regarded with contempt – the figures were regarded as absurdly exaggerated by manipulation, with even some Nazis complaining that the results were devalued by such methods.

These reports suggest that the reoccupation of the Rhineland had paid off in terms of domestic politics but that the victory was not as complete as it seemed. Hitler had once again made foreign policy serve domestic politics and domestic politics reinforce foreign policy. He saw himself as the saviour of the nation and felt he had been renewed in his mystical mandate to lead. Public opinion rallied to the condemnation of Versailles and Bolshevism, and the argument that the economic difficulties came from the peace treaty had some success. There was also a feeling that Hitler's method of springing surprises was justified after years of negotiation under the governments of the Weimar Republic had apparently achieved little. But underlying contradictions remained. It would be increasingly difficult to gain foreign policy success with the slogan of equality and peace. The basic problems of the German economy – the competition between 'guns and butter' – remained unsolved. And with each coup, Hitler's promise to be a man of peace lost some of its credibility. His successes in his first three years of office were undeniable, and they were successes for his policy rather than that of his officials. But as his programme unfolded, the risks of war were bound to increase.

5 Preparing for War: From Rhineland Occupation to *Anschluss*

The two years from the occupation of the Rhineland in March 1936 to *Anschluss* with Austria in March 1938 saw the Third Reich move from defence to offence. Having removed the sanctions imposed by Versailles, the next decision was whether to go for expansion or stability. It was a moment of truth. Was Hitler serious about the conquest of an empire with all the risks involved? Or would he settle for a process of negotiation to achieve gradually those limited gains which could be justified by self-determination – Austria, revision of the Polish frontier, the acquisition of the mainly German Sudetenland region of Czechoslovakia – and perhaps some colonies?

Hitler later referred to 1937 as 'the year of awareness' (*Erkenntnis*).[1] A decision had to be made between maintaining the pace of rearmament which would eventually require a grab for new resources of raw materials and labour, or slowing rearmament down to boost exports to pay for imports through the normal process of trade. And in foreign policy a decision had increasingly to be made between siding with Italy or Britain, since their interests clashed in the Mediterranean. Hitler reluctantly began to accept that Britain did not see its role in the way he did. It was also a time of parting of the ways between the regime and some of its most important professional advisers: Schacht lost power to Göring in control of the economy from 1936 and eventually resigned as Minister of Economics in November 1937. Neurath, Blomberg and Fritsch were forced out in February 1938, followed by Beck who resigned in July. Ribbentrop replaced Neurath and Hitler himself took over Blomberg's position as Minister of Defence. Those who wanted to know could see that the regime was now heading for a European war.

This is also a period over which interpretations divide. The same evidence can be explained in different ways. Was the priority of

rearmament and expansion a result of Hitler's decision, as 'intentionalists' claim? Or was the choice already determined by the momentum
of the regime which made his decision inevitable, as 'structuralists'
argue? Did Hitler suffer from indecision and an inability to focus on
complex matters like the economics of rearmament? What was the
role of other Nazi leaders, particularly Göring and Ribbentrop? And
did mere chance play a significant part, for instance the unintended
consequences of Blomberg's marriage to a former model for porno-
graphic photographs? In this chapter an attempt will be made to review
the evidence in the light of these different approaches and to strike a
balance between them.

A brief outline of the main events is necessary to provide the
context for the interpretations. In July 1936 a new conflict opened in
Europe with the Spanish Civil War. Germany and Italy both sided
with the rebel forces of General Franco against the Popular Front
government in order to prevent, as they saw it, a Communist victory
in Spain. After its conquest of Abyssinia which was completed by
May 1936, Italy's involvement in Spain caused renewed antagonism
with Britain and France. That in turn meant that Italy continued to
look to Germany for support. In October 1936 Hitler offered the
Italian foreign minister (who was also Mussolini's son-in-law), Galeazzo
Ciano, a free hand in the Mediterranean provided Germany was given
a free hand in the east and in November Mussolini referred publicly
to the Berlin–Rome 'axis'. Inevitably Italy's greater dependence on
Germany meant a weakening in its support for Austria. In July 1936,
Mussolini had already encouraged Austria to reach an agreement with
Germany which maintained Austria's formal independence but aligned
it more closely with Germany. Representatives of parties in favour of
union with Germany were allowed into the Austrian government and
economic links between the two states were strengthened. It looked
as though there would be a gradual *Gleichschaltung* or parallel development of the two states, though in fact *Anschluss* came about in a hastily
improvised fashion in March 1938.

Success in Germany's relations with Italy was matched by failure
with Britain. In August 1936 Ribbentrop was appointed ambassador
to London with Hitler's instruction (as recalled later by Frau von
Ribbentrop) to 'bring me the English alliance'.[2] He soon found that
anti-Communism was not a sufficient basis on which to build the kind
of alliance Hitler wanted. Instead Ribbentrop turned to Japan with
whom he negotiated the so-called anti-Comintern (i.e. Communist

International) pact in November 1936 which Italy joined a year later. The pact was intended to increase the pressure on the Soviet Union, though Hitler vetoed the formal military alliance which Japan wanted and instead the signatories were bound only to remain neutral in the event of a Soviet attack on any of them. The anti-Communist rhetoric was also intended to appeal to Britain. At the same time, in Ribbentrop's mind, the alignment of Germany with Italy and Japan – which could threaten the British empire from the Mediterranean and in the Far East – was a warning to Britain that Germany and its allies could, if necessary, turn against the empire.[3] In 1937 Hitler also allowed a public campaign for the return of German colonies, another way of putting pressure on Britain.[4]

HITLER'S INTENTIONS

There is no lack of material on Hitler's intentions. The Goebbels' diaries make frequent references to conversations where Hitler commented on international developments and the opportunities these created for Germany. Three themes stand out for the period from 1936 to the beginning of 1938: the hostility between Italy and Britain over Abyssinia and Spain, and the weakness of British policy; Japanese expansion in China and the threat it posed to the Soviet Union; and the way in which Germany could exploit these developments to seize a continental empire with the first steps being Austria and Czechoslovakia.

On 8 June 1936 Hitler discussed foreign policy with Goebbels, Papen and Ribbentrop. Goebbels recorded:

> Führer sees conflict coming in the Far East. And Japan will thrash Russia. And this colossus will start to totter. And then our great goal is there. Then we must secure land for a 100 years. Let us hope that we are ready then and that the führer is still alive. So that action will be taken.[5]

On 20 October, Hitler told Goebbels of his intention to take sides publicly with Japan, Italy and the Franco regime in Spain. He would sign the anti-Comintern pact with Japan, negotiated by Ribbentrop, and:

That will change the whole position when it is published in three weeks. Our corn is beginning to ripen. He [Hitler] will then summon the Reichstag, recognize Manchukuo [the Japanese puppet regime in Manchuria] and Abyssinia [i.e. Italy's conquest], also the Spanish National Government [i.e. Franco's regime in Spain]. Create clear fronts. Air in the stifling atmosphere.[6]

There are frequent references to Hitler's increasing doubts about Britain (whose support for a policy of non-intervention during the Spanish Civil War was regarded as weak and hypocritical) and, conversely, increasing respect for Italy which was successfully using force in defiance of the League of Nations. On 13 November, for instance, Goebbels recorded after meeting Hitler the previous day that the Italian Foreign Minister Ciano had made a good impression, adding:

Italy is cleverly led. England on the other hand very badly. In the long term even a global power cannot survive that....The Führer complains very much about England. It cannot make up its mind. Its leadership has no instinct.[7]

And on 12 July 1937 similarly:

The führer discusses England's position in the world. Sees it as very weakened. The Empire is at a standstill if not in decline. England cannot attack Italy.[8]

Over lunch on 27 January 1937, after Blomberg had given a three-hour presentation of a defence ministry study of war between Germany together with 'its fascist allies' against Russia, Czechoslovakia and Lithuania, Hitler thought aloud about the future:

[H]e explains rearmament, lays out Russia's strength, considers our possibilities, describes England's bad political leadership but warns against drawing the conclusion that the English people are of poor quality, describes also Italy's more heroic enthusiasm, hopes still to have six years time but will not let a very favourable opportunity slip if one arises. Russia is driving violently towards world revolution. It knows that every year strengthens our power. But its hysterical shouting is also sending us allies again. For example the greatest part of the Little Entente. Romania, Yugoslavia and more and more Poland too. France would probably like to be reconciled as well, but that can only come finally when we are strong enough.[9]

On 22 February, Hitler was in an expansive mood, discussing with Goebbels for two hours policy towards the churches, the nature of Christianity and Judaism, and Marxism. Interspersed was the comment:

> The führer describes his great work as: 'I have taught the world to distinguish method from purpose again.' Purpose is the life of the nation. All the rest is method. He expects in 5–6 years a great world conflict. In 15 years he will have liquidated the peace of Westphalia. He develops magnificent prospects for the future. Germany will either be victorious in a coming conflict or not survive.[10]

On 14 March, Hitler talked to Goebbels until deep into the night and for the first time in more specific terms:

> He speaks of Austria and Czechoslovakia. We must have both to round off our territory. And we will get them too sometime.[11]

And on 2 August:

> In Austria the führer will one day create a tabula rasa. Let's hope we all still experience it. He will go the whole hog then. This state is no state. Its people belong to us and will come to us. The führer's entry into Vienna will one day be his proudest triumph. Czechoslovakia too is no state. She will be overrun one day.[12]

What conclusions should be drawn from such evidence? An 'intentionalist' can reasonably argue that it shows Hitler restlessly striving to find ways of achieving the goal of expansion. All his comments assumed that Germany would start a great war by 1943 at the latest. He saw international developments in terms of the opportunities they created for a successful war. Other states were judged according to their ability to upset the status quo. Japan, Italy and Franco's Spain, the authoritarian regimes which successfully defied the democracies and the League of Nations were the rising powers. Britain, on the other hand, emerged as weak and ineffective despite its global reach – poorly led, unable to bring itself to side with Germany and also incapable of defeating Italy, pointing to a revision of the views he had expressed in *Mein Kampf*.[13] The Soviet Union, as in *Mein Kampf*, was still seen as at risk, despite its size ('this colossus'), because of the threat from Japan. The timetable was vague – the great conflict was to be in 1942 or 1943 but action might be taken earlier if circumstances were favourable. In 1937 Hitler began to talk about taking Austria and Czechoslovakia. Given that Austria was annexed in March 1938 and Czechoslovakia dismantled that October and then over-run in March 1939, the 'intentionalist' case certainly looks plausible. But is it convincing?

Hitler's remarks, as recorded by Goebbels, show the way he was thinking but that is not the same as planning. The fact that some events, notably the occupation of Austria and Czechoslovakia, did occur more or less as he predicted may give a false impression of coherence between Hitler's conversation and actual policy. Other events did not follow as or when he had predicted, for instance the idea that Poland and France were coming to accept war with the Soviet Union, and that the great conflict would take place in 1942 or 1943 (by when German rearmament was expected to be complete).[14] In fact, Hitler's remarks suggest that he had very little idea at this time as to how he was going to get into a position to attack the Soviet Union. Does that mean that these remarks should not be taken seriously? Were they no more than day-dreaming, in the way A. J. P. Taylor understood Hitler, and in the way depicted in Chaplin's film *The Great Dictator* where Hitler played with the world as a toy balloon?[15]

To dismiss these remarks as no more than fantasies, however, is to make as much of a mistake as to read into them the existence of firm plans. What Hitler said was perfectly consistent with his goal of expansion given the date and contexts in which he was speaking. He was expecting the great war when German rearmament was ready in five or six years time. He did not know exactly what the position would be then but the way in which Italy and Japan were already revising the peace settlement by force showed that it could be upset. And although Britain was not proving receptive to German overtures for an alliance, Hitler was starting to revise his estimate of Britain by emphasizing its weakness, suggesting that an alliance might not be a necessary condition for German expansion after all. And he was already thinking about taking the first steps, namely Austria and Czechoslovakia, if favourable conditions presented themselves.

There is, however, a deeper challenge to be made to the 'intentionalist' argument. It accepts that these were Hitler's intentions but questions how much they mattered. The argument is about the nature of his leadership.[16] On this thesis Hitler is seen still as essentially a propagandist, someone who shied away from decisions and whose intentions were therefore not turned into plans. Because he had no clear idea in this period how the great war was to come about, let alone how 'living space' once conquered was to be exploited, he left a huge area of policy vacant for others to fill. He was, to take the main example, drawn only with the greatest reluctance into discussion of the rearmament programme and the conflicts it generated. That created political space for other leaders, and their ideas were not always the same as his. Göring who became increasingly influential in this period did not share Hitler's racial philosophy though he too wanted to see German domination in central Europe and expected war with the Soviet Union. Ribbentrop also ceased to be simply Hitler's mouthpiece and became increasingly anti-British, looking to construct an alliance which could threaten the British empire rather than the Soviet Union. Hitler did not withdraw entirely from decision making. His word remained the ultimate authority but he often authorized parallel and conflicting policies – notably in economic matters where he did not want to commit himself. When he did give a lead it was only at the level of slogans or propaganda, laying down the priority of expansion and living space but not getting involved in detailed administration. He could be driven to take a decision in a crisis but then it bore all the hallmarks of improvisation rather than planning. So the structuralist case is that as a result of Hitler's kind of leadership – or rather lack of leadership – the Third Reich lurched from crisis to crisis. There was no coherent development based on Hitler's intentions. We will now consider these arguments in the light of specific examples.

INTERVENTION IN THE SPANISH CIVIL WAR

The Spanish Civil War is a good example of Hitler reacting to a development he had not foreseen. The request for German assistance reached him while he was enjoying the Wagner opera festival at Bayreuth in July 1936.[17] It came from the rebel general Franco in Morocco who urgently needed transport planes to get his troops to Spain. The request came through a German businessman, Johannes

Bernhardt, and reached Hitler via the Nazi party *Auslandsorganisation* (which cultivated links with Germans abroad) and Rudolf Hess, bypassing the Foreign Ministry which wanted Germany to maintain strict neutrality. Hitler received Bernhardt on the evening of 25 July after a performance of *Siegfried* and seems to have decided at once to agree to what was asked. His motives appear to have been straightforwardly political. If Spain went Communist, as the Foreign Ministry had reported was possible, then with a Popular Front government already elected in France (which was dependent on Communist support), Germany would be sandwiched between the Soviet Union and a Communist Western Europe.[18] If, on the other hand, the Spanish Nationalists could be helped to an early victory by a few camouflaged transport planes the situation would be reversed and France would be isolated between Germany, Italy and a Nationalist Spain. According to Ribbentrop's later account Hitler told him the following day that (in Ribbentrop's words) 'Germany could under no circumstances tolerate a Communist Spain.'[19] It would seem that the economic potential of Spain with its mineral resources was at this stage only a secondary consideration, though once the decision had been taken Göring exploited the opportunity to the full.[20]

Partly because of the way the decision was taken, the sources for it depend on the later recollection of those involved and must be treated with caution. But it is obvious that Hitler took the decision immediately and himself before consulting Göring and Blomberg and against the advice of the Foreign Ministry. Ribbentrop who was uneasy about the impact on Britain also made no impression. Indeed Hitler may have made up his mind immediately in order to pre-empt criticism from his advisers.[21]

The initial commitment of transport planes was in any case a limited one though of crucial importance to Franco. Goebbels commented: 'We are taking part a bit in Spain. Planes etc. Not clear. Who knows what it's good for. Still no decision. But the nationalists are making progress.'[22] With no victory in sight, however, Hitler agreed to increase the German commitment in the summer and autumn. At the end of October it was decided to send a substantial force, the Condor legion, consisting of 92 aircraft, and eventually some 5000–6000 troops together with tanks, anti-aircraft guns and other equipment. Already, at the beginning of October, Göring had set up the organization designed to turn Spain into virtually a German colony supplying vital raw materials, especially iron ore, in return for German military support and equipment.[23] In November Germany and Italy recognized the Nationalist government, although Madrid was still held by Republican forces.

However, when in December the German military representative to Franco, General Faupel, asked for the deployment of one or more German divisions, Hitler refused.[24] That decision was supported by Blomberg, Fritsch, Neurath and probably Göring. It would have been a provocative act since German involvement in Spain was still unofficial. Formally Germany subscribed to the British policy of non-intervention and was a member of the Non-Intervention Committee which was supposed to uphold that policy. The danger of a full-scale commitment of German troops leading to war with the western powers was too great. Such a commitment would also be at the cost of the rearmament programme. So long as Hitler's minimum aim – to prevent a Communist-supported victory of the Spanish Republic – was achieved, Spain was not a vital theatre. Germany was able to benefit from the fact that Mussolini took the opposite decision and committed some 40 000–50 000 troops to the conflict. Hitler could see the advantage of allowing Italy to bear the main burden and, indeed, of the Spanish Civil War being allowed to drag on. That would increase Italian dependence on Germany and, with their attention concentrated on Spain, the other powers would be less able to resist German expansion in Central Europe.[25]

The example of the Spanish Civil War shows different sides of Hitler's leadership. He reacted swiftly and on his own initiative, over-riding the objections of the Foreign Ministry. He stuck to the policy until the main aim was achieved. However, he was also shrewd enough to set a limit to German involvement and to extract the maximum advantage from the way the war developed into a long conflict, ending with the fall of Madrid to Franco only in April 1939.[26] Hitler's initial decision to intervene can be regarded as in part ideological, based on a rather simplistic view that the victory of the Spanish Republic and a Popular Front government in France would mean a 'Communist' Western Europe. In fact the Communists were only one element in a broad left of centre alliance of parties in both Spain and France. However, his refusal to become more heavily committed in December 1936 revealed a more realistic and cynical appraisal of the way in which the war, and heavy Italian involvement in it, could be exploited. So long as the war continued, Franco was also in a weak position to resist Göring's pressure for vital raw materials. The whole episode shows that despite his haphazard method of taking decisions, Hitler cannot be dismissed simply as a fanatic or a propagandist. He was also capable of cool calculation and the successful adjustment of means to ends.

THE FOUR YEAR PLAN

The weakest area of Hitler's leadership was over economic policy. Yet the economy was obviously vital to achieving the goal of expansion. The basic problem was simple. Germany depended on imports of food and raw materials. The growth in public spending on infrastructure and the rearmament programme increased demand for both. With the increase in employment from the low point of the depression, consumers had more money to spend. The rearmament programme meanwhile required constantly increasing quantities of steel, rubber, oil and other raw materials. Despite efforts to increase exports, including paradoxically arms exports, the trade gap led to severe shortages of foreign exchange. Attempts to get over this problem by making trading partners accept German goods in return for their supplies, for example the vital supply of oil from Romania, met increasing resistance. Another expedient was to produce substitute raw materials by chemical processes in Germany, for instance oil from coal by hydrogenation, and accept the extra cost that involved, but not all Germany's requirements could be met in that way.[27]

The basic problem that too much was being expected too fast of the economy led to fierce competition between rival authorities.[28] Schacht as Reich Minister of Economics imposed drastic controls on the allocation of foreign currency and argued that measures to boost exports should be given priority over synthetic production and, by 1936, that no extension of the rearmament programme was feasible. Carl Goerdeler, the Lord Mayor of Leipzig, who had been appointed Commissioner to control prices in 1935, also thought that the only solution was to increase exports at the cost of slowing down the rearmament programme. Walter Darré, who was in charge of agricultural production through the Reich Food Estate, pressed for foreign currency to be allocated to imports of fats and animal fodder where German production was insufficient. The military naturally pressed for allocations for the rearmament programme which, with Hitler's encouragement, was becoming ever more ambitious, and the three services also competed among themselves. Göring, who was determined on a rapid expansion of the Luftwaffe, was quite prepared to act independently in securing foreign trade deals. To promote synthetic production, a special agency had been set up in 1934 under an industrialist member of the Nazi party, Wilhelm Keppler. In addition, the great chemical concern, I G Farben, succeeded in 1933 in securing through one of its directors, Carl Krauch, the Feder–Bosch agreement which gave it a guaranteed price and market for synthetic oil for ten years. Krauch energetically promoted the cause of synthetic materials and by 1936 Göring became increasingly receptive to his ideas.

The conflicts between his subordinates led to increasing pressure on Hitler to take decisions both about the policy to be pursued and the way it was to be organized. Hitler was reluctant to do either.[29] Perhaps realizing that there were no easy solutions and that any decision would damage his reputation, he temporized. In August 1935 he appointed Göring to arbitrate in a dispute between Schacht and Darré over foreign currency but he refused Göring's requests to take over the allocation of petrol and rubber. He also turned a deaf ear to appeals from Schacht and Blomberg to sort out the rival competencies of the different economic agencies and he took no action on complaints from Darré and Keppler against Schacht.

The situation changed in April 1936 when Hitler received a joint approach from Schacht and Göring for the latter to be appointed Commissioner for foreign currency and raw materials. Hitler agreed, perhaps not fully understanding the scope of the new appointment and, in any case, probably content to be presented with a joint proposal – particularly as Blomberg was also supposed to support it – rather than the usual bickering. Schacht's motive in supporting Göring was to relieve the pressure on himself. He was confident that Göring would be unable to solve the underlying economic problems and would therefore divert criticism by the party from Schacht onto himself. Göring, however, moved rapidly to capitalize on his new position. He made his 'führer's commission' public (although it was supposed to have been kept confidential) and set up a special 'Raw Materials and Foreign Currency' office. Schacht and Blomberg realized the danger too late. Göring ignored their protests and put his authority behind a joint programme to boost both exports and the production of synthetic materials. According to Göring, Schacht tried to persuade Hitler to take back the appointment but Hitler refused telling Schacht that he 'did not want to have anything more to do with these things'. Göring continued to expand his staff appointing specialists for particular areas, including numerous experts from I G Farben. He also used his position as head of the Prussian government to provide himself with a second power base and he extended its scope by inviting the most important Reich ministers to attend meetings of its cabinet. Although he had no new solutions to the basic economic problems, by the early summer of 1936 Göring was well on the way to winning the power struggle. The British ambassador, Sir Eric Phipps, speculated that he might be appointed Reich Chancellor.

It was in these circumstances that one of the most famous documents of the Third Reich came to be written – a memorandum by Hitler which survived only in a copy given by him to Albert Speer in 1944 who gave it the title 'Memorandum by Adolf Hitler on the Tasks of a Four Year Plan.'[30] According to Speer, Hitler explained that he had composed the memorandum because of 'the lack of understanding of the Reich Ministry of Economics and the opposition of the German business world to all large-scale plans'. He had therefore decided to carry out a Four Year Plan and to put Göring in charge of it, giving him a copy of the memorandum.

What appears to have happened is that Göring pressed Hitler in July 1936 for a confirmation of his authority over that of his rivals and suggested that he (Göring) should make a speech on the subject of the economy to the Nuremberg party rally in September.[31] Hitler decided to make the speech himself but asked Göring to supply him with the necessary material. Although only some of the experts' reports were available in time Hitler went ahead, composed the memorandum at the end of August and in his speech to the Nuremberg rally gave an outline of the new 'Four Year Programme' which soon became known as the 'Four Year Plan'. He still seemed unsure, however, about how the plan was to be implemented. Meanwhile Göring, lost no time in asserting his authority.[32] He revealed the contents of the memorandum – which was supposed to be secret – to a meeting of Prussian ministers together with Blomberg and Schacht on 4 September and claimed that he was responsible for putting it into effect. Only on 18 October, however, did Hitler sign a decree setting out Göring's powers and that was worded in a way which suggested that Hitler wanted him to coordinate the other bodies involved rather than to be in charge of them. The result was that conflict and confusion continued between Göring's Four Year Plan organization, Schacht at the Economics Ministry and

Blomberg representing the military. Hitler was unwilling to arbitrate and simply urged them to agree among themselves. Göring, however, was able to use his position to push through the policies he favoured, including promoting synthetics over Schacht's opposition and even founding an enormous new industrial concern – the Hermann Göring Company – with public finance to overcome the opposition of private industry to using low-grade German iron ore. By the summer of 1937 Schacht realized that he had lost control of economic policy and Hitler eventually accepted his resignation in November.

How important was Hitler's memorandum? Should it be seen as one of the key documents of the Third Reich? The simple answer is that it is important but because it reveals both sides of Hitler's leadership – its weaknesses as well as its strengths.

Hitler arranged his argument to reach the conclusion he wanted. He started with ideology: 'Politics is the conduct and the course of the historical struggle of nations for life.' That led on to the threat of Bolshevism and 'world-wide Jewry'. Germany because of its position was the key to resisting Bolshevism – of the other powers only Italy and Japan could be regarded as 'firm in the face of the world peril'. It was not the aim of the memorandum 'to prophesy the moment when the untenable situation in Europe will reach the stage of an open crisis' but 'this crisis cannot and will not fail to occur'. As 'a victory of Bolshevism would lead not to a Versailles Treaty but to the final destruction, indeed to the annihilation, of the German people...all other considerations must recede into the background as completely irrelevant.'

From this premise, Hitler proceeded to discuss Germany's defensive capacity. He gave pride of place to the German people, its 'impeccable political leadership', ideology and military organization. Military capacity depended on the new army: '*The extent of the military development of our resources cannot be too large, nor its pace too swift.*' Everything else was secondary.

> It is a major error to believe that there can be any argument on these points or any comparison with other vital necessities. However well-balanced the general pattern of a nation's life ought to be there must at particular times be certain disturbances of the balance at the expense of other less vital tasks.

Only then did Hitler move on to the principal subject of the memorandum, economic policy. The opening paragraph made it clear that

'The nation does not live for the economy, for economic leaders or for economic or financial theories' but rather the reverse. There then followed the basic proposition of *Mein Kampf*: 'We are overpopulated and cannot feed ourselves from our own resources.' What was necessary was to bring about:

a *final* solution for the *future* and a *temporary* easing of conditions during the *transition* period. The final solution lies in extending our living space, that is to say, extending the sources of raw materials and foodstuffs of our people. It is the task of the political leadership one day to solve this problem.

Hitler then addressed what could be done in the meantime, drawing on some of the material which Göring had given him. He was firm on two points: the absolute priority of rearmament and in that connection the equally absolute priority of producing arms and ammunition rather than accumulating reserves of foreign currency and raw materials for use during a war – as he claimed the First World War had shown. The problems of further rearmament once war had broken out were 'not an *economic problem* but solely a *question of will.*' He then set a programme for 'economic rearmament' which was to be conducted 'with the same ruthlessness' as military and political rearmament. This was for the production of synthetic materials wherever possible – fuel, rubber, iron, industrial fats – and in all of these cost was 'irrelevant'. The Ministry of Economics was told not to interfere and industry was warned that either

it will grasp the new economic tasks or else it will show itself incapable of surviving any longer in this modern age in which a Soviet State is setting up a gigantic plan. *But in that case it will not be Germany that will go under, but at most a few industrialists.*

Hitler also threatened businesses which kept foreign exchange abroad 'with the death penalty for economic sabotage' and proposed a law to make German Jews liable for the damage they had inflicted on the economy. He closed by giving figures for the annual production of various synthetic materials which could have been achieved over the previous four years with the right policies and then 'set the following tasks: (1) The German army must be operational within four years. (2) The German economy must be fit for war within four years.'

The strength of Hitler's argument was that it set clear priorities: there would be a war with the Soviet Union; the needs of the military came first; so far as the economy was concerned, Germany needed an extension of its living space; until that was achieved domestic production should be boosted wherever possible; military and economic preparations for war must be completed within four years; nothing and nobody would be allowed to stand in the way.

The weaknesses are equally apparent. Hitler made no serious attempt to demonstrate the need for war with the Soviet Union or where living space was to be acquired, what resources it would contain and how they were to be exploited. War and the need for living space were simply assumptions of his argument, ideological idées fixes. He treated Germany's trade gap as confirmation of the need for living space whereas it was, in large part, a result of his preparations for war.

Even accepting his assumptions, there were still important flaws in his argument. In August 1936 he still had no clear idea of how war with the Soviet Union would come about. He did not know what the position of other powers would be – Britain or the United States, for example. He therefore planned simply for a continental war and demanded the largest possible military force in the shortest possible time. That was logical given that he was committed to expansion. Germany could succeed only by extending its resource base early before it was committed to a long war against potentially superior powers, for instance an alliance of Britain, the United States and the Soviet Union. The grab for new resources by over-running weaker opponents was the obvious and indeed the only strategy to follow. To that extent Hitler was right in rejecting the ideas of those like Schacht and the chief of the Defence Ministry's Economic staff, General Thomas, who argued for rearmament in depth.[33] Germany would never win a long war of attrition against powers with superior economic might – that had indeed been a lesson of the First World War. However, Hitler failed to take account of the effects of German rearmament on the policies of other powers. He was not prepared to face the objection that his policies might themselves precipitate a long war against superior opponents before an expanded Germany was secure. Since he reasoned that Germany could not stand still, he had to take that risk. He resembled a gambler whose instinct was always to go for broke. But as the international situation developed, he found that the rearmament plans were not adequate and could not easily be altered to allow for the risk of war with Britain or the United States.

The programme he demanded for production of synthetic materials was itself designed to reach its full capacity only by the mid-1940s. The result was serious gaps in provision for the war Germany in fact faced in September 1939.

Equally Hitler was not prepared to argue seriously about the best economic policies to pursue before war broke out. Having established the priority of rearmament at any cost he could leave the rest to experts. But the objections of those who disagreed with him were already dismissed in the memorandum with a combination of bombast and threats. Difficulties both before and during war were to be solved by will-power. If German industrialists and economic experts did not have the will – a will which incidentally he was able to argue had been shown by the Soviet five-year plan – the National Socialist state would supply it.

ELITE AND PUBLIC ATTITUDES

Hitler's memorandum shows therefore both his strengths and weaknesses as a leader – a clear sense of what he wanted and ruthless determination to get it, while ignoring objections both to his irrational goals and also to the way he intended to achieve them. Since his arguments would not have survived sustained criticism, he had no alternative but to dismiss such criticism in advance and threaten those who gave it with being pushed aside or treated as criminals. How was it that in these circumstances he continued to enjoy the co-operation of his military leaders, civil servants, German industry and the wider public?

The military leaders are the easiest to understand. For them rearmament was a goal they shared with Hitler.[34] Their programmes escalated with Hitler's encouragement. They also changed in character from the defensive purpose of the first years – to be able to resist foreign intervention – to what General Fritsch called in 1935 'offensively conducted defence'.[35] This development was a result of calculations about how to conduct a war on several fronts and the possibilities now opened up for mobile warfare using armoured divisions of tanks. The idea of tank warfare, pioneered by Colonel Guderian, was accepted enthusiastically by Hitler in July 1935 and developed by the Chief of the General staff, General Beck, in a key memorandum in December 1935. In this he argued that 'strategic defence...[would] only be successful if it were able to be carried out in the form of an attack'. He proposed that within the plan for a 36 division army, already decided, there should be a doubling of the number of armoured brigades to 12. After the reoccupation of the Rhineland, the total size of the projected army was again increased in June 1936 to a field army in wartime of 102 divisions which Beck intended to be completed by the autumn of 1939. That matched Hitler's instructions in the Four Year Plan. In the words of General Fritsch, in submitting the plan to Blomberg in October 1936: 'According to the Führer, a powerful army is to be created within the shortest possible time.' This was indeed achieved. On the outbreak of war, the German army mobilized 3 737 000 men, compared to 2 147 000 in August 1914.

The dedication with which the army chiefs set about achieving such astonishingly rapid rearmament shows that they saw no conflict between their aims and Hitler's. They concentrated on solving the problems of size, speed and equipment given the danger of war on several fronts. They were not put off by the consequences of their programme for German finances or the economy. Rearmament was to have priority: it was for others to solve the problems it created. This led to the extraordinary situation, as their own experts pointed out, that armaments factories would have to be sustained by minimum purchases after 1940 to maintain their capacity for wartime needs even though the armed forces would have no use for these purchases in peacetime. As Major General Fromm pointed out in August 1936 in that situation the only other alternatives would be to go to war or to reduce the level required for the army's operational readiness. Fromm asked the central question, whether there was 'any firm intention of employing the armed forces at a date already fixed'. To this he got no answer.[36]

The implication of the preparations was a war in 1940 which though thought of as a defensive war – arising from the threat of combined French, Soviet and Czech attack – would be fought offensively as the only available strategy. In June 1937 new operational plans for possible future conflicts were drawn up by the Defence Ministry. These included both a two front war concentrated on France (Case Red) and a two front war concentrated on the Soviet Union and Czechoslovakia (Case Green). In the latter case, Germany would forestall an 'imminent attack' by carrying out a 'surprise attack on Czechoslovakia'. These plans were made subject to both the favourable attitude of other powers, in particular the non-intervention of Britain and Poland, and the completion of Germany's preparations for tank warfare and its defensive capacity in the west. The plans therefore depended on the international situation and the success of the rearmament programme by 1940–41.[37]

Like Hitler, the army chiefs took no account of the effects of their programme on the plans of other powers. In a circular argument they simply assumed that the reaction of other powers necessitated Germany's own rapidly escalating programme. They thus abdicated part of their responsibility. Although aware of the demands of total war on the economy and the dangers of Germany's strategic position, they continued to see rearmament as the opportunity to achieve the recovery of German power which had been a dream since 1919.

What was true of the army was equally true of the Luftwaffe. With Göring at its head, it was in any case led by someone committed to the goal of expansion and the second most powerful man in the Third Reich. The initial purpose of the air force was to create a deterrent sufficient to prevent foreign intervention while Germany rearmed. The first two years were remarkably successful with rapid expansion of the aircraft industry and the creation of a fleet of 270 bombers, 99 fighters and 303 reconnaissance planes and a much larger number (1300) of machines for training the pilots for the new fleet. The whole process was efficiently managed by Erhard Milch, a former squadron commander from the First World War and director of *Lufthansa*, who became state secretary in the new air ministry. In July 1934 a new programme was adopted with Hitler's approval to produce a much larger fleet by March 1938 of 2225 fighters, 2188 bombers, 699 dive bombers and 1559 reconnaissance aircraft as well as nearly 9000 training machines.

From 1936, however, problems emerged which were typical for the regime. First the type of aircraft produced quickly became obsolescent and new prototypes required time to develop and test. Second, the purposes of the air force expanded to include not only operations against France and Poland or Czechoslovakia but also from 1938 against Britain. Operations against Britain required aircraft with a longer range and higher bombing payload and also created new problems of command and control and training of crews for operations over longer distances. Demands by Göring and Hitler for massive production increases of five times the existing programme could not overcome these basic problems, which only time could solve. The result was that there was actually a sharp decrease in the number of aircraft produced in 1938 and Germany was not equipped for the air war against Britain in 1939. This failure, however, was a reflection of the difficulties inherent in meeting the escalating targets rather than any lack of will on the part of the air force chiefs.

The German navy is interesting in that initially Hitler did not see any purpose in naval rearmament – in line with his plan for an alliance with Britain – and had to be won round by the naval leadership under Admiral Raeder. Raeder argued for a navy which could create bargaining power for an alliance without actually being used against Britain. In 1934 a programme was adopted to construct a fleet of eight battleships, three aircraft carriers, 18 cruisers, 48 destroyers and 72 submarines by 1949. The aim was to achieve parity with France, as part of plans for a war with France and Poland which did not involve Britain. That remained the basis on which the Anglo-German naval agreement was concluded in June 1935, setting the German fleet at 35 per cent of the Royal Navy. However, both Raeder and Hitler understood that war with Britain might occur at some time in the future and they discussed that possibility as early as June 1934. For both of them however, at that date, it was only a distant possibility. Raeder knew that war with Britain would be beyond the capacity of the German navy in the near future and Hitler was perhaps thinking in terms of a final conflict involving Britain and the United States once the continental war had been won. Although naval planning continued to exclude war with Britain therefore, Raeder regarded the Anglo-German naval agreement as setting only a temporary limit to German naval expansion which might be reached as early as 1938.

By 1937–8, as the British alliance failed to materialise, the danger of war with Britain was taken more seriously. In June 1938, having received indications from Hitler of a changing assessment of the British threat, the naval command considered more closely what would be required. The results were alarming, requiring not only major new construction programmes but the occupation of at least the whole French side of the Channel coast. At the same time there were serious delays of, on average, a year in the existing programme for all types of ship. In October 1938 a new programme was drawn up with a substantial increase, among other categories, in the number of submarines with which to harass British shipping though it was unclear how much of this could be achieved by 1942–3 at the earliest. Hitler, meanwhile, pressed for extra battleships – in January 1939 he ordered that six be built by 1944 – and gave naval rearmament priority over other programmes. He was still presumably thinking in terms of a fleet which would act as a deterrent to British intervention, once the continental war had been won, and allow Germany to prepare for the final struggle for global power.

The outbreak of war in September 1939 found the German navy unready for its main enemy and Raeder complained that the surface ships were so far behind Britain that 'they could demonstrate only their readiness to die honourably'. As with the air force, however, that was a result not of unwillingness on the part of naval leaders to go along with Hitler's plans. Rather they had planned for a war without Britain on the assumption either that Hitler would make good his promise of a British alliance or that if war with Britain followed a continental war, they would have had time to build a sufficient fleet for that purpose. Neither of these assumptions was realistic and in their desire to find a glorious role for the navy, they failed to question them. As with the army chiefs, they abdicated part of their responsibility with disastrous results.

The rearmament plans also required the co-operation of officials and industrialists. That the object was war and expansion was hardly a secret. In his first address to the Prussian cabinet about the Four Year Plan on 4 September 1936, a meeting also attended by Blomberg, Schacht and the Reich Finance Minister, Schwerin von Krosigk (a conservative Prussian nobleman and former civil servant), Göring was explicit. Explaining Hitler's memorandum, he said that it started 'from the basic premise that the showdown with Russia is inevitable'. He then read out the whole memorandum and concluded the meeting by observing that 'All measures must be taken as if we were actually at the stage of imminent mobilization.'[38] Göring had no difficulty in recruiting officials (particularly from his own Prussian cabinet staff and the air ministry) and industrialists (particularly from I G Farben) for his Four Year Plan organization which soon had a staff of over a thousand. It was presided over by a former state secretary from the Prussian cabinet office and included the state secretaries from the Ministries of Labour and Agriculture, thus effectively co-ordinating those departments. When Schacht resigned as Minister of Economics, he was replaced by a non-entity thus also removing that Ministry as a rival. It is noticeable that Göring preferred to appoint officials and industrialists rather than Nazi party activists, showing his desire for an independent power base.[39]

How does one explain the willingness of so many able and experienced people to go along with a development which obviously carried a high risk, if not a certainty, of war? Many factors were at work. It was still possible to think of rearmament as a necessity in view of the threat from the Soviet Union and its French and Czechoslovak allies, as indeed Hitler presented it. The specific risks of expansion did not yet have to be faced and when they did, in 1938–9, more opposition surfaced. There were also significant costs to opposition as Hitler's threats in the Four Year Plan memorandum showed. Göring had no hesitation in accusing those industrialists who did not wish to co-operate of sabotage and his police and intelligence organization ensured that their every move was known to him.[40] In these circumstances a solid front in any organization was hard to achieve. Göring successfully employed the tactic of divide-and-rule, first to gain influence in the banking community and later to overcome opposition from heavy industry to exploiting low-grade iron ores.

There were also gainers as well as losers.[41] The Four Year Plan organization became itself a powerful bureaucracy. Between 1936 and 1942 its projects absorbed half of total industrial investment with I G Farben among the beneficiaries. Once Schacht had lost the power struggle and resigned in November 1937, industrialists could no longer look to the Ministry of Economics to defend their interests and had to accept the terms set by the Four Year Plan organization in an economy where raw materials, wages, prices and labour were increasingly controlled. There were also spoils to be shared. In 1938 when Jewish businesses were expropriated, it was possible to make profitable acquisitions. As the Reich expanded, there were similar opportunities in the occupied countries. Many industrialists would have preferred to be left alone to run their businesses in the traditional way, once the influence of unions had been curbed. Even those who benefited from the rearmament programme were nervous of the dependence it created on state contracts which might not continue. It has been suggested that there was a division between the generation of industrialists who owned their family firms – the Krupps for instance – and a younger generation of managers and technicians who were more disposed to co-operate with the state.[42] Whatever the differences, however, German industrialists were manoeuvred from their original acceptance of the Third Reich step-by-step into increasing dependence and complicity, the latter most obvious in the conditions of the millions of slave labourers in German factories during the war.

There were examples of resistance. Hugo Junkers tried to prevent the Nazi takeover of his company, was arrested on charges of treason and compelled to sell.[43] Fritz Thyssen, head of one of the great Ruhr firms and an important early supporter of the Nazis, became increasingly disillusioned and fled abroad in 1939.[44] There was also disillusionment within government. Schacht, as we have seen, resigned in 1937. Goerdeler, the lord mayor of Leipzig, saw like Schacht the dangers of the rearmament programme and became in time a fundamental opponent of the regime and a member of the wartime resistance.[45] A notable example from within the civil service was Fritz-Dietlof Count von der Schulenburg. A Prussian nobleman and official in the Ministry of the Interior, he joined the Nazi party in 1932 but in 1937 criticized the way in which orderly government was being undermined by party agencies and the way in which civil servants were abused by the party.[46] He too later became an active member of the wartime resistance.

What is notable, however, about the industrialists and officials is that opposition remained an individual matter – there was a lack of institutional or group solidarity. The deepest reason for this failure was the same as that which had led such people to support the regime from the beginning. They had never felt at home in the Weimar Republic. They had not overcome the trauma of defeat and revolution in 1918–19. They feared the spread of Soviet-led Communism in Europe, a fear increased by the Spanish Civil War. These feelings left a deep reluctance to break with the Third Reich and a willingness to be carried along with its central policy of rearmament and war. They wanted to see Germany restored to a leading position in central Europe. Even most of those who made the transition to resistance carried over their hostility to democracy and their hopes for Germany as a great power into their plans for the future giving those a highly conservative character.[47]

The only mainly middle-class organizations which did offer a form of institutional opposition were the Christian churches. Here through the parishes there was the potential for communities to unite around an ideology which offered an alternative to Nazism and a basis on which resistance could form. The primary motive which led the churches (though the Protestant church was internally divided between pro-Nazi 'German Christians', those opposed to the 'German-Christians' in the 'Confessing Church' and a large third uncommitted group) into conflict with the state was simply the desire for self-preservation –

their freedom to organize, to preach and to teach. The churches did not seek political conflict and church leaders overwhelmingly shared the authoritarian and patriotic beliefs of their class. But the increasingly total claims of the Nazi state meant that the independence of the churches was bound to be seen as unwelcome and unacceptable – evidence that the ambition of Nazism to create a new nation in its image had failed. Nazi ideology – racism, glorification of Hitler, and in time euthanasia and mass murder – also directly challenged Christian belief. The churches responded to attacks, for instance the show trials of Catholic clergy on charges of sexual immorality, with condemnation of the regime's ideology, most impressively in the papal encyclical 'With burning concern' which was smuggled into Germany and read from the pulpits on Palm Sunday, 21 March 1937. The conflict with the churches also caused concern among other groups, for instance the officer corps. But among churchmen, as elsewhere, the transition from criticism to opposition to wartime resistance was made only by individuals. Once again there was a reluctance to break with the regime on issues of war and peace, since church leaders were instinctively patriotic and anti-Communist (especially given the news of atrocities committed by Republican forces during the Spanish Civil War and religious persecution in the Soviet Union). But the churches did provide a place to think differently and, as we shall see, the threat of war played some role in motivating their opposition.[48]

Attitudes within the working class were also mixed. The initial demoralization after 1933 in conditions of mass unemployment, the division of the working class movement and the destruction of its parties and trade unions had given way by 1936 to a different picture. There was full employment and indeed an increasingly serious labour shortage in agriculture, construction and the armaments industries. As a result labour regained bargaining power and a wave of absenteeism, strikes and other forms of pressure for better conditions followed. How far did this unrest reflect alienation from the regime and how far simply an attempt to exploit more favourable economic conditions? There was certainly discontent. Although jobs were easy to get, wages were held down (only reaching their 1929 level again in 1938) and there were frequent shortages of food and other consumer goods as the regime gave priority to rearmament. On the other hand, the regime provided some welfare benefits, arranged holidays at the seaside or even abroad through the 'Strength through Joy' organization, and tried to broaden its appeal by populist propaganda about the 'national community' with attacks on elite groups – such as civil servants – as well as more obvious targets such as Jews, homosexuals, shirkers and other so-called 'asocials'. Terror continued against known opponents with Himmler extending his control from the political police, which he had exercised since 1934, to the whole force in 1936.[49] In these circumstances working-class attitudes appear to have ranged from dislike (among former SPD or KPD activists), to indifference and attempts simply to make the best of the situation, through to those who were willing to concede at the very least grudging recognition to the regime for its achievements – and often a mixture of these.[50]

How did foreign policy and war fit into the general picture? This is a subject which deserves more attention than it usually receives. On the evidence of the reports of the SPD organization in exile, fear of war became a dominant theme of conversation in the second half of 1936.[51] That was hardly surprising. During the Olympic games, which were held in Berlin in August, the regime was careful to put forward a peaceful image for foreign visitors. But as one SPD informant from Upper Silesia commented, 'After the Olympics – war?'. The preparations were not hard to find: the increased pace of rearmament with the Four Year Plan, the extension of military service from one to two years in August, the issuing of mobilization instructions to the adult population, the emphasis on anti-Soviet propaganda (a main theme of the Nuremberg party conference in September, including Hitler's speech), the anti-Comintern pact with Japan, military exercises in frontier areas, preparations for air attack, and the existing commitment of German 'volunteers' in Spain. It was natural that expectations of war, sooner rather than later, were rife. The monthly reports from different parts of the Reich again describe the atmosphere as one of 'war psychosis'.[52]

What effect did fear of war have on attitudes to the regime? Here the picture is varied. Some believed that the preparations were necessary and that there was a real danger of attack by the Soviet Union through its Czech ally.[53] Others thought Germany was preparing for war but was not yet ready. Others again speculated on German plans for a local war to relieve its shortages of food and raw materials. In January 1937 it was already suggested that there might be a 'lightning type' (*blitzartig*) attack on Czechoslovakia.[54] Fear of war did not translate immediately into opposition. Rather the mood was one of fatalism and indeed the regime may have benefited as people were distracted from daily discontents by the looming prospect of war. The reports repeatedly emphasize that there was no parallel to the euphoria of 1914. There was admiration for the thoroughness of German preparations but only some young people and dedicated Nazis were confident of victory. On the other hand anti-Nazis saw no hope of getting rid of the regime without war and looked forward to its defeat. These circles were also critical of the democracies for their weakness and short-sightedness in not standing up to Hitler.

The reports for 1937 show an initial lessening of tension after Hitler declared in his speech to the Reichstag on 30 January that 'the time of so-called surprises' was over, a speech that failed to inspire even party members.[55] This lessening of tension was identified in some reports as itself a danger to the regime – the party needed excitement to maintain its momentum. A justification for continued rearmament could be found in the rearmament of other states, including Britain from 1937. Some still thought that the shortages of raw materials would make it impossible for Germany to go to war but others thought that the arms race would itself lead to war and that Germany (and Italy) would have to act before they were overtaken. The differences between Schacht and German industrialists on one side and Göring on the other were reported together with the view on the part of some industrialists that the Nazi economy would make sense only in war. Germany's lack of colonies was also played up by the regime as an explanation for its economic difficulties. Nazi propaganda was effective with some: they accepted that Germany needed more land if it were not to starve and that if other states refused to allow German expansion, war would be inevitable. Nevertheless there was a growing tide of criticism which extended to Hitler himself. The regime badly needed another foreign policy success. In 1937 unlike 1935 (the Saar, conscription) or 1936 (the Rhineland), there was no dramatic event to celebrate. The intervention in Spain was slow to succeed and unpopular – the relatives of German conscripts deployed (and some killed) in Spain were not even allowed to know they were there because officially Germany subscribed to the policy of 'non-intervention'.

By the summer of 1937 there was again a general feeling of mounting tension and the regime positively encouraged that mood as a way of asking for greater sacrifices for rearmament. Czechoslovakia was considered the most likely target with party members claiming that it would be simply 'overrun'.[56] But by the end of the year, according to one report, rumours of an imminent *Gleichschaltung* of Austria as a first step towards further expansion were giving the party the impetus it needed.[57] The replacement of Blomberg and Fritsch in February 1938 was seen as a further step towards a more radical policy – following 'the inherent laws of fascist dynamism'.[58] The annexation of Austria which followed in March provided the excitement and ultimately triumph which the regime needed.[59] As one report observed:

> Hitler's domestic political power has rested for years only on his foreign policy successes. Whenever the domestic unrest has risen to the highest pitch, a so-called great foreign policy success has come. And the more the tensions increased inside the Reich, the greater was the daring that Hitler showed. Austria is, seen from this standpoint, the greatest success for Hitler so far.[60]

The SPD reports are valuable precisely because of the range and variety of opinion which they record.[61] They help to show the way in which public attitudes were formed and the part played by foreign policy and war in that process. There was clearly lively, if surreptitious, discussion as people nervously followed the evident preparations for war and speculated on the outcome. Many of their views anticipated later debates between historians, particularly about the relationship between rearmament, shortages of food and raw materials and the need for the regime to demonstrate dynamism and success. Together these provided the domestic political context for foreign policy. War was not popular but fear of war helped to hold regime and people together and foreign policy triumphs without war were the best cement of all. How did this context affect Hitler's decision making?

DECISION MAKING, NOVEMBER 1937–MARCH 1938

By the autumn of 1937 Hitler was under pressure to give a lead which went beyond mere lunchtime conversations. The pressure came from various quarters. There were first the continuing problems with the rearmament programme. They came to a head when at the end of October Raeder threatened resignation, telling Blomberg that cuts in steel allocation to the navy (for which he blamed Göring's preferential treatment of the Luftwaffe) were such that he could no longer take responsibility for the programme; he requested an immediate decision from Hitler.[62] At the same time Schacht was also pressing his resignation, though perhaps hoping that Hitler might yet reverse strategy to one of slower rearmament, foreign trade, and seeing what could be achieved by negotiations with Britain and France for the return of colonies and revision of European frontiers.[63] Hitler had no intention of doing any of these things and was preparing to part with Schacht, something which he had previously shied away from since it would give clear confirmation to the professional and business elites that policy was moving to a new and more radical course.

Those who favoured seeing what could be achieved by negotiation included Neurath and the head of the political department in the Foreign Ministry, Ernst von Weizsäcker, and among the military commanders, the Chief of the General staff, General Beck. Even Göring was nervous of a strategy which risked ending in a war with Britain on the side of France and the Soviet Union.[64] Neurath and Göring pressed Hitler to meet a British cabinet minister, Lord Halifax, in November in the hope that a basis for agreement could be found. Hitler however, partly influenced by Ribbentrop, had come to the conclusion that Britain would not be prepared to help Germany expand to the east and at most might offer Germany the odd colony, probably from another country's empire. He suspected that British offers to negotiate were a ruse to make it possible for Britain to concentrate its forces against Italy in the Mediterranean. Mussolini would be forced to withdraw and would then redirect Italian ambitions back to South Eastern Europe, leading to a renewed clash with Germany in Austria. At that point Britain, having split the axis, would revert to indifference and Germany would have gained nothing.[65]

Hitler also felt under pressure to plan for action before German rearmament was overtaken by its potentially stronger enemies, particularly once Britain embarked on rearmament in 1937. Action necessarily involved deciding on the first steps and when they were to be taken. These first steps, as Hitler had already indicated in conversation, were to be the annexation of Czechoslovakia and Austria, which would bring Germany important strategic and economic gains.

There were also other pressures for decision. Having aroused expectations by forcing the pace of rearmament and constant propaganda about Germany's lack of living space and the evils of Bolshevism, it was necessary to deliver some tangible success. Otherwise the party would lose momentum and the regime would lose prestige. That would be dangerous since, apart from coercion, the regime depended for support on its reputation for dynamism. Promises of a glorious future for Germany were what it used to justify present sacrifices, particularly where rearmament was concerned. Hitler also felt under personal pressure to move quickly, worrying about his health, in particular he feared he had cancer which had caused his mother's early death.[66]

When confronted with Raeder's ultimatum and Göring's complaints against Schacht, Hitler decided to take the initiative and set out his views at a meeting summoned to discuss the rearmament issue on 5 November 1937.[67] Those present included Blomberg, the commanders-in-chief of the three services, Fritsch, Göring and Raeder, and Neurath. These were the people whom Hitler needed to give effect to his policies. The only other member of the audience was Colonel Friedrich Hossbach, the senior military adjutant on Hitler's personal staff. Since no secretary was present and since he was impressed by the importance of what Hitler had to say, he took notes in his diary which he wrote up on 10 November.[68] This document, the 'Hossbach memorandum', is a unique record of the moment when Hitler moved from generalities to setting out objectives and a timetable. The interpretation of this event is also controversial between those who see Hitler as in control of foreign policy and those who stress the structural constraints and doubt his capacity to give coherent leadership. It is therefore a good place at which to assess these interpretations.

Hitler started by restating the basic ideas of *Mein Kampf* about Germany's need for greater living space. He warned that without expansion the German race would decline, not only in Austria and Czechoslovakia but in Germany itself. Hossbach recorded Hitler as referring to the loss of dynamism, 'Instead of increase, sterility was setting in…since political and ideological ideas remain effective only so long as they furnish the basis for the realization of the essential vital demands of a people.' Hitler then reviewed the economic evidence arguing in the usual way that autarchy (self-sufficiency) within the existing boundaries was impossible and that reliance on foreign trade also offered no solution since vital imports, including food, would be cut off in war. 'The only remedy, and one which might appear to us as visionary, lay in the acquisition of greater living space…' and this could 'only be sought in Europe, not, as in the liberal – capitalist view, in the exploitation of colonies'. Expansion necessarily involved risk: 'The question for Germany ran: where could she achieve the greatest gain at the lowest cost.'

Hitler then considered the opposition – which he identified as the 'two hate-inspired antagonists, Britain and France, to whom a German colossus in the centre of Europe was a thorn in the flesh, while both countries were opposed to any further strengthening of Germany's position either in Europe or overseas'. Britain, he said, after its loss of prestige over Abyssinia would be prepared only for a token colonial concession, such as the Portuguese colony of Angola, and France would take a similar line. However, he then launched into a lengthy account of why he 'did not share the view that the Empire was unshakable'. He gave various reasons, the fact that Britain could not defend its empire without allies, the problems it faced in Ireland and in India, the threat of Japan in the Far East and Italy in the Mediterranean, and the unfavourable proportion of Britons to the total imperial population, itself a warning for Germany to heed in its own expansion. The French empire was in a better position but France suffered from internal political difficulties.

Hitler then turned to the all-important questions of the ' "when" and "how" ' of expansion. He discussed three possible cases. The first was 1943–45. That was the last possible time since thereafter Germany's 'relative strength would decrease in relation to the rearmament which would by then have been carried out by the rest of the world'. Any year could then bring the food crisis which would be a 'weakening point' of the regime. 'Nobody knew today what the situation would be in the years 1943–45. One thing only was certain, that we could not wait longer.' There was also the problem of 'the aging of the movement and its leaders'. 'If the Führer was still living, it was his unalterable resolve to solve Germany's problem of space at the latest by 1943–45.' The second and third cases were for earlier action should a domestic crisis in France or French involvement in a war with another state make the French army unable to act against Germany.

Hitler then discussed specific objectives. In the event of war, Germany's 'first objective...must be to overthrow Czechoslovakia and Austria simultaneously in order to remove the threat to our flank in any possible operation against the West.' If the Czechs were overthrown, Poland would remain neutral should war follow between Germany and France. In fact, however, Hitler thought that 'almost certainly Britain, and probably France as well, had already tacitly written off the Czechs'. Britain was unlikely to act and France would not act without Britain. The 'annexation of Czechoslovakia and Austria would mean an acquisition of foodstuffs for 5 to 6 million people, on the assumption that the compulsory emigration of 2 million people from Czechoslovakia and 1 million people from Austria was practicable'. Annexation would also mean shorter frontiers and the possibility of creating an additional 12 divisions. Italy was not expected to object about Czechoslovakia but its attitude over Austria was still uncertain and depended on whether Mussolini was still alive. Poland and Russia would be kept in check by the speed of German action; in addition Poland would be deterred from intervening by the fear of Russia at her rear and Russia would be deterred by Japan. Hitler considered that an opportunity for action might arise from the tensions in the Mediterranean over the Spanish Civil War as early as 1938, which he described in some detail – probably influenced by his talks with Mussolini who had paid a state visit to Berlin at the end of September.[69] Hitler argued that Germany's interest was for the Spanish War to be prolonged to maintain the tension. Given a favourable opportunity, Czechoslovakia should be attacked 'with lightning speed'.

In the discussion that followed Hitler's statement, it was noticeable that no-one supported him. Blomberg and Fritsch 'repeatedly emphasized the necessity that Britain and France must not appear in the role of our enemies'. They estimated that French forces would be superior to German defences on the western frontier, even if France was also engaged in a war with Italy. Blomberg also warned about the strength of Czech defences which he likened to the French Maginot line. Neurath did not think that an Anglo-French-Italian conflict was as close as Hitler seemed to assume – in reply Hitler suggested the summer of 1938. Even Göring thought that in view of what Hitler had said they should think of withdrawing their forces from Spain, to which Hitler agreed while reserving the decision over timing.

It is easy to fit the Hossbach memorandum into an argument for Hitler's control of foreign policy.[70] His statements about the vital necessity of conquering living space were consistent with his earlier views and the Four Year Plan memorandum. He had adjusted his view of Britain but remained intent on expansion nevertheless. He set out a timetable for the future and specified the objectives of Austria and Czechoslovakia, talking of 1938 as a possible first date. His views clearly alarmed Blomberg, Fritsch and Neurath who made their opposition plain. Nevertheless military plans were altered in December to give 'an offensive war against Czechoslovakia' for 'the solution of the German problem of living space' (Case Green) priority over preparations for war with France (Case Red), though the generals were careful to add that the war would be undertaken before Germany's full military preparations were ready only if neither Britain nor France was likely to intervene.[71] Austria was to be incorporated at the same time though without the use of military force if possible. When a scandal erupted over Blomberg's marriage in February 1938, Hitler proceeded to get rid of the doubters – Fritsch and Neurath as well as Blomberg. In March, Austria was annexed and pressure soon mounted on Czechoslovakia leading to its dismantling in October and destruction in March 1939. Things did not work out exactly as Hitler had suggested at the meeting recorded by Hossbach but nevertheless there is sufficient consistency for one to assume that he meant what he said and that he was in charge.

Doubts have been raised, however, about this interpretation both of the significance of Hitler's statement on 5 November 1937 and the sequence of events that followed. Some of these doubts deserve to be taken more seriously than others. One that can be dismissed is the allegation that the text of the Hossbach memorandum was tampered with by the allies for the Nuremberg trials, where it was used as evidence for the charge of 'conspiracy to wage aggressive war'. It is true that Hossbach's original did not survive the war, together with other secret documents which were deliberately burnt by the German officer in charge of them before the capitulation. However, a copy had been made of it in November 1943 by a member of the military history section of the German army, Graf Kirchbach, and entrusted to his brother-in-law, Viktor von Martin, who handed it over to the British military government in October 1945. From there it went to the War Office in London and it is now in the National Archives in Kew.[72] Interestingly, a copy of Kirchbach's copy had already reached the Foreign Office in London and the State Department in Washington from the intelligence section of allied military headquarters in May 1945 and that was the copy used at Nuremberg. It is not known who made that copy or how it fell into allied hands.[73] But the important thing so far as the authenticity of the text is concerned is that it is identical with Kirchbach's original in London. There is therefore no basis for the allegation of forgery.

There are better reasons for questioning whether Hitler's statement should be taken at face value. The meeting was called to settle an argument about the allocation of steel between the armed services. Instead of dealing first with the business in hand, Hitler launched into a two-hour harangue about foreign policy. Might that not have been a convenient and typical way of evading a decision between his military chiefs and softening them up so that they would be willing to reach agreement themselves? Rearmament was discussed at the end of the meeting and the navy's steel allocation increased.[74] In other words, Hitler's discussion of the timetable for expansion can be seen as simply a smokescreen, made more impressive by describing the subject as too important to be divulged to the cabinet and asking for it to be regarded as his 'testament' in the event of his death. Göring argued in his defence at Nuremberg that these were Hitler's tactics and that the meeting had no deeper significance.[75] It is noticeable that Hitler did not think it necessary to have his statement recorded by a secretary – hence Hossbach's memorandum – and also that Hitler twice refused to read Hossbach's record saying he had no time.[76] That can be seen as further evidence that he was not serious.

Hitler may also have had another purpose in mind. As we have seen, he had come to accept the necessity of dropping Schacht and he knew that Schacht's views were influential with conservative elites. He needed therefore to persuade the military chiefs and Neurath that Schacht's policies were unrealistic. That would make sense of the way he emphasized his arguments against foreign trade and colonies and also the lengthy passage designed to show both that Britain would not surrender significant colonial possessions and equally that Britain was not in a position to intervene in a European war and could therefore be discounted. Schacht, the military chiefs and the Foreign Ministry were not inclined to write off Britain so easily. In his attempt to win over his audience he may perhaps have exaggerated the possibilities of early expansion in Europe, without in fact being committed to them. On this view he was presenting an argument against Schacht rather than revealing his real intentions. As A. J. P. Taylor put it, 'The conference was a manoeuvre in domestic affairs'.[77]

If one takes Hitler's talk of expansion seriously, there is also an important difference in the argument compared to *Mein Kampf* and other statements by Hitler. He did not mention the Soviet Union as the ultimate source of living space.[78] Although he spoke of the need to secure living space for 'about one to three generations' and of an annual population increase of 560 000, the only targets for expansion he mentioned – even in relation to his final date of 1943–45 – were Austria and Czechoslovakia. But on his figures they would provide food for at best six million people, so less than 11 years of population growth. He did describe the overthrow of Austria and Czechoslovakia as 'our first objective' in any war in order to remove the danger of attack in the rear if Germany was involved in war in the West. But he did not speak of further campaigns against the Soviet Union. How does one account for this omission?

In addition, the connection between the Hossbach meeting and the dismissal of Blomberg, Fritsch and Neurath in February 1938 is at best indirect.[79] Hitler could not foresee Blomberg's marriage and there is no sign that he intended to dismiss him until it happened. Indeed, on the evidence of Goebbels' diary, he was shocked and distraught at Blomberg's behaviour. Goebbels described what followed as 'the worst crisis of the regime since the Röhm affair'. In the ten days from 25 January to 4 February while Hitler decided what to do, Goebbels described him as looking 'like a corpse', 'utterly pale and grey', 'completely knackered', 'with tears in his eyes' and as having 'trusted him [Blomberg] blindly'.[80] The situation was not improved by Hitler becoming convinced on investigation that a previous (trumped up) charge against Fritsch of homosexuality was also true. In the end, a major rearrangement of posts took place, in Goebbels' words, 'to cover the whole affair with a smokescreen'.[81] Hitler took over from Blomberg as commander-in-chief of the armed forces himself, in the process thwarting Göring's ambition for the post – Göring was fobbed off with promotion to the rank of Field Marshal. Apart from Blomberg and Fritsch, 12 generals and 51 other senior officers were removed. And in addition to the replacement of Neurath by Ribbentrop as Foreign Minister, new appointments were made to four senior ambassadorial posts. But none of this had been planned as a result of the doubts expressed about Hitler's ideas at the meeting in November 1937. On the contrary, it was directly a result of the Blomberg scandal and the need to cover it up. Another sign of the improvised nature of the reshuffle was that Ribbentrop did not see eye to eye with Hitler at the time and was temporarily out of favour.[82] Like Hitler, he had come to the conclusion that Britain would not be Germany's ally but, unlike Hitler, he thought Britain might well resist German expansion. Indeed he regarded Britain as Germany's 'most dangerous enemy' and wanted to reorient German foreign policy against the British empire.[83] The appointment of Ribbentrop as Foreign Minister reflected therefore less an identity of views with Hitler than the lack of any more suitable candidate.

Similar arguments apply to the *Anschluss* which followed in March.[84] That can also be seen as prompted by the need for foreign policy success to distract attention from the internal crisis. Hitler did not expect an immediate union (*Anschluss*) of the two states. When he saw the Austrian Chancellor Schuschnigg on 12 February, at a meeting which had been postponed because of the Blomberg crisis, he bullied Schuschnigg into taking Nazis into his government. He wanted to be able to include the achievement of closer relations with Austria in his speech to the Reichstag which had also to be postponed from 30 January (the fourth anniversary of Hitler's appointment as Chancellor) to 20 February because of the crisis. Hitler now regarded Austria as little more than a satellite but he still thought in terms of final union occurring in 'the evolutionary way'.[85] No preparations were made for invasion. The situation was transformed by Schuschnigg's decision, announced on 9 March to hold a referendum, which was carefully worded to achieve a vote for Austrian independence, on 13 March. That forced Hitler to react and set in train the process of ultimatums for Schuschnigg to call off the referendum and resign which were backed by the threat of military force. Even though the Austrian government eventually complied with the ultimatums the invasion, described as a 'friendly visit' of German troops, went ahead on 12 March. Mussolini acquiesced, to Hitler's huge relief, and France and Britain, as he had anticipated, did not intervene. Hitler followed the troops, greeted by cheering crowds, initially to his boyhood town of Linz. It was only once there, carried away by the reception for the German invasion and with foreign newspapers already declaring that *Anschluss* had occurred, that he decided on the final step. Legislation for the 'reunion' of Austria was drafted on 13 March and formally accepted by the Austrian government. Hitler now made the most of his success with a triumphal entry into Vienna the next day, a speech to the Reichstag in Berlin on 18 March and new elections on 10 April which produced majorities of over 99 per cent for union in both Germany ('the old Reich') and Austria. As usual there was manipulation of the results but once again there can be no doubt that success in foreign policy had boosted popular support for the regime. But equally the need for a foreign policy success to distract from the domestic crisis had itself set off the final train of events which led to *Anschluss*. The outcome was not the result of careful planning but of hasty improvisation along the way.

How far do these various arguments about the Hossbach memorandum and its consequences undermine the picture of Hitler as a leader in control of foreign policy setting out his plans for the future? Let us take the objections in turn. The fact that the meeting was called to discuss rearmament and that Hitler used it for a lengthy statement of foreign policy, in the process repudiating Schacht's ideas, is not in itself a reason for thinking that Hitler was not serious. On the contrary, if his plans were to be carried out it was essential that the rearmament problems were solved and that he persuaded the people on whom he relied, to support his views. The fact that no secretary was present was typical of Hitler's informal method of rule which could certainly be a source of weakness but was not a reason for thinking he was play-acting. His refusal to read through and correct Hossbach's memorandum could be explained by the opposition he had encountered at the meeting and a desire to avoid taking responsibility for decisions which did not command full support. Again this was a source of weakness in policy making but that is not the same as saying that he did not mean what he said.

The objection that he did not discuss further stages of expansion against the Soviet Union is more interesting. His words implied that there would have to be further stages if the needs of future generations were to be met. His military chiefs and Neurath were used to Hitler's argument that war with the Soviet Union would be inevitable at some time, possibly triggered by the Soviet Union coming to the aid of Czechoslovakia in the event of German attack. However, there was an essential difference between Hitler's view of war with the Soviet Union and theirs. He thought in terms of a racial war for living space. They thought in terms of a defensive war to protect Germany's central European empire – an empire that would be formed by annexing Austria, destroying Czechoslovakia and frontier revision with Poland. Hitler apparently chose to confuse the difference between these two concepts at the meeting by talking of living space in Austria and Czechoslovakia. This may have been simply because these were the first stage. But it may also have been because he sensed that agreement would be easier to achieve if he limited the discussion to these two cases. He was right in that his audience raised objections to the practicality of what he proposed but not to the principle. General Beck, who wrote an important criticism of Hitler's arguments, did not accept the feasibility of Hitler's goal of 'living space' and may not have understood that Hitler intended to expel or eliminate whole populations to achieve it.[86] Their mentalities were too far apart. Had Hitler launched into an argument for a racial war against the Soviet Union, he would have met more fundamental resistance. Obscuring the difference between his ideas and those of his senior advisers may well therefore have been deliberate.

The connection between the Hossbach meeting and the February purge is clearly not one of cause and effect. However, once Hitler recovered from his shock and embarrassment at Blomberg's marriage (at which he had been a witness), he did make changes which brought the armed forces directly under his control. In addition, despite his differences with Ribbentrop, putting him in charge of the Foreign Ministry was a warning to conservative diplomats – about whom he had frequently complained – against obstructing the new course.[87] Similarly, *Anschluss* was not a direct consequence of the Hossbach meeting but nor was it simply an accident resulting from the Blomberg crisis. Pressure to undermine Austria's independence had been a constant of Nazi foreign policy. There were differences within the leadership over tactics. Hitler was more sensitive to Mussolini's concerns than Göring, who pushed harder and more consistently for *Anschluss* though he too was taken by surprise at the way it eventually occurred.[88] But both he and Hitler expected it to be achieved sometime as a result of their pressure. *Anschluss* had deeper causes than the Blomberg crisis though that crisis helped to set off the final stage of the process.

What conclusion does this suggest about Hitler's leadership? The argument really turns on what is meant by control of foreign policy. No leader acts in a vacuum. Policy must always be constructed in relation to the distribution of power between states and within each state. Hitler was no exception. He showed a politician's sensitivity to the likely reactions of other powers and of his own elites and people. Looked at in this way Hitler's statement, recorded in the Hossbach memorandum, and the events that followed show neither complete control nor someone at the mercy of events. The picture is, as one would expect, more mixed. It shows a revolutionary leader wedded to the goal of expansion, looking for opportunities despite opposition at home and abroad. Hitler was aware of the risks, of economic failure, of loss of public support, of the rearmament programme being overtaken by that of its enemies, of domestic opposition from Schacht and his like. He was also coming to terms with a fundamental change in his strategy. He no longer expected alliance with Britain to open the way to continental expansion. On the other hand he calculated on the weaknesses of the British empire and predicted that Britain would not intervene over Czechoslovakia. He was no doubt disappointed at the reaction of his senior advisers on 5 November – Hossbach later recorded that Hitler's expression showed he knew that he had failed to persuade them.[89] Characteristically he drew back, refusing to read Hossbach's memorandum and allowing the generals to make an early attack on Czechoslovakia conditional on a situation in which neither France nor Britain would intervene. Again Hitler did not foresee the Blomberg crisis but, once he had recovered his confidence, he used the crisis to impose his authority on the armed forces and the Foreign Ministry. He then intensified the pressure on Austria to get a foreign policy success to distract public attention and rebuild support. Again he did not expect it to lead to *Anschluss* then but, when challenged by Schuschnigg's referendum proposal, he was prepared to authorize military intervention – accurately assessing the risks of foreign intervention. Carried along by the enthusiasm for union in Austria unleashed by these events, he scored a triumph he had not expected so soon.

Putting the Hossbach memorandum and the events that followed into the context of foreign and domestic politics certainly adds a great deal to our understanding of Hitler's leadership. Each element – public morale, the rearmament crisis, Schacht's resignation, the failure to get the British alliance – is important, but none by itself provides the whole explanation. Hitler's intentions are also only part of the explanation but an important part. To put those intentions into practice he had to confront real obstacles and take risks. His preferred style of leadership, when he met resistance, was to allow a crisis to build up and then to use it as the opportunity to move to a more radical solution. He responded to the rearmament crisis by proposing a timetable for expansion in November 1937. He was rebuffed by his senior advisers but regained the initiative in February–March 1938. Once again risk taking paid off. The weakness of the western powers and nationalism in Germany and Austria gave him an easy victory. But his leadership, crude and simplistic though it was, had also been effective. He had no doubt that his tactics were right – maximum rearmament to seize opportunities for the initial stage of expansion before the advantage of Germany's lead was lost. For the time being he could still mask the differences between his vision of a racial empire in the east and traditional ideas of restoring Germany's place in central Europe. He could also force his critics on the defensive by emphasizing their lack of a realistic alternative. Their opposition was to do with the risks not the objective of frontier revision. And with *Anschluss* he demonstrated his superior assessment of the risks, and achieved the first major annexation – a real change in the balance of power which the peacemakers at Versailles had tried to prevent. Given his nature and that of the regime, however, each success could only be the stepping-stone to the next move. And with each move he had to weigh the risk that he might no longer be able to carry the elites and the German people with him.

6   To War in Europe: From *Anschluss* to the Invasion of Poland

From March 1938 to September 1939 Hitler moved from preparation for a great war to deciding the where and when of expansion. That involved a new degree of risk. It was no longer a question of undoing Versailles: union with Austria had accomplished the last major goal of that kind in Europe where Hitler's aims were shared by most Germans. Increasingly, he faced the problem that his aim of empire in the east would be made more difficult to achieve by simply revising the Versailles frontiers in line with self-determination. He continued to make use of that principle but a return to the frontiers of 1914 – even extended to include the German populations of the former Habsburg monarchy – was not what he wanted. He was not fundamentally interested in the Sudetenland (where most of the 3 million strong German minority in Czechoslovakia lived) or Danzig (with its German population) and the Polish corridor or Memel (another German port on the Baltic which had been ceded by the treaty of Versailles and subsequently annexed by Lithuania). He was interested in these only in so far as they served his larger goal. The puzzle for Hitler was how to make use of them as a pretext. He needed them as justification both for German public opinion, which was nervous as the risks increased, and to stave off foreign intervention – from France, Britain and possibly the Soviet Union – before Germany was strong enough for full-scale European war. But he did not actually want mere frontier revision in line with self-determination to occur. That would deprive him of the pretext, making it harder to maintain support at home and increasing the risk of foreign intervention as he went beyond frontier revision to empire. The interest of the period from March 1938 to September 1939 is to see how Hitler manoeuvred to destroy his opponents singly, gambling successfully on the reluctance of Britain and France to go to war again and mesmerizing German elites and public opinion by his compulsive risk-taking. By September 1939 he had exhausted the possibilities of this tactic and the European war broke out.

THE CRISIS OVER CZECHOSLOVAKIA AND OPPOSITION TO WAR

Hitler's mood just after the *Anschluss* is captured by Goebbels describing an afternoon with him in the Reich Chancellery:

> Then study of the map: first it's Czechoslovakia's turn. We will share it with the Poles and the Hungarians. And indeed with no half measures at the next opportunity. Memel we wanted to bag now if conflict had broken out between Kaunas [the Lithuanian capital] and Warsaw [i.e. Poland]. Fortunately, however, that did not happen. We are now a boa constrictor which is digesting.
>
> Then there is still the Baltic, [and] part of Alsace-Lorraine. Let France sink ever deeper into its crisis. Only no false sentimentality.
>
> The führer is wonderful: wide-ranging and constructive. A true genius. He sits over the map for hours and broods. It's moving when he says he would like to experience the great German Reich of the Teutons (*Germanen*) himself.[1]

From brooding, Hitler turned to planning. The first target was Czechoslovakia, an enemy because it was allied to France and the Soviet Union, posing as Hitler put it 'a threat to our flank in any possible operation against the West' and, because of its geography, 'an aircraft carrier in the heart of Germany'.[2] In addition, it was a democracy and Hitler had an ingrained dislike of the Czechs as a subversive influence in the Austria–Hungarian empire of his youth. In November 1937 Hitler had thought of wiping out Czechoslovakia before or at the same time as accomplishing union with Austria. Now it was clearly next on the list and there was a general expectation in Germany, and fear outside Germany, that it would be.

Hitler, however, did not want to act too fast. Austria had to be 'digested' and fortifications on Germany's western frontier – the West wall – completed to counter the danger of French intervention. His tactics were to use the Sudeten issue to isolate Czechoslovakia so that he could overrun the whole country without France and Britain intervening, and either achieve another bloodless triumph or give the German people its first taste of victory. In this tactic, he had the advantage that Poland and Hungary also had ambitions on Czechoslovak territory and the Slovaks were themselves restless under what they saw as Czech rule. Hitler saw the leader of the Sudeten German party, Konrad Henlein, and his deputy on 28 March 1938 and explained that he intended to solve their problem 'in the not-too-distant future'. Henlein's instructions were to make demands which the Czech government would be unable to accept. Hitler also encouraged him to repeat a successful visit to London which he had made the previous October to win over British opinion. Henlein did as he was told and on 24 April demanded autonomy for the Sudeten Germans within Czechoslovakia.

Meanwhile, Hitler puzzled over the diplomatic and military situation. On 21 April he saw General Keitel, who had become his chief of staff at the Armed Forces High Command after Hitler had taken direct control in February. He told Keitel that an attack 'out of the blue' was not possible because the effect it would have on world opinion 'might lead to [a] serious situation'. That left open two possibilities: either 'action after a period of diplomatic discussions which gradually lead to a crisis and to war' or 'lightning action based on an incident (for example the murder of the German Minister [i.e. envoy] in the course of an anti-German demonstration)' – ordering the murder of a German diplomat clearly raised no problem for Hitler. Keitel was told to prepare military plans for these two contingencies which he did without protest. The plans were to be for an attack by land and air to create a *fait accompli* in the first four days which would prevent foreign intervention. Even so, preparations should be made to defend the western frontier against France should that prove necessary.[3] Next Hitler made sure of Mussolini's acquiescence during a visit to Rome at the beginning of May. He regarded Italian support as a precondition for success, as it would help to prevent French and British intervention.[4] Hitler now spoke of taking action that year since the international situation might later be less favourable.[5] On 20 May Keitel sent Hitler a draft directive for the invasion of Czechoslovakia, couched in the language of their discussion on 21 April, that it was not Hitler's intention 'to smash Czechoslovakia by military action in the immediate future without provocation', unless developments within Czechoslovakia forced the issue or political events in Europe created an opportunity which might never recur.[6]

Hitler, however, was already moving towards action sooner rather than later.[7] The exact stages of this process are uncertain. His usual instinct was to be bold and use the advantage of surprise to prevent foreign intervention: that had worked in the Rhineland crisis and the *Anschluss*. Yet in April he had accepted that such tactics would be too dangerous in relation to Czechoslovakia, risking a European war prematurely. But in May he revised his view. Keitel's draft directive, issued on 30 May, was changed to read: 'It is my unalterable decision to smash Czechoslovakia by military action in the near future.'[8] Mussolini's support was one reason for the change. In addition, Hitler may have grown apprehensive about the consequences of delay. It would give the British and French time to concert their reaction. If, as was already starting to happen, they made support for Czechoslovakia dependent on the Czechs giving the Sudetenland autonomy, and the Czechs bowed to the pressure, that could deprive Hitler of his pretext for war, making an attack on Czechoslovakia more likely to lead to a European war and more difficult to justify at home.[9]

If Hitler was already thinking on these lines, two incidents served to underline the dangers. On about 12 May he was shown part of a memorandum by the Chief of the General staff, General Beck, which argued that Germany could not survive a European war, that it would not be possible to solve the Czech question that year with the exclusion of France and Britain and, on the other hand, that agreement with Britain over Czechoslovakia was possible.[10] If, Beck argued, Britain was turned into an enemy over Czechoslovakia it would be able to form an alliance with France and Russia with the support, if only at first in material terms, of the United States. That alliance would be more powerful than Germany and its ideological allies (i.e. Italy). The first two parts of Beck's memorandum were withheld from Hitler – for fear of his reaction – by the commander-in-chief of the army, General von Brauchitsch. He had replaced Fritsch in February and, unsure of his position, had consulted General Keitel about what he should do. Even so, what Hitler read was enough to provoke his anger. If he allowed Beck's views to prevail, it would mean that he would have to abandon all hope of a German continental empire and settle for such frontier revision as Britain would allow. Beck's memorandum may also have made him more determined to force the pace against Czechoslovakia, before he became ensnared in British attempts at a negotiated settlement, which he knew would have support among the professional elites.[11]

The second incident, which took Hitler by surprise, was the 'weekend crisis' of 20–22 May.[12] Routine German troop movements near the Czech border set off partial Czech mobilization and the belligerent tone adopted by Ribbentrop to the British ambassador, Sir Nevile Henderson, in turn alarmed the British Government. The Foreign Secretary, Lord Halifax, instructed Henderson to tell Ribbentrop that France would intervene if Czechoslovakia was attacked and Germany should not count on Britain standing by. The message provoked another tirade from Ribbentrop.[13] However, Hitler was not ready to act and his failure to do so in the face of diplomatic warnings from Britain and France was seen as a climbdown. Determined to recover the initiative, he now used the crisis as a further argument for speeding up German preparations.

On 28 May, he addressed his senior military and diplomatic advisers.[14] Hitler repeated much of his argument from 5 November 1937 – the imperative of acquiring living space, the unavoidable risk in doing so, the enmity of France and Britain but also their vulnerability, and the key role of Czechoslovakia as 'our most dangerous enemy in the event of war in the west'. However unlike his position in November 1937, he was now forced to accept that Britain might intervene in a continental war. He described the objective of the war in the west, which he expected in three to four years time, as the 'extension of our occupation of the coast (Belgium, Holland)'.[15] The purpose was obviously to forestall British intervention, an aim further underlined by Hitler's instruction to Raeder the previous day to speed up the construction of battleships and submarines.[16] Before action could be taken in the west, Czechoslovakia had to be destroyed. That could not happen immediately as the method of overcoming the Czech fortifications had still to be worked out and the protective barrier of the west wall completed. Nevertheless, action should be taken swiftly while Czech fortifications were still incomplete, the attitude of Italy, Poland and Hungary favourable, British and French intervention unlikely with their rearmament still years from completion, and Russia incapable of attack. The task of the military was to strengthen to the utmost the fortifications in the west and to prepare 'a lightning invasion of Czechoslovakia'. These instructions, in turn, became the new military directive of 30 May 1938, with the deadline set in a covering note from General Keitel as 1 October 1938 'at the latest'.[17]

Hitler had made his position plain. He would embark on a war of conquest for living space despite the risk. Because of their inevitable opposition, he expected war with the western powers in three to four years time. To prepare the way and protect Germany's flank, he would destroy Czechoslovakia in the autumn of 1938. He did not expect French and British intervention but he was prepared to take that risk, which might lead to a European war. At the same time Hitler started to take a close personal interest in the details of the preparations, laying down what was required in the western fortifications and giving precise instructions for the way in which the invasion of Czechoslovakia was to be conducted.[18] That showed a confidence in himself as a military commander which had been lacking in other areas of policy, for instance the economy. It also heralded a new dimension to his decision making. He was not content to be simply the political leader; he also intended to be an active supreme commander of the armed forces.

It was possible to believe that Hitler was engaging simply in a giant bluff, calculated to produce a negotiated solution to the Sudeten issue. The recently promoted State Secretary in the Foreign Ministry, Ernst von Weizsäcker, initially thought that was the case though he feared that war might result nevertheless.[19] General Beck, however, had no doubt that Hitler was intent on war. During the summer he did his utmost to prevent that happening before resigning in August in despair. As the most determined opponent of Hitler's policy in the senior ranks of the military, his attitudes and the methods he adopted are very revealing for the ways in which conservative elites differed from the Nazis.

Beck did not accept Hitler's basic premise of 'living space'. In his written refutation of Hitler's address in November 1937, he accepted that there was a 'problem of space' but he did not believe that 'far-reaching changes' could be made in Europe where its populations had stabilized over a thousand years 'without the most difficult upheavals, whose duration was impossible to forecast'.[20] Small changes, however, were possible which should not be allowed to threaten German national unity or its racial core. It is not clear whether Beck understood that Hitler intended to expel conquered peoples and resettle the land but he clearly rejected the idea of major change in population distribution on the European continent. In the same way, though not claiming to be an expert on the economy, he associated himself with the ideas of Schacht that autarky could provide only a temporary stopgap and that participation in the world economy, as actively as possible, would always be necessary.

Beck did not, however, dispute the objective of 'resolving the Czech (and possibly also Austrian) issue if an opportunity offered'.[21] In comments on Hitler's speech of 28 May 1938, he accepted that Czechoslovakia was 'a source of danger' for Germany which should be eliminated by war if necessary.[22] But although that was a legitimate strategic objective, he did not accept that the conditions to carry it through successfully had been achieved. His main theme remained that the war could not be isolated: 'We face the fact that military action by Germany against Czechoslovakia will lead automatically to a European or a world war [and] that such a war...will end not just in a military but a general catastrophe for Germany.'[23] He also doubted whether Hungary, Poland and Italy could be relied on to give the support Hitler expected. In addition, he deployed a range of arguments against the invasion itself, including the rejection of what would be seen as an unnecessary war by the German people and their fear that it would lead to general war, a mood that was to be found also in the army, the time it would take to overwhelm the Czech defences before troops could be redeployed to protect the western front from French attack, the damage to morale if there were initial setbacks, increased Czech preparations for a German 'surprise' attack and the lack of German experience with combined land and air operations.[24] He made a series of increasingly desperate attempts to persuade Brauchitsch (the commander-in-chief) that it was the responsibility of the army leadership to prevent war. He later said that he had only one thought in these months, 'how do I avoid a war'.[25]

Beck is particularly interesting because of his clarity and strength of character. He later developed into a leading figure in the military opposition and was killed after the failure of the plot in July 1944.[26] What is important for our purposes is that his memoranda in 1938 allow one to define precisely what divided the conservative elites from Hitler. Beck accepted that there could and should be changes to the Versailles peace settlement. And this was not just a question of frontier change in accordance with self-determination, for instance *Anschluss* or revision of the Polish frontier. Beck also, as we have seen, accepted the strategic objective of the elimination of Czechoslovakia by war if necessary – because of its geographical position and its pacts with France and the Soviet Union it was considered a potential threat. Like other conservative nationalists Beck wanted to see Germany secure in central Europe with an influence amounting to informal empire over the states of eastern and south-eastern Europe. They would look to

Germany as the leading economic and military power in the region rather than to the Soviet Union or France. It was similar to the old German concept of 'Mitteleuropa'. That was emphatically not the same as Hitler's idea of a racial reconstruction of Europe to establish German dominance deep into Russia, but nor was it simply about self-determination.

By 1938 Beck, and those who thought like him, faced a dilemma.[27] He had taken a prominent part in achieving the most rapid possible rearmament for Germany. That, together with Hitler's risk-taking over conscription, the Rhineland and *Anschluss*, had alarmed the other European great powers into starting rearmament of their own. Beck was now convinced that a surprise attack on Czechoslovakia would lead to a European and even a world war which Germany was bound to lose. That lay at the heart of his opposition in 1938. But, if that was true, how could Germany achieve the revision of the Versailles settlement which Beck thought necessary? He hoped it would be possible with the consent of Britain and France. As the appeasement policy of the British and French governments showed in 1938, that was not a foolish hope. Britain and France were prepared to concede the Sudetenland to Germany which also undermined Czech defences and therefore could be considered as having achieved Beck's strategic objective in relation to Czechoslovakia. But would Britain and France have been willing to go so far without the immediate threat of war from Hitler which Beck thought so unwise?

That illustrated another weakness in Beck's position. Britain and France were not at all certain to go to war over Czechoslovakia, as Beck insisted they would. He was not completely wrong. There were days at the end of September 1938, as we shall see, when it seemed likely that war would break out. But the British Prime Minister, Neville Chamberlain, was determined to go to the absolute limit to find a negotiated settlement. In addition, Beck was wrong about some of the military facts. A war game undertaken by the German general staff in June showed that it would take only 11 days to overrun Czechoslovakia, not three weeks as Beck had maintained.[28] In this situation it is not surprising that Brauchitsch, and other senior army commanders, hesitated to challenge Hitler's authority on the issue.

That brings us to the issue of how Beck thought the army should stop Hitler. Initially, in May 1938, he limited himself to memoranda for Brauchitsch. He used what he saw as the 'intolerable' interference of Hitler in military planning to pursue a long-standing ambition to strengthen the position of the army command in relation to the central Armed Forces High Command (which came directly under Hitler and had responsibility for all three services).[29] At the same time he wanted the army to be in a position to counter what he regarded as the irresponsible 'radical' influences around Hitler. Radical influences included the secret police and the SS, the people who had been responsible for forcing Fritsch's resignation in February with the false allegation of homosexuality and also those in Hitler's circle, like Ribbentrop, who were pressing for war. Believing as he did in the joint responsibility of the army with the political leadership for decisions on war and peace, he was not prepared to accept a subordinate role as simply the executant of Hitler's decisions. Beck received only weak support from Brauchitsch, however, who feared for his position with Hitler. By the middle of June it was clear that Hitler had rejected Beck's views on a reorganization of the war ministry and was proceeding with planning for war that autumn. Beck now attempted more extreme measures. In further memoranda and an oral presentation to Brauchitsch in July, he emphasized the responsibility of the military leadership for the whole people in the age of mass armies. He proposed a meeting of all the senior army commanders, and consultation with the other commanders-in-chief, and their collective resignation if they were unable to reverse the decision for war: 'If they all act with a united will, it will be impossible to carry out the war. They will have saved their fatherland from the worst, from destruction.'[30] In a further note he suggested how they should deal with the radical elements of the party, particularly the SS, in the conflict which would inevitably follow. He insisted that action taken by the military should be regarded as 'for the führer' and that there should be not 'even the slightest suggestion of a plot'.[31] Their slogans should be: 'For the führer. Against the war. Against the party bigwigs. Peace with the church. Freedom of opinion. An end to the methods of the Cheka [i.e. the Soviet secret police]. Justice again in the Reich. Halving all contributions. No building of palaces. Living accommodation for comrades. Prussian simplicity and uprightness.' To cope with the inevitable reaction from radical elements, Beck suggested that contact should be made both with the commanding officer of the Berlin district and the city's police chief.[32]

Nothing came of these ideas in the short term. Without the support of Brauchitsch and finding that his judgement over Czechoslovakia was not universally shared by other senior commanders, Beck drew the inevitable conclusion and resigned on 18 August. He even agreed to Hitler's request that his resignation should not be made public for the time being. However, he had shown the kind of alternative which a determined member of the conservative leadership might have offered to Hitler.

Beck was unusually forceful but his reservations about the regime, his view of Germany's proper place in Europe and his fear of a new European war were widely shared by people of his class and background. Another example was Ernst von Weizsäcker in the Foreign Ministry.[33] He agreed with Beck that Czechoslovakia should be dismantled and that a European war should be avoided at all costs. He favoured what he called a 'chemical process of dissolution' through the detachment of the Sudetenland which would undermine Czech defences. He thought that economic pressure could hasten the process. He also thought that a negotiated settlement with Britain and France was possible. Indeed, he believed that war would play into the hands of the Czechs by bringing the western powers to their rescue and saving them from the otherwise natural process of dissolution of their state. Weizsäcker tried to persuade Ribbentrop (who had been appointed Foreign Minister in February) but Ribbentrop preferred to curry favour with Hitler by insisting that Britain and France would not fight for Czechoslovakia. Getting nowhere with Ribbentrop and recognizing in August that Hitler was serious about war, Weizsäcker tried to act as a restraint by influencing others. He warned the Hungarians, to whom Hitler was looking for support, of the dangers of a European war. In particular he tried to influence Britain, on the one hand to accept the detachment of the Sudetenland, but on the other to warn Hitler privately that, in the event of war, France and Britain would become involved. He was also in touch with military circles who were, like him, thinking of ways to stop war and even, if all else failed, of a coup. A message was sent covertly through the Kordt brothers (Erich who worked in the Foreign Ministry and Theodor who was in the London embassy) to the British Foreign Secretary, Lord Halifax. Theodor Kordt went further than Weizsäcker intended, asking Halifax for a public warning to Hitler and explaining that the army leadership was prepared to use force if such a warning was given. Weizsäcker was doubtful about the success of a coup and still hoped to rescue the peace by diplomacy. Chamberlain's visits to Hitler ultimately enabled him, bypassing Ribbentrop, to help to dissuade Hitler from war. Looking back in 1939 he said he had experienced perhaps 'no happier day' than that of the Munich agreement.

As the action of the Kordt brothers shows, there were others who were prepared to go further than Beck or Weizsäcker.[34] Admiral Canaris, the head of military intelligence, gathered around him a group of people, like Hans Oster, who saw that the regime could not be reformed but had to be overthrown. They had the support of younger men like Hans von Dohnanyi (who compiled a dossier of Nazi crimes against political opponents), Hans Bernd Gisevius and the Kordt brothers. Beck's successor as chief of the General Staff, Franz Halder, was more cautious than the younger group but was also prepared to contemplate a coup to prevent war. In September 1938 preparations were made involving the military commander in the Berlin district, General von Witzleben, and contact was made with the Berlin police authorities. Even Brauchitsch was in the know and seems to have adopted a passively permissive attitude. Key installations in Berlin were to be occupied and counter-measures by the SS prevented. Shock troops were organized to seize Hitler in the Reich Chancellery under the command of a former free corps veteran, Friedrich Heinz.[35] There were, however, important differences among the conspirators between those like Gisevius who pressed for action, and those like Halder who insisted that they would have support only once they were seen to be preventing Hitler taking Germany into war. There were also differences about what was to happen to Hitler, whether he should be put on trial, declared insane or shot (as Heinz and the more radical conspirators believed). There was also a lack of clarity as to what kind of regime would follow the coup, whether a transitional military dictatorship, a new alliance of conservative groups with a Nazi party purged of its radical elements, or the replacement of the Nazi regime by a regency under a Hohenzollern prince leading to a constitutional monarchy.[36] All these raise doubts about whether action would have been taken and whether it could have been successful, even if the crisis had not been resolved peacefully.[37]

What in the event proved fatal, however, was that everything depended on the western powers making clear that they would go to war for Czechoslovakia. By relying on others to provide the occasion for the coup, the conspirators lost control of the process. They hoped that if Britain and France took a hard line and Hitler backed down at the last moment, his prestige would suffer such a blow that the coup would succeed. What would be the situation, however, if he did not back down? Could a coup at the last moment prevent war breaking out? Would Britain and France offer a post-Hitler government the kind of terms – for instance over the Sudetenland and revision of the Polish frontier – which the conspirators wanted and which would popularize the new regime? In fact the western powers were not prepared to threaten war in the hope that a coup would succeed. Indeed, the British government treated the various emissaries of the opposition with suspicion. The prospects of the coup were regarded, reasonably enough, as uncertain and what the conspirators asked for in terms of frontier revision for the Sudetenland and also the Polish frontier and perhaps colonies seemed to go further than Hitler was demanding. The conspirators were seen (in many ways correctly) as a throwback to Wilhelmine Germany, lacking legitimacy and (quite wrongly) as offering no advantage over Hitler as a partner for peace. In addition, there was concern in Britain that an unsuccessful coup might be followed by a communist revolution. However, despite the total lack of encouragement they received from abroad, the conspirators continued to make preparations right up to the last nerve-racking days of September as the prospects of war breaking out ebbed and flowed. But, when the news came on the 28th that agreement had been reached to hold a conference in Munich the following day, it put an end both to the international crisis and the conspiracy.

Although nothing came of the coup, it is worth asking how representative the conspirators' views were of German opinion. There is overwhelming evidence that fear of war was widely felt in the summer and autumn of 1938. The reports of the SPD in exile show that similar fears from previous years intensified as the crisis over Czechoslovakia deepened.[38] What gave this crisis a different edge was the feeling that the western powers and even, in some cases, the Soviet Union would be more likely to go to war than previously.[39] British and French warnings during the false alarm in May and Hitler's apparent humiliation suggested that this crisis would be different. Some thought that Hitler could not be so crazy as to want war given the economic difficulties. Many thought he was bluffing but some feared that, when the bluff ceased to work, he would go to war as there would be no other way out. Others feared that because he had lost prestige in May he could not afford another climbdown and therefore war would result.[40] Attitudes to the Sudeten Germans were divided. Some were impressed by Goebbels' propaganda and felt the injustices to the German minority should be put right.[41] But, as the crisis deepened, many felt little sympathy for them – bolder spirits suggesting that they were better off not being 'liberated' by the Third Reich. In any case there was a strong feeling that their cause did not justify a European war.[42] Some young people and convinced Nazis remained confident that there would be just 'a short fresh, happy war' and some of these accepted the official line that Jews were to blame for the crisis.[43] But most – one report from South Germany spoke of 80 per cent – of the population regarded war, and the preparations for it which were increasingly evident and oppressive, with foreboding.[44] A report from the Ruhr in September spoke of 'giant unrest', saying that if war came it would be 'as unpopular as possible' and predicting that 'With this people, Hitler will not win a war.'[45] In the Saar a frequently expressed view was that in the event of war 'civil war would break out'.[46] Several reports noted a new willingness to criticize the regime openly, as in one from Silesia which said 'One hardly recognizes the people any more, so openly do they speak out against Hitler and the whole system.'[47]

These reports were no doubt coloured by the sympathies of the authors and their relief at seeing opinion turn increasingly against the regime. But there are many other sources which point in the same direction. The military's economic staff, reporting on the morale of the population on 1 October, stated bluntly that there was 'a general war psychosis'.[48] Party sources were equally aware of the problem and sensitive to any public demonstration of popular feeling.[49] When the more radical wing of the Protestant opposition 'Confessing Church' issued a prayer for peace and repentance in September, Reinhard Heydrich, the head of the SS security service, described it as calculated to spread 'fear and unrest'.[50] Despite the official boasts of overwhelming support for the government, Goebbels' diary entries at the end of August show that he knew better: 'There is serious unrest in the country because of the position. Everyone is talking of war', 'the war psychosis is growing', 'The mood of the country is numb. Everything is waiting for what will happen.'[51] Even Hitler sensed the atmosphere. At the height of the crisis on 27 September, he ordered a motorized division to parade through Berlin but the lack of enthusiasm of the Berliners was a shock to him.[52]

The evidence for the unpopularity of war in 1938 does not of course show that a coup would have been successful. It would have been hard for a new government to establish its authority. Its origins as a seizure of power by the army would have given it only doubtful legitimacy. It would have been easy for the Nazis to portray its leaders as a reactionary clique. Some prominent civilians associated with it like Schacht, and (although he did not know about it in advance) Goerdeler, would have lent it plausibility but what the results would have been of elections can only be guessed at. It is also possible that if war had broken out in September, opinion would have rallied to the troops despite the reservations people felt. And a quick victory over Czechoslovakia might have led to a new sense of triumph, as was to happen in 1939–40. Nevertheless, it is clear that Germany was, at the very least, deeply divided at the prospect of war in 1938. The regime had not succeeded in convincing the public that a war for living space was worth the risk. On the contrary there was a strong feeling that Hitler's incessant brinkmanship would end in disaster.

Hitler reacted angrily to the opposition of Beck and the scepticism of other army commanders. He had no intention of being diverted from his course. For him, the destruction of Czechoslovakia was the essential next step to the defeat of France and the occupation of the channel ports to deter or prevent Britain from intervening. Victory in the west was, in turn, the essential precondition for empire in the east. That was not something on which he could compromise without giving up the whole purpose of being in power. Hitler was no mere ideologue or propagandist. He was intent on turning his ideas into reality.

During the summer, he had several encounters with army commanders.[53] At a meeting on 13 June which had been called to resolve the Fritsch affair, he appealed to his audience to unite behind him in view of the dangers of the international situation, thus evading pressure to restore Fritsch to office despite the fact that he had been completely cleared. Hearing in August that there had been a meeting of senior commanders to discuss Beck's views, Hitler vented his fury on Brauchitsch. In further meetings, Hitler tried to win over some of the younger senior officers and then again the top commanders, in both cases arguing that the western powers would not declare war for Czechoslovakia. He also clashed with generals who dared to tell him that the west wall was inadequate to resist French attack. Despite these efforts the army leaders remained unconvinced though, unlike Beck, they were not prepared to try to force Hitler to change course. Hitler knew that he had not overcome their doubts and within his own circle he let his displeasure show, talking of the 'old generals' with whom he would still have to deal with Czechoslovakia but implying that they would be replaced before the war in the west in four to five years time.[54] On another occasion, prompted by Himmler, Hitler referred to the 'old fossilized army command' which would have to be 'dismantled as soon as possible'.[55] In August 1938, the limits on the size of the SS armed sections were removed and they were made wholly independent of the regular army. Another sign that the regime was moving in a more radical direction was an intensification of measures against the Jews, forcing Jewish businesses to close and confiscating their property and culminating in the November 1938 pogrom – 'the night of glass' – when, at Goebbels' initiative and with Hitler's approval, synagogues were set on fire across Germany, Jewish property wrecked, Jews beaten up and some hundred killed.[56]

Hitler deliberately stoked up the crisis over Czechoslovakia in the autumn, telling the Sudeten German leaders to create incidents, trying (unsuccessfully) to persuade the Hungarians to take action with Germany, and finalizing the plans for invasion on 1 October.[57] Regardless of the fact that the Czech government, under pressure from France and Britain, had in fact offered the Sudeten Germans autonomy, Hitler was determined on war. On 12 September he gave the closing speech at the annual Nuremberg rally, billed as the first of 'Great Germany' including Austrian delegates.[58] That gave him the cue to launch an attack on the alleged suppression of the Sudeten Germans and the hypocrisy of the so-called democracies in supporting the Czech government, even in alliance with the Soviet Union. In the interests of 'European peace', he made it clear that Germany was no longer prepared to accept this situation and that it no longer had reason to fear foreign intervention – he made a point of emphasizing the extraordinary progress that had been made on the west wall.

Hitler's calculations were upset by the British Prime Minister, Neville Chamberlain. In an attempt to stop the build-up to war, he flew to see Hitler on 15 September. Chamberlain succeeded in getting Hitler to agree that if the principle of self-determination for the Sudeten Germans was accepted, they could discuss how it would be put into practice and he would not use force in the meantime. That was a crucial concession. Hitler had been induced to accept a position where his pretext for war might be taken from him. The alternative would have been to make it clear that he was intent on war with Czechoslovakia, whatever concessions were made on the Sudetenland. That would have increased the likelihood of British and French intervention which, despite his bluster, was not a risk he wanted to take.

Two days later, Hitler explained to Goebbels that Chamberlain's visit was 'not very convenient' and the solution of a plebiscite 'does not suit us entirely'. But if it was proposed seriously, then they could not very well refuse. However, he went on to say that even that way 'Czechoslovakia will end well' and 'we will have for the real thing an incomparably much better military position'. Nevertheless, he added, 'Prague remains for the present intransigent. All the better. For then there will be the total solution.'[59] From these remarks it is clear that Hitler's preference had not changed. He was still hoping for war with Czechoslovakia alone. If the Czechs refused to cede the Sudetenland despite British and French pressure, then the western powers would leave Czechoslovakia to its fate. However, he was beginning to consider a possible alternative, namely acquiring the Sudetenland peacefully with all the advantages that would bring in relation to getting behind the Czech defences and subsequently taking the rest.

Over the next week, before Chamberlain returned to report on what he had been able to achieve, Hitler's attitude hardened. To Goebbels, he described the whole process as a war of nerves. He drew up a map of the area to be ceded. He thought the Czechs would not submit, then – when news came that they had – he was relieved, but subsequently when he thought they wanted to negotiate over procedure, he became suspicious that they were trying to stall in the hope that international opinion would turn in their favour. He became adamant that his terms would have to be accepted unconditionally. These were for an immediate evacuation by the Czechs of the area claimed by Germany, made as extensive as possible, and its occupation by German troops within eight days (when the German army would be ready). If the area was disputed, then a plebiscite could be held before Christmas. The clear advantage was that if it came to war subsequently, the German army would already be established behind the Czech defences. As a safeguard against having to guarantee the remainder of Czechoslovakia, that was made conditional on Hungarian and Polish claims also being satisfied.[60]

At their next meeting on 22 September, Chamberlain was able to report that he had secured French and Czech agreement to the principle of self-determination for the Sudeten Germans. Hitler, however, now presented his terms as to the procedure to be adopted which were in effect an ultimatum with a deadline of 28 September. Chamberlain was naturally affronted at this change of position. He tried to get Hitler to withdraw the demand for the German army to occupy the area but Hitler insisted, saying he could not trust the Czechs to keep their word. At a second meeting the following day, during which news of Czech mobilization arrived, Hitler made a slight concession, extending the deadline for Czech withdrawal from 28 September to 1 October (the date which he had anyway fixed for the invasion). Chamberlain made clear his disappointment but said he would act as a mediator and put the terms to the Czechs.

There followed a second war of nerves when it seemed quite likely that real war would result. The British cabinet decided not to press the Czechs to accept Hitler's terms and to send a representative, Sir Horace Wilson, to warn Hitler that in the event of a German invasion, Britain and France would support Czechoslovakia. Hitler flew into a rage, saying that he was 'completely indifferent' to the threat.[61] Nevertheless in a speech the previous evening in the Berlin *Sportpalast*, he was still concerned to 'build golden bridges' for Britain and France and to strengthen Chamberlain's position.[62] He still, in other words, hoped to isolate Czechoslovakia. The speech contained vicious attacks on the Czech president, Eduard Beneš, accusing him of driving the Sudeten Germans out of their villages 'with grenades and gas'. To appease the western powers, however, he promised that the Sudetenland would be Germany's last territorial demand in Europe and that, once the Hungarians and Poles had been satisfied, he would have no interest in the remainder of the Czech state.[63]

Hitler's mood swung between exaltation and doubt. Would it be better to hold out for his maximum terms in the hope that war with Czechoslovakia would result, even at the risk of general war, or should he relent, negotiate to get the Sudetenland and then polish off the rest of Czechoslovakia more cheaply later? He still appeared to prefer the former – what he called 'the radical solution' and he continued to hope that it could be kept a local war.[64] But doubts remained. After the scene with Wilson and Czech rejection of the ultimatum, Hitler mused to Goebbels about the 'power of faith' and his 'sleepwalker's certainty about his mission' and he spoke with admiration of Mussolini who had 'embarked on his Abyssinian adventure against the whole world – the act of a madman, as it was thought – but in the end he won'.[65] Yet he chose to send a reasoned reply, drafted by Weizsäcker, to Chamberlain, rather than listening to Ribbentrop who argued that Czech acceptance of the German ultimatum would be 'the worst thing that could happen to us'.[66] That night, however, with Ribbentrop and Weizsäcker present, he again declared his intention 'to destroy Czechoslovakia now'.[67]

The following day, 28 September, shortly before the deadline for ordering mobilization, Hitler gave way and agreed to Italian mediation and a four-power conference to meet the following day at Munich. 'The change is incomprehensible', noted one of the officers involved in the conspiracy.[68] It is impossible to be certain what led at the last moment to Hitler's reversal, amid chaotic scenes in the Reich Chancellery, to what he had previously regarded as second best.[69] The British and French made final representations offering to secure the immediate evacuation of the Sudetenland, starting on 1 October. Like Chamberlain's original intervention, this was hard to refuse and, if refused, might lead to general war. France had mobilized 14 divisions and on 28 September the news arrived that the Royal Navy was being mobilized. Hitler also knew from the reaction to the military parade that there was no real enthusiasm for war in Germany. In his immediate circle there were influential voices opposing Ribbentrop – Göring who knew that the Luftwaffe was not ready for war with Britain, Goebbels who knew the state of public opinion and Neurath, who forced his way in, and, according to Goebbels, 'stood up to Ribbentrop and his pig-headed policy courageously'.[70] But the key influence was probably Mussolini. Hitler had always regarded Italian support as essential. When Mussolini made himself the spokesman for moderation, Hitler was offered a way out which, coming from his brother fascist dictator, he could accept with honour. His resistance to a negotiated settlement was finally overcome.

The Munich conference quickly settled the terms of Czechoslovakia's demise. Göring and Weizsäcker prepared the draft, bypassing Ribbentrop, and it was communicated through the Italian ambassador to Mussolini who presented it as his own, thus saving face all round.[71] Under its terms, which were essentially those of Hitler's ultimatum and the final British and French proposals, the Sudetenland was to be transferred to Germany in phases between 1 and 10 October with an international commission to determine where, in areas of mixed nationality, plebiscites should be held and to fix the final frontiers. The remainder of Czechoslovakia would be guaranteed by Britain and France, and Germany and Italy would join the guarantee once Polish and Hungarian claims had also been satisfied.

Reactions to the Munich agreement were mixed. According to SPD reports, there was a general feeling that Munich had been 'a hundred

per cent success for Hitler' and the Nazis, who had been losing confidence as war threatened, were again triumphant – for them Hitler was
'the ruler of the world'.[72] Among the public at large, there was huge
relief that war had been avoided qualified by the sense that it would be
only a matter of time before the next crisis.[73] Opponents of the regime
felt bitter about the failure of the democracies to stand up to Hitler.
As the editor of the SPD reports commented, the Munich agreement
'shook the opposition to Hitler at its core, in its faith that in the end
right would prevail and that truth and faith would be re-established in
the world. Where should opponents of dictatorship draw the spiritual
strength to risk their lives for these ideals, if the democratic world
powers betrayed the ideals to buy an illusory peace?'[74]

From exile Thomas Mann wrote, 'The history of the betrayal of
the Czechoslovak Republic by the European democracies...belongs
among the shabbiest acts that have ever been performed.'[75] The
conspirators who had hoped to use Hitler's determination for war as
the springboard for a coup were devastated. As one of them put it
later 'Chamberlain saved Hitler'.[76]

Hitler's reactions were also mixed. Goebbels describes him as
returning to a triumphant reception in Berlin with 'his whole face
shining with joy'. He boasted of how he had managed the conference
as 'a meeting of the real world powers' with the Czechs excluded.[77]
He later described his satisfaction when he toured the Czech defences
and saw 'what it means to capture 2000 kilometres of fortifications
without having fired a shot'.[78] On the other hand, he had not wanted
the conference or the agreement. He had been persuaded into it and he
disliked ever surrendering the initiative to others. He started to suspect
that the British would not have fought and had cleverly bought time
for rearmament.[79] He resented the role played by Göring in bringing
about the settlement and listened increasingly to Ribbentrop instead.[80]
He was also uneasy about the obvious desire for peace among the
German people and the way in which Chamberlain had been cheered
by the Munich crowds.[81] To a meeting of newspaper editors on 10
November 1938, he spoke of the danger of people being led to assume
that 'the present regime really identifies itself with the determination to
preserve peace at all costs.... It was only out of necessity that for years
I talked of peace.' For the future, though he accepted that it could not
be done in a year or two, the German people must be taught 'to believe
in final victory so *fanatically* that even if we were occasionally defeated,
the nation would regard it from an overall point of view and say: This

is a temporary phase; victory will be ours in the end!' To achieve that the press should 'hold blindly to the principle: the leadership is always right!' Perhaps thinking of the discussions before Munich, he said there would sometimes be disagreement about a decision but what mattered was not whether the decision was 'absolutely right' but that people united behind it.[82]

FROM MUNICH TO THE OCCUPATION OF PRAGUE

Hitler was less sure of the future after Munich. It was as though, having once been sidetracked from his preferred course, he had lost the sleepwalker's confidence in the next step. In speeches he rehearsed the successes of his first six years in power to emphasize his ability to make the right decisions at the right time.[83] To Goebbels, he spoke of taking a rest.[84] There was good reason for uncertainty. As he moved from dismantling Versailles to domination of the European continent – liquidating the 1648 peace of Westphalia by 1948, as he put it to Goebbels – the stakes were much higher.[85] More worrying, his original plan for an alliance with Britain based on sharing the world between the British overseas empire and a German continental empire had proved unworkable. Already in November 1937 he had ranked Britain alongside France as an enemy but he had predicted that neither would fight over Czechoslovakia. During 1938, in the May crisis and again in September, he had been forced to accept that they might. Even if after Munich he reverted to his original view and thought he had been out-bluffed by the western powers, he knew that he had to prepare seriously for war in the west in the future. That was confirmed by British rearmament moving into high gear. Hitler claimed that British rearmament would not begin to be effective until 1941–42, but he also believed that after 1943–45 Germany's relative strength would decline.[86] That was why in November 1937 he had declared that Germany's 'problem of space' had to be solved by 1943–45 'at the latest'.[87]

Hitler's strategy for dealing with Britain, was to occupy the channel ports and to deploy a navy large enough to deter Britain from intervening on the continent. In November 1938 he authorized the Armed Forces High Command to prepare discussions with Italy for:

War by Germany and Italy against France and Britain, with the object first of knocking out France. That would also hit Britain, as she would lose her bases for carrying on the war on the Continent and would then find the whole power of Germany and Italy directed against herself alone.[88]

However, his plans for naval construction – even when in January 1939 they were given priority over every other rearmament – would not reach completion before 1944. In other words, having neglected the threat from Britain until 1938 he lacked a convincing strategy for deterring, let alone defeating, Britain before British rearmament – perhaps with support from the United States – turned the tables on Germany. Like the Kaiser's Germany he would have to accept the risk of a naval war together with the continental war, something which in the 1920s he (like many others) had regarded as the fatal error which had led to Germany's defeat. To Goebbels he hinted at the problem:

> He foresees further away in the future a very tough conflict. Probably with Britain which is preparing for it methodically. We must face up to it and the hegemony over Europe will be decided by it.[89]

Given the risks, and also the lack of enthusiasm for war among the German public, it would have been rational to settle at this point for what could be achieved by negotiation. Revision of the Polish frontier and a return of German colonies could still have been presented as legitimate demands. In addition Germany could bring its economic weight to bear to extend its influence in eastern Europe and the Balkans. But Hitler was not a rational statesman. He was not interested in being fêted as a peace-maker at home and abroad – the role Chamberlain had forced on him at Munich. He was intent on domination whatever the risk. Since the war in the west would be decisive for control of the continent, his thinking was now shaped by that priority.[90] The Soviet Union, meanwhile, attracted less of his attention. He hoped that fear of Japan would keep the Soviet Union on the defensive in Europe. In any case, Stalin's ruthless purge of the military in 1937 did not suggest that the Soviet Union was a serious threat. If France could be defeated and Britain contained, then the opportunity might come to turn on the Soviet Union. Hitler may even have started to wonder whether the war against the Soviet Union might have to be postponed to a more remote future, if victory in the west proved difficult and led to full-scale war with Britain. Ribbentrop, whose influence increased after Munich, held to the view that Britain was 'our most dangerous enemy' and could be contained or defeated only by an alliance of Germany, Italy and Japan together threatening the British empire in the British isles, the Mediterranean and the Far East.[91] Hitler was not convinced that war with Britain was inevitable, and on occasion sharply disagreed with Ribbentrop on the subject, but he knew he had to prepare for it.[92]

This he did in three ways. He demanded, as we have seen, ambitious (and ultimately utopian) new air force and naval programmes. He also allowed Ribbentrop to pursue his alliance strategy for 'the Berlin-Rome-Tokyo triangle'. And in eastern and south-eastern Europe, he looked to construct a series of satellites states which would offer no threat as Germany became involved in war in the west and which would act as a buffer against the Soviet Union.

Ribbentrop set about turning the Anti-Comintern Pact with Japan and Italy into a full military alliance. However, the interests of Japan and Italy were not as easily aligned with Germany as he imagined.[93] Despite the support of the Japanese ambassador in Berlin, Hiroshi Oshima, Japanese governments – already heavily committed in China and with no desire on the part of the navy to be drawn into war with Britain – were prepared to offer only an alliance directed against the Soviet Union. Initially, he also had no success with the Italians who declined to be committed to what Ribbentrop declared was an inevitable war with the west in a few years. Only in January 1939 did Mussolini, fearing isolation, change his position and seek a bilateral pact with Germany. That eventually led to the 'Pact of Steel' on 22 May 1939. However, the Italians acted on the understanding that the two powers would consult each other fully and that war would not occur for at least three years, an understanding which neither Hitler nor Ribbentrop had any intention of honouring.

Attempts to impose satellite status to the east and south-east of Europe enjoyed more success. Hitler wasted no time in preparing the final elimination of Czechoslovakia. On 21 October 1938, the armed forces were directed to be ready for a surprise attack to occupy the Czech lands of Bohemia and Moravia and cut off Slovakia. A further directive on 17 December stipulated that it must appear as 'a peaceful action and not a warlike undertaking'.[94] In other words a way should be found to eliminate 'the rump Czech state' without triggering the Anglo-French guarantee. No deadline was stipulated but meanwhile the Czechs were forced to accept their dependent status. The

Germans dictated the frontiers of the Sudetenland to the international commission and Hitler made clear to the Czech Foreign Minister, Chvalkovsky, that his country was 'in the German sphere' and that British and French guarantees were 'worthless'.[95] The ambitions of the other regional powers, Poland and Hungary, to share in the spoils by asserting claims on behalf of their own minorities added to the pressure.[96] Poland took the disputed area of Teschen, bordering on Silesia, immediately after Munich with Hitler's approval. Hungary, on the other hand, which had resisted Hitler's demand for joint action before Munich, was now punished by being told that Germany could no longer support its claim to the whole of Slovakia. With German and Italian arbitration, it did receive in November a substantial redrawing of the frontier in its favour. However, Hitler decided that Slovakia – which had successfully claimed autonomy from the Czech state – could be a useful satellite. In addition, the easternmost region of Czechoslovakia, the Carpatho-Ukraine, could be a bargaining tool with the Hungarians and Poles. The Hungarians wanted it while the Poles feared that, if it became independent, it might inflame Ukrainian nationalism and attract their own Ukrainian minority. Hitler's attitude to the disposal of these territories was governed by pure expedience. The purpose was to ensure the submission not only of Czechoslovakia but also of Hungary and Poland. Germany could then extend its influence south to Romania, the Balkans and even Turkey. For that reason it was better to avoid final decisions until each of the intended satellites was prepared to accept German hegemony. As Hitler gave Goebbels to understand immediately after Munich, 'In general, clear and guaranteed frontiers in central Europe are not today in our interests. One day we will swallow this Czech state. The way to the Balkans must be made open.'[97]

Hitler's tactics were effective with Hungary which joined the anti-Comintern pact. Poland, however, was not willing to give up its independence. It wanted Hungary to be given the Carpatho-Ukraine to prevent that region becoming a centre of Ukrainian nationalism. But German proposals for what Ribbentrop called 'a general settlement of all possible points of friction between Germany and Poland', incorporating the return of Danzig (though with rights of access for Poland to the port), an extra-territorial motorway and railway across the corridor (which separated East Prussia from the rest of Germany) and for Poland to join the anti-Comintern pact were politely refused.[98] Despite their efforts between October 1938 and January 1939, neither Ribbentrop nor Hitler was able to persuade the Polish Foreign Minister, Josef Beck, to agree to their terms. It was clear that Poland was not willing to submit to German leadership.[99]

By the end of January, Hitler was planning his next coup. Goebbels noted that he was going to his Alpine retreat 'to think over his next foreign policy moves', adding:

> Perhaps it will be the turn of the Czech state again. Because this problem is of course only half solved. But he is not yet completely clear about that. It could also be the Ukraine.

The following day, over lunch, Goebbels observed Hitler's restless scheming:

> The führer speaks almost only about foreign policy now. He is mulling over new plans again. A Napoleonic nature![100]

What was in Hitler's mind?[101] The uncompleted action against the Czechs still rankled, although they were defenceless and bent over backwards to appease him. The obduracy of the Poles made further pressure on them by whatever means attractive. Control of the rest of Czechoslovakia would mean that Poland could be threatened from the south as well as the west. Encouraging Ukrainian nationalism would be another option against both Poland and the Soviet Union, though for Hitler the real attraction of the Ukraine was as rich agricultural land to be re-settled in time by German farmers.[102] A further possibility, which the military had also been told to prepare for in the directive of 21 October 1938, was to take back the Baltic port of Memel from Lithuania, an action which could be justified in terms of its majority German population and would also increase the pressure on Poland and create a bridgehead for action against the Baltic states.[103]

There were other considerations. The German economy continued to suffer the effects of escalating rearmament – shortages of labour and raw materials, growth of consumer spending and an escalating budget deficit.[104] These were problems which could not be overcome by will power alone. They were obvious to the Nazi leadership. Göring admitted that the financial situation was 'very critical' and Goebbels noted that it was 'catastrophic'.[105] In December Hitler ordered a temporary reduction in military expenditure.[106] But when in January

Schacht warned of the dangers of a new inflation – a nightmare for Germans since the hyperinflation of 1923 – Hitler dismissed him from his post as president of the Reichsbank.[107] The economic pressures in themselves did not point to a particular solution. Göring favoured expanding trade with south-eastern Europe.[108] But the Czech lands of Bohemia and Moravia contained an advanced industrial economy and extensive military equipment (which later proved enough to equip 20 divisions), a strong incentive to taking direct possession.[109] Hitler may also have felt the need to maintain the momentum of expansion, asserting his authority and showing the Nazi leadership, his conservative opponents and the German public, that there would be no turning back.

Hitler soon decided on the most obvious move, the occupation of the Czech lands. Since Chamberlain's surprise intervention the previous autumn, he had always thought of this as completing what had been begun with the annexation of the Sudetenland. On 16 January, he suggested to the Hungarian foreign minister that they should work for 'a politico-territorial solution' together with Poland and he indicated that March would be the earliest time when military action would be possible.[110] On 21 January, by contrast he was coldly dismissive to the Czech Foreign Minister, Chvalkovsky, complaining that his countrymen still hoped 'for a turn in European politics' and warning that such a turn would lead at once to 'the annihilation of Czechoslovakia'.[111]

Once he had decided on the goal, Hitler did not have to look far for the means. The obvious pretext for intervention would be a conflict between the Czechs and Slovaks enabling Germany to intervene on the side of the Slovaks.[112] German agencies were already active encouraging nationalist movements in Slovakia and the Carpatho-Ukraine. The Slovak leaders in fact resisted mounting German pressure to declare independence. But when the Czechs tried to pre-empt the threat by deposing the Slovak government on 9 March, Hitler saw his opportunity. 'Shouting for joy', he ordered an invasion of the Czech lands on 15 March and, with Goebbels, prepared an announcement that the Slovak government had already requested German assistance before its deposition – Hitler remarking about this fabrication that 'one cannot make history with lawyers'.[113] The Slovak leadership remained stubbornly slow to do what was expected of it and Goebbels began to worry about how to create another pretext for the invasion since the Czechs also refused to be provoked.[114]

Brutal methods were resorted to: the Slovak Prime Minister, Tiso, was brought to Berlin on 13 March and given an ultimatum to declare independence and put Slovakia under German protection, or face the consequences which would be Hungarian occupation. When the Slovak government complied on 14 March, the elderly Czech President, Hácha, and Chvalkovksy tried to stave off the inevitable by travelling to Berlin and appealing direct to Hitler. When he deigned to receive them in the early hours of 15 March, they too were bullied mercilessly into capitulation. Hácha ordered Czech troops not to resist the German invasion and agreed to accept a German protectorate. On the same day, with German encouragement, the Hungarians occupied the Carpatho-Ukraine. Czechoslovakia had ceased to exist. Hitler set off immediately to Prague to seal the triumph in person. To complete the immediate agenda, the Lithuanian government was told to return Memel or suffer the military consequences and the territory was returned to Germany on 23 March.[115]

Public reaction in Germany to this latest coup was again divided. Unlike the *Anschluss* and Munich, it had happened very suddenly without an anxious period of increasing tension leading up to the crisis. Judging by the reports of the SPD in exile there was again a feeling that Hitler had got away with it, indeed that he could now do what he liked without the western powers intervening.[116] Others feared that it marked another step towards an inevitable war, though some were swayed by the revival of an old propaganda theme from before the First World War that Germany was encircled by hostile powers and had to break out.[117] Sceptics grumbled about the cuts in food allocations, blaming the occupation and complaining that now they would have to feed Czech gypsies. Others thought that foreign coups were simply a way of distracting attention from domestic difficulties. There was also the basic feeling that 'the Czechs are not Germans' and would become a source of unrest; in contrast there was support for the return of the German population of Memel. Hundred per cent Nazis were reported as expecting a quick victory over the democracies to be followed by the invasion of Russia. To the objection that Napoleon had come unstuck in Russia, they replied that in the age of the aeroplane distances could be swiftly overcome. Critics of the regime feared that it was heading in the same direction as Bolshevism, citing what had happened to Jews in the November pogrom. There was also scepticism about the value of Italy as an ally.

FROM THE OCCUPATION OF PRAGUE TO THE INVASION OF POLAND

Hitler knew that he had broken the spirit if not the letter of the Munich agreement. Technically it could be argued that Czechoslovakia had ceased to exist at its own request and therefore the agreement was void. Indeed the British and French governments reacted at first, in the way Germany expected, with protests. As public opinion in the democracies quickly began to harden against Germany, however, Hitler became aware that he had pushed their toleration to the limit. Despite appearing to Goebbels at first 'relaxed' and 'totally calm' in face of the hostile reaction, in a rare admission he subsequently spoke of 'allowing a period of calm to begin in order to restore trust again' and then broaching the colonial question.[118] This is an interesting moment. The demand for the return of colonies had been kept alive in a minor key as a warning to Britain not to interfere on the continent. Although Hitler never regarded colonies as a substitute for continental expansion, they might provide an acceptable interim gain to be negotiated with Britain, which had earlier shown a willingness to discuss the subject. Talking like this, Hitler was clearly not expecting a European war to break out the same year.[119]

Hitler was, however, no longer in control of events. When, at the end of March, Ribbentrop renewed the demands on Poland for Danzig and a German road and railway link through the corridor to East Prussia, Hitler was still prepared to 'bite on the sour apple and guarantee Poland's frontiers' in return.[120] But the Polish government saw no need to accept such terms. Rather it was able to take advantage of a major shift in British policy to guaranteeing states which were seen to be at risk from Germany or Italy. Poland became the first beneficiary of this policy when alarm at German intentions led Chamberlain to guarantee Polish independence in the House of Commons on 31 March. Further guarantees followed on 13 April to Romania which, under pressure, had agreed to a trade treaty securing German oil supplies, and Greece following the Italian invasion of Albania. In addition, the American President Franklin Roosevelt asked Hitler to give an undertaking that he would not attack any of a whole list of European and Middle Eastern countries in the next 10 or 25 years. The Soviet Union was also drawn into discussions for a security pact and, on 17 April, proposed a military alliance with Britain and France. To Hitler these developments were wholly unacceptable, reviving the threat of 'encirclement' to prevent German domination of the continent.

To regain the initiative, he moved from trying to reach agreement with Poland prior to the war with the western powers to making preparations to eliminate Poland. As with Czechoslovakia in 1938, he expected to be able to achieve this without western intervention but he was in any case prepared to take the risk. And, as with Czechoslovakia, he did everything possible to isolate Poland from its allies. In this policy he had the full support of Ribbentrop who consistently encouraged him to believe that, when it came to the point, Britain and France would not fight. In turning against Poland Hitler was also able to draw on broad support among the German people. The Versailles settlement of the frontier giving parts of Prussia to Poland, separating East Prussia by the corridor and making Danzig a Free City under the League of Nations had always been resented more than any of the other frontier provisions, certainly more than the Czech frontier where the Sudetenland had not previously belonged to Germany. In addition there was a history of animosity of Germans toward the Poles, similar to that felt in some circles in Britain towards the Irish. It is noticeable, however, that Hitler's propaganda was directed not just against Poland but also against the western powers and, in particular, Britain. Its themes were living space, contrasting the ratio of 135 people per square kilometre in Germany with less than 10 in the democracies (including their empires), and the arrogance of their claiming the right to interfere against Germany in what it saw as its region of central Europe while Germany made no claim to interfere in their empires – for instance during the brutal coercion of the Palestinian Arabs by Britain. These themes were clearly intended to prepare the German people not just for war with Poland but also for the larger conflict to come.[121]

On 25 March, Hitler ordered the army to study the Polish question though at that date he still hoped to prevent Poland becoming aligned with Britain.[122] On 3 April, however, he ordered the armed forces to be ready for war against Poland at any time after 1 September as 'a precautionary complement' to the main objective of preparing for war with the western democracies.[123] The political leadership (i.e. Hitler) would try to isolate Poland if possible. That would be easier to achieve if the attack started 'with sudden, heavy blows' which achieved rapid success. On 28 April, in a polemical but effective speech to the Reichstag, Hitler replied to Roosevelt.[124] He presented himself as peacefully overcoming the sources of conflict in Europe which resulted from Versailles – the Saar, Austria's separation from Germany, the Sudetenland, the artificial state of Czechoslovakia and lastly through his generous offers to resolve the problems of the Polish frontier, which the Poles had misguidedly rejected. The democracies which constantly tried to upset these peaceful developments, accusing Germany of aggressive intentions, were themselves disturbers of the peace. He poured scorn on Roosevelt's suggestion that conflicts be solved by conferences and disarmament – Germany had once trusted in President Wilson's promises of that kind and, as a result, had become the victim of a dictated peace with loss of territory, all its colonies, and total disarmament. Hitler declared that he, an unknown worker and soldier without the advantages of the President of the United States, had restored his country from impotence and mass unemployment to order and strength. And he believed that by serving his people alone, he would continue to make the best contribution to the peace of the world. He also used the opportunity to announce the cancellation of the naval agreement with Britain (which Germany was in any case already breaking) and the non-aggression treaty with Poland. He claimed that the Anglo-Polish alliance, directed as it was against Germany, had already broken these treaties.

Unlike the crisis over Czechoslovakia there was no significant opposition from the military leadership. A combination of anti-Polish feeling, confidence that victory would be easy and acceptance that Hitler's judgement about the democracies had proved right before led to an unwillingness to question his authority.[125] On 23 May Hitler explained the situation to his most senior commanders.[126] He opened with the fundamental need for living space and the inevitability of conflict with the established powers to achieve it. He then spoke of Poland, declaring that it would be an enemy in any conflict and also that the issue was not Danzig but rather 'expanding our living space in the East and making food supplies secure and also solving the problem of the Baltic States'. He then related Poland to the 'showdown with the West' arguing that since Poland would try to prevent a German victory in the west it must be attacked 'at the first suitable opportunity'. There would be war, unlike 1938, and they would try to isolate Poland. Confusingly however, according to the notes of the meeting, Hitler added the rider that if it was not certain that Poland had been isolated then the war would be primarily against England and France – 'it is better to fall upon the West and finish off Poland at the same time'. He went on to discuss the position of other powers: Japan whose interests he saw as to move against Russia, Russia which he hinted might be interested in improving relations with Germany and willing to accept the destruction of Poland, and Britain with whom he did not expect a peaceful settlement but rather a 'life and death' showdown for hegemony. To defeat Britain, Dutch and Belgian air bases would have to be occupied and (he later added) France defeated. Britain could then be cut off from supplies of food and oil which would force its capitulation. The aim should be to deal the enemy 'a smashing blow or *the* smashing blow at the start' but that would be possible only if they did not 'slide' into war with Britain over Poland. They should also prepare for a long war (elsewhere he spoke of one lasting 10–15 years) where with their occupation of France and the Low Countries, 'Time will decide against England.' These were the lessons of the world war. There is no evidence that any of those present questioned Hitler's argument. They may have been reassured by his statement, in reply to Göring, that the completion date for the armaments programme was to remain 1943–44. That suggested that, whatever the plan for Poland, Hitler did not expect the showdown with the western powers in the immediate future.

Isolating Poland meant persuading Britain and France not to fight. Hitler tried the same method as he had used with the Sudetenland, putting Poland in the wrong by emphasizing his attempts to reach a peaceful solution over Danzig and the corridor. During the summer, propaganda mounted about Polish 'terror' and the desire of Danzig to 'return to the Reich'. The destruction of Czechoslovakia in March 1939, however, meant that the western powers were not going to fall for this tactic again. Hitler recognized the difficulty and, in any case, did not want another Munich – he wanted the destruction of Poland. Given that he expected war with the western powers at some time, it was really a question of whether that war could be postponed to a time of his choosing, preventing it breaking out with the Polish war or as a result of a 'slide' from one to the other. There was, however, not much he could offer the western powers other than trying to persuade them of his willingness to reach a separate agreement with them but equally of his determination to smash Poland should Poland resist what he presented as his reasonable demands. He also wanted to demonstrate that Germany was fully prepared for a European war should it come about. Both formed part of a conversation on 11 August with the League High Commissioner in Danzig, Carl Burckhardt, which Hitler knew Burckhardt would pass on to the British and French governments. Hitler declared that there was no need for war over Poland: all he demanded was a free hand in the east for corn and timber and he suggested that a special English envoy should be sent for discussions, someone like Lord Halifax or General Ironside.[127]

A more promising tactic soon attracted the attention of Ribbentrop. It was to prevent the Anglo-French commitment to Poland being complemented by an Anglo-French-Soviet alliance which was now the subject of negotiation following the proposal by the Soviet Union in April. If the Soviet Union could be detached then Germany would no longer face war on two fronts once Poland was defeated, and British and French intervention would become less likely. Ribbentrop eagerly interpreted what were in fact non-committal remarks by Soviet representatives as signs of willingness to reach an understanding.[128] He was not concerned by the contradiction between his new policy and the anti-Comintern pact – for him Britain remained the enemy that mattered and any strengthening of Germany's position against Britain had priority.[129] Attempts to make progress with trade talks were stalled in June but reopened in July and in August moved on to political questions with the German side offering to discuss Poland and the Baltic states and renounce any interest in the Ukraine. The Soviet preference remained a military alliance with Britain and France but in August those negotiations broke down over the refusal of Poland and Romania to allow Soviet troops to cross their territory. At that point Stalin turned to Germany. Ribbentrop achieved his dramatic coup with the conclusion of the Nazi–Soviet pact on 23 August, a non-aggression treaty with a secret proviso that in the event of any change in their frontiers, the Baltic states beyond the northern frontier of Lithuania, and eastern Poland (the area which Poland had occupied in 1921 to the east of the frontier suggested at the Paris peace conference) would be considered as belonging to the Soviet sphere of interest.

Having fixed the date for the invasion of Poland as 26 August, Hitler had arranged to address a group of some 50 senior officers on the 22nd.[130] When the time came he already knew that Stalin had agreed to Ribbentrop's visit to conclude a non-aggression pact. That made him more confident that Britain and France would not intervene. Hitler began by explaining that he had intended to fight the war in the west in a few years time and only then move east but that Poland's attitude had forced a change of plan. He gave various reasons for immediate action. First there were 'personal factors': himself and his political talents – 'probably no one will ever again have the confidence of the whole German people as I have' – and he could be assassinated at any time, Mussolini who kept Italy loyal to the alliance and Franco who ensured Spain's benevolent neutrality, while on the other side there were no outstanding personalities – later he described them as the 'small fry' he had seen at Munich. Given the economic constraints which meant they could hold out only for a few more years Germany had to act, whereas the others had much to lose. Then there was the favourable political situation with the British empire weak and threatened and a balance of power favourable to Germany and Italy in the Balkans (Yugoslavia internally divided, Romania threatened by Hungary and Bulgaria, and Turkey lacking leadership). It was also time for the German military machine to be put to the test. Meanwhile the relationship with Poland had become 'unbearable': 'The power of initiative cannot be allowed to pass to others' and with the compromises that were being suggested 'There was a danger of losing prestige.' And for the present 'the probability is still great that the West will not intervene'. There was as always in such decisions 'great risk' requiring 'iron nerves'. But neither the British nor the French were in a position to fulfil their commitments to Poland. Their only means were blockade, which would be ineffective because of German supplies from eastern Europe, or attack in the west, which Hitler thought would be impossible directly from France while he did not believe either that the western powers would violate Dutch, Belgian or Swiss neutrality to attack Germany: 'Thus in actual fact England cannot help Poland.' Then Hitler produced his trump card, the impending non-aggression pact with the Soviet Union together with the trade agreement under which Germany would receive grain, cattle, coal, lead and zinc in return for manufactured goods. The impact would, he predicted, be 'a bombshell'. In a further address, after lunch, Hitler made no secret of the kind of war he was about to unleash: 'Close your hearts to pity. Act brutally. Eighty million people must obtain what is their right.'

Despite his show of confidence, Hitler was still unsure. He summoned Goebbels to his Alpine retreat on the Obersalzberg and discussed the situation with him on 23 August. Goebbels noted in his diary that destroying Poland would not take much effort but whether the west would intervene was more difficult to say: 'London is more firmly committed than in September 1938. We must therefore proceed very cleverly. England certainly does not want a war at the moment. But it cannot lose face.' On the other hand, Hitler seemed confident that Italy, although not 'enthusiastic', would act with Germany as it had 'scarcely any alternative', and he was untroubled by the fact that Japan had been alienated by the Nazi–Soviet pact.[131] The following day, he was surprised at the lack of reaction abroad to the pact, which he had been counting on to weaken the determination of the western powers.[132] The next day, 25 August, with Hitler back in Berlin, events reached a crisis. The order for the attack on Poland to start at 4.30 AM the following day was given at the last possible time, just after 3 PM, but rescinded at 7.30 PM.[133] Hitler had lost his nerve. The reason was the receipt of a message from Mussolini at 5.45 PM that, if the western powers intervened, Italy would not take part in the war since, as it had previously made clear, it would not be ready until 1942.[134] Goebbels noted: 'That changes the whole position.... For the time being everything remains in the balance. The führer broods and thinks. That is a bad blow for him.'[135]

Without Italian support, it became more important to prevent British and French intervention. Late on 26 August, Hitler authorized an intermediary used by Göring, a Swedish industrialist Birger Dahlerus, to offer the British government a settlement under which Germany would guarantee the Polish frontiers and the British empire in return for British support for the return of Danzig and the corridor and German colonies. Hitler explained to Goebbels that his minimal demands were Danzig and 'the corridor in the corridor', an apparent reference to the idea of a German rail and road link to East Prussia and conversely, if after a plebiscite the corridor returned to Germany, Poland having a right of access through it to the sea.[136] Britain replied on 28 August reaffirming its guarantee to Poland but proposing that Germany should negotiate directly with Poland. Hitler agreed, provided negotiations started immediately. The Polish Foreign Minister, Beck, also agreed to negotiate. Goebbels noted: 'Everything is still in the balance. London certainly knows of the precarious situation in which we find ourselves.... We must try everything to come out of it with a success. The reckoning in its final form can be caught up with subsequently.' This suggests that Goebbels, at least, may have been starting to think of destroying Poland in two stages as had happened with Czechoslovakia. Later the same day, after seeing Hitler, he noted: 'He is very serious and somewhat worn out. That is no wonder given the nervous strain.' In the evening, he added that Hitler did not regard the offer for Beck to hold negotiations in Berlin as sufficient.[137] Of the events of the following day, 29 August, Goebbels recorded that Hitler would propose a plebiscite in the corridor and added: 'He hopes in this way perhaps still yet to prise London apart from Warsaw and find an occasion to strike.' Beck was to be allowed to come to Berlin. Goebbels thought they could lean on the willingness of Britain to allow negotiations but he saw a danger that Beck's arrival might set off 'an unstoppable wave of optimism here and thus undermine our whole position.'[138]

He need not have worried. Though Hitler toyed with the idea of negotiations his purpose was, as he told Göring, to separate Britain from Poland and also, as Schmidt heard him say, to show the German people that he had done everything possible to preserve peace.[139] German mobilization continued throughout the crisis and Italian efforts at mediation were rejected. On 28 August, the same day as he agreed to negotiate, Hitler set a provisional new date for the invasion as 1 September. On the evening of 29 August he insisted that Polish plenipotentiaries would have to come to Berlin the next day. When the British government refused to put pressure on the Poles to comply and suggested that German proposals be submitted in the normal way through the Polish ambassador, Hitler lost interest. Ribbentrop refused even to give the British ambassador, Sir Nevile Henderson, the text of the German proposals which were to be used now only for propaganda. On 31 August the order was given for the attack to begin at 4.45 AM on 1 September. A pretext was found by faking attacks on German positions by the SS in Polish uniforms and killing concentration camp inmates to serve as casualties.

Hitler had decided on war. He may have felt that he had no alternative – the imperative of living space, the inevitable opposition of the powers that already possessed so much of the world, the need to act while Germany still had a lead in rearmament, the economic constraints to which he could see no solution other than expansion, his age, his determination to keep the initiative, his fear of loss of prestige at home and abroad, all impelled him forward. But the pressures were a product of his own attitudes. He knew the risks but he was determined (as he told Göring) to go for broke.[140] In fact, events were already beyond his control. He had concluded a pact with the Soviet Union in the hope that it would isolate Poland. The manoeuvre failed. As Victor Klemperer predicted on seeing the photograph of Ribbentrop hand in hand with Stalin: 'A politics that is too immoral turns into political stupidity.'[141] By 3 September, Hitler found himself at war with the western powers whom he had not intended to fight before 1942, in a pact with the Soviet Union which was to have been the object of living space, and having alienated Japan and been left in the lurch by Italy. It was not what he had planned.

Given the risks, why did nobody stop him? Within the Nazi leadership there were the usual divisions. Ribbentrop egged him on to think that in the end Britain and France would climb down.[142] Göring and Goebbels were more inclined to take the threat of western intervention seriously but they offered no challenge to Hitler.[143] Some, like Rosenberg, were unhappy at the Nazi–Soviet pact but accepted that it was necessary given the decision to attack Poland.[144] The military leadership had its reservations about Hitler's leadership, and fumed when the original order to attack was reversed, but its will to resist – which had never been strong – had been broken in 1938.[145] The groups which had then planned a coup took no initiative other than sending warnings to Britain.[146] Inside the *Auswärtiges Amt*, Weizsäcker found Hitler erratic and irrational and tried, as in 1938, to steer events by warning Britain to take a strong stand and by co-operating with the Italian ambassador to get Hitler to draw back but this time Hitler was not to be deterred.[147] And for reasons already explained, both the military and the diplomats were much more receptive to the idea of war with Poland than they had been to war with Czechoslovakia. The same was true of the German public. As the SPD in exile noted, anti-Polish feeling was easily aroused.[148] Fear of war seems to have been less marked than in 1938, perhaps because of the expectation that Hitler would succeed in bringing off another peaceful triumph.[149] After all why should Britain fight for Poland, when it had allowed Czechoslovakia to be carved up? Nazi propaganda about Polish 'atrocities' and the increasing emphasis on encirclement and the opposition of the 'have' nations to German demands for a fair share of the world's resources also had an effect. Once war had broken out there were frequent reports of anti-British feeling, reminiscent of the hostility at the beginning of the First World War. Nevertheless, in comparison to 1914, the mood was one of resignation and fatalism not enthusiasm.[150] There was also at the beginning an air of unreality as people hoped that peace might yet return if a solution could be found for Poland. A Christian author, Jochen Klepper, noted in his diary on 4 September: 'People do not grasp the reality of the war, it seems distant, reversible. Just depression, just seriousness, just worry – apart from a few stupid expressions of the old, general chauvinist kind.'[151]

7 To World War: September 1939–December 1941

The invasion of Poland marked the beginning of the European war. The rapid defeat of Poland was followed by the occupation of Denmark and Norway in April 1940, the invasion of Holland, Belgium, Luxembourg and France in May, the battle of Britain from August to October, the invasion of Greece and Yugoslavia in April 1941 and the campaign in North Africa in which the Germans supported the Italians from February 1941, the invasion of the Soviet Union in June and, following the Japanese attack on Pearl Harbor, the declaration of war on the United States on 11 December 1941. It is possible to argue that each escalation of the conflict followed from the invasion of Poland. But each also required a decision by the German leadership and the willingness of Germans to fight, to administer the occupied territories, to produce the weapons for victory and to maintain morale on the home front. A study of Germany and the origins of the Second World War cannot therefore stop in September 1939. From the invasion of Poland, justified by a deeply felt frontier dispute, to war with the western powers which revived memories of a struggle since the 1890s for Germany to be the equal of the great powers, to the invasion of the Soviet Union which drew on both anti-Communism and specifically 'Jewish Bolshevism', Hitler found the support he needed. Germany, which had been fearful and divided at the prospect of war in 1938 and unenthusiastic in 1939, became Germany in occupation of much of the European continent by 1941, and moreover an occupation in Poland, parts of the Balkans and the Soviet Union of extraordinary ferocity and ruthlessness. How did it happen?

There are many kinds of explanation. Once war broke out attitudes hardened. Even opponents of Nazism felt the call of simple patriotism. Jochen Klepper, who was to commit suicide with his wife and stepdaughter in 1942 when they were about to be transferred to a concentration camp, wrote in his diary on 3 September 1939: 'We cannot from bitterness against the Third Reich wish for Germany's destruction, as many do. That is quite impossible.'[1] Germany's stunning victories in 1939–40 and the way its armies swept into the Soviet Union in 1941 were a natural cause for celebration for all but dedicated opponents of the regime and appeared to confirm Hitler's genius as a war leader.[2] The effect of the years of preparation for war, the propaganda, the glorification of war in education and culture, the military training of conscripts and party formations, like the SA, the SS and the Hitler Youth, is more debatable. But there is much evidence of a generational divide with young people being more influenced than those who had experienced the previous war. And many of the older population who feared a new war nevertheless also resented the Versailles Treaty, shared in some degree the racism and anti-Semitism of the Nazis and were prepared to support Hitler so long as he was successful. Although, as many contemporaries noted, the euphoria present in some circles in 1914 was not there in 1939, that by itself may be misleading. After what had happened in the First World War, it was hardly to be expected. A quiet determination to do one's patriotic duty with greater realism about what war meant might actually help to stabilize the home front in the trials to come.[3] Goebbels interpreted the mood in this way, saying in January 1940 that it was 'firmer and better for the war to come than 25 years previously'.[4] A parallel could be drawn with the mood in Britain at the same time, united and determined rather than elated.

The occupation regimes, particularly those in Poland, the Soviet Union and parts of the Balkans, require a different kind of explanation. These were the regions that suffered the worst Nazi experiments. The SS, trained as ideological warriors, were responsible for many though by no means all of the atrocities. Part of the explanation lies in institutional rivalries and lack of planning, leading to unforeseen crises and improvised solutions eventually culminating in systematic mass murder. Part of the explanation may also lie in the escalation of war on the eastern front, as it became a desperate struggle for survival, a genuine 'total war' where soldiers no longer felt bound by legal or moral norms. Another factor was the memory of the food shortages caused by the British blockade in 1917 and the damaging effect it had on morale: this was to lead in 1941–2 to the requisitioning of supplies from Poland and Russia regardless of the millions who starved as a result. But the deeper cause was the power of racial ideology, the central inspiration of Nazism, which allowed people to

think in terms of superior and inferior races and the right to depop-
ulate whole regions in order to resettle them with Germans and to
engage in mass murder. What Hitler called 'a racial reconstruction of
Europe', was not an idea confined to Himmler and a small circle of
the Nazi elite.[5] It influenced a significant number of university gradu-
ates in the 1920s, scientists, geographers, economists and historians
among others.[6] Their willing co-operation in the occupation regimes
helped to turn Hitler's crude concept of what would now be called
'ethnic cleansing' into brutal reality, a process at first chaotic and
haphazard but ultimately performed with clinical efficiency. The belief
that the laws of race had their own compelling morality, overriding
humanitarian scruples, had deep roots. It was to be found in the
irrational mysticism of Nazi ideologues, epitomized by Alfred Rosenberg's *The Myth of the Twentieth Century*, but also in the eugenic ideas
of modern medicine. In a way typical of Nazism, it combined the
irrational with the scientific, revealing what has been called 'the dark
side' of modernity.[7] And as the occupation regimes and the war on
the eastern front showed, such ideas were not confined to Germany.
Indeed, outside Poland and the Russian heartland of the Soviet Union
the occupation depended not only on coercion but also degrees of
acceptance and collaboration.[8] Romanians, Hungarians, Lithuanians,
Ukrainians and Croats among others all took part in atrocities against
those they saw as their racial or ideological enemies.

Germany was carried from the European war to world war by
many different currents. Victories continued to bind the regime to
the people, as had the foreign policy successes of the 1930s, despite
the privations of war as the economy became increasingly subject to
immediate military requirements. Hitler did not, as was previously
thought, try to spare consumption to sustain civilian morale in the
first two years of the war. Rather he wanted the economy mobilized
for a total but a short war, calculating accurately that Germany could
not win a long war against enemies and potential enemies (including
the United States) with greater resources.[9] Driven on by the need for
a decisive victory, he kept increasing the stakes until he was at war
with all the great powers apart from Italy and Japan. The occupation
regime in the Soviet Union meanwhile turned the possibility of a
war of liberation from Stalinism into its opposite, the mobilization of
the Soviet peoples behind Stalin against the Nazi conqueror. When
Hitler declared war on the United States, he admitted he did not yet
know how to defeat America.[10] The twin characteristics of Nazism,

the escalation of goals to be achieved by war and the crude racism that made enemies of all Slavs, ensured not only that the European war would become a world war but also that it would end in Germany's defeat.

POLAND: FROM WAR TO RACIAL EMPIRE

The invasion of Poland was the first occasion on which the armed forces of the Third Reich had been required to fight. With overwhelming strength on the ground, in the air and at sea, victory was swiftly achieved. The tactics of rapid penetration by motorized divisions supported by air attack proved their worth. Within four weeks effective Polish resistance was at an end, overwhelmed by the Germans from the west and south and, after two weeks hesitation, also by the Red Army from the east. Poland was occupied and divided between its conquerors.[11] Germany took some 90 000 square kilometres with 10 million inhabitants – 80 per cent of whom were Poles – into the Reich, extending East Prussia and Silesia and creating the new provinces of Danzig-West Prussia and Posen, or the Warthegau, as it was renamed in January 1940. The future status of the remainder of German occupied Poland, a further 96 000 square kilometres, was initially left unclear with the possibility of some sort of Polish state under German control being allowed there. As the 'General Government' it became an area to which Poles and Jews were deported from the incorporated territories. In July 1940, however, it was given the status of an 'adjunct territory' with the prospect of eventually developing its own 'German racial core'. Meanwhile the Soviet Union occupied the east of Poland, and under a revision of the Nazi–Soviet pact on 28 September transferred Polish territory to German control in return for German agreement that the whole of Lithuania should be regarded as in the Soviet sphere.

The German occupation of Poland was marked by a high degree of improvisation and terror. Before the summer of 1939, as we have seen, Hitler had not expected to have to conclude a pact with the Soviet Union against Poland. Now he found himself at war with Britain and France and dependent on the Soviet pact to avoid war on two fronts and to provide vital raw materials. Policy towards Poland reflected his anger that the Poles should have dared to cross him and also, perhaps, the fact that the great experiment of living space in the east, in the Baltic states and western Russia, was blocked for the time being. Poland became the helpless victim of Nazi racial doctrine. The extension of the Reich by the directly incorporated territories and the brutal treatment of the subject population in the General Government made it clear that no basis for an independent Polish state was to survive. The Nazi Gauleiter of the incorporated areas were allowed to begin deporting their Jewish and Polish populations with total disregard for their welfare or even survival. The SS was given the authority to enforce the deportations and resettle Germans from the Baltic states and Soviet occupied Poland in place of those evicted. After some protests from the armed forces against the atrocities that accompanied the occupation, Hitler transferred authority from military government to the new civilian administration on 26 October. Himmler was appointed Reich Commissioner for the Strengthening of German Nationality on 7 October and, not content with a mere deportation programme, embarked on a complex screening of the Polish population into different categories to determine those suitable for Germanization.

The German occupation of Poland was an experiment in every sense. Policies were inconsistent and varied between regions. Racial policy, championed by Himmler, and economic policy led, among others, by Göring were in conflict. Deportation of Poles and Jews into the General Government was stopped and restarted and stopped again as the 'Governor General', Hans Frank, protested that he could absorb no more and the army objected to the use of badly needed transport for the purpose. When the programme was suspended in March 1941 as preparations were made for the attack on the Soviet Union, some 365 000 Poles (including Jews) had been deported and further large numbers had fled to escape deportation but Himmler had been intending to deport another million in 1941 alone. Economic policy towards the General Government also shifted from initially stripping the region of its assets to exploiting its productive capacity though these conflicting priorities were never fully resolved.[12] Germany's need for Polish labour to replace Germans called up into the armed forces – a million were wanted according to Göring in January 1940 – was met by any method that came to hand, by recruitment and the use of prisoners of war and when that proved inadequate by conscription, seizure and deportation. The system of classifying Poles into various categories of eligibility for Germanization also varied: in West

Prussia the Gauleiter entered villages with 80 per cent Polish populations as 'German', whereas in the Warthegau the sifting into different
categories was much stricter. There was also inconsistency in the policy
of deporting Jews into the General Government from other parts of
the German empire. Deportations from Austria (the Ostmark) and the
former Czech lands (the Reich Protectorate of Bohemia and Moravia)
and elsewhere were begun but then suspended, first when priority was
given instead to deportations within Poland, then when the idea of
deporting Jews to Madagascar was seriously considered after the fall of
France in 1940, and subsequently when attention turned to planning
the attack on the Soviet Union.[13]

Faced with conflicting priorities, the German authorities resorted to
ever higher levels of coercion. For the overwhelmingly Polish populations of the Warthegau and the General Government, life under
German occupation was – and was intended to be – that of people
treated as sub-human, without rights, deprived of culture, religion
and all but elementary education, and with inadequate food; all this
tempered only by expedience, corruption and occasional humanity
from elements of the occupying forces. For Jews the experience was
even worse, driven into ghettos in the major cities, deported into work
camps, kept on starvation rations, put to work in conditions where they
were not expected to survive and killed when they were considered
unfit for work. It is estimated that six million people – about 18 per
cent of the population – about half of them Jews died over the whole
course of the occupation.

What light does this throw on the German experience of war and
the degree to which Hitler was able to carry the German people with
him into the kind of war he intended and put into practice? Hitler
made his views clear to those who needed to know, though the detailed
application was left to them. Before the invasion he had told his senior
commanders to close their hearts to pity and act brutally.[14] To his
immediate circle he was blunt about what he had seen in Poland
after the invasion. Rosenberg recorded him as saying: 'The Poles: a
thin germanic layer, underneath frightful material. The Jews, the most
appalling people one can imagine.'[15] To Goebbels he described the
Poles as 'More animals than humans...' adding that had the medi-
aeval ruler of Saxony, Henry the Lion, conquered the east the result
would have been 'a heavily slavified German mongrel race' but 'Now
at least we know the laws of race and can apply them'. A few days
later he added 'Asia begins already in Poland.'[16] At a meeting with

senior figures involved in the administration of the General Government, Hitler made it clear that there would be 'a hard ethnic struggle
which would not permit any legal restrictions' adding that it should
be possible to use the area 'to purify the Reich territory also of Jews
and Polacks [a derogatory term for Poles]' and describing it as 'The
devil's work'.[17] In public he used different language but the sense was
the same. In a speech to the Reichstag on 6 October, celebrating the
victory, he referred to 'the most important task' following the disinteg-
ration of Poland as 'a new ordering of ethnographic relationships, that
is a resettlement of nationalities' not just in Poland but on behalf of
German minorities in the whole of eastern and south-eastern Europe.
Germany and the Soviet Union were, he said, undertaking this work
jointly, making good the failures of the Versailles settlement which
had ignored the problem.[18]

Those entrusted with carrying out the work were, in the first
instance, the SS in the form of the Security Police and the intelligence service (SD) under Reinhard Heydrich. Plans had already been
made in August for special task forces (*Einsatzgruppen*) to carry out a
'Fundamental cleansing: Jews, intelligentsia, clergy, nobles'.[19] Similar
task forces had already been used against Jews and political opponents
after the occupation of Austria and Czechoslovakia and they were to
be used again in the Russian campaign in 1941. For the invasion of
Poland one force of some 400–600 men was allocated to operate in
the rear of each of the five German armies. It is estimated that they
killed some 60 000 people. They were helped by so-called self-defence
organizations of ethnic Germans in Poland, who had suffered discrimination from the Polish authorities and themselves been the victims
of violence during the invasion. In addition atrocities were committed
by regular troops of the German army, though – unlike the SS – their
commanding officers regarded these atrocities as a breach of discipline
to be punished.[20] Two senior commanders also protested against the
actions of the SS, describing them as counter-productive, dishonour-
able and brutalizing. Hitler dismissed their objections saying 'one can't
fight a war with Salvation Army methods'.[21]

At the end of October 1939, authority was transferred from military
government to the civilian authorities. This meant the party and the SS
with its responsibility for security, deportation and resettlement. The
party was represented by dedicated Nazi Gauleiter in each area and
their staffs. These thousands of officials were chosen for their party
loyalty rather than their administrative competence and ruled their

districts as racial conquerors, sometimes incidentally for private profit. The worst conditions were in the Warthegau where its Gauleiter, Arthur Greiser, wanted to turn it into a model of how Germany itself would be ruled when the war was over, and the General Government, under Hans Frank, where the SS in effect established a state within a state.[22] It should not be assumed, however, that the German occupation depended simply on over-promoted party officials and thugs with an appetite for mass murder. It also depended on experts with doctorates who willingly advised on racial background, population policy, and economic organization, some of whom worked for Göring in the Four Year Plan organization, some were academics and some worked directly for the SS and supplied the leadership of the *Einsatzgruppen*.[23] They were united in the belief that Poland suffered from overpopulation and inefficiency and that it was their duty to deport millions of Poles and Jews and replace them with Germans who would farm the land productively. This was the morality of racial imperialism: there was not enough land for everybody; it was the duty of Germans to protect the German race; if that meant deporting and even eliminating millions of others so be it. The cold logic of the experts was parallelled by the emphasis in the SS on discipline, toughness and incorruptibility in carrying out tasks which were seen as necessary though unpleasant. As Frank declared in December 1941, discussing the killing of 'a few thousand Poles', 'Gentlemen, we are not murderers', though he admitted that it was 'a fearful task' for those who had to carry it out.[24] In fact the strains of mass executions by shooting – Himmler himself nearly fainted when witnessing one event – had already led by December 1941 to other methods being tried. Gas vans were used to kill Jews in Chelmno in the Warthegau and the first extermination centre using a gas chamber was planned at Belzec in the General Government.[25]

The occupation of Poland saw the transplanting from Germany of the most radical elements of Nazism without the constraints which still existed in Germany itself. The SS and the security police already had experience of the concentration camps and the cumulative persecution of Jews and other unwanted groups to draw on. The Four Year Plan organization already had experience of expropriation of Jewish businesses and conscription of labour. A board to organize emigration of Jews had already been active under Adolf Eichmann in Vienna. Even mass killing, including the use of gas, had already been pioneered in the euthanasia programme against the mentally and incurably sick.[26]

In each case these could be applied with a new freedom in Poland and allowed Nazis like Greiser to experiment with policies – for instance eliminating the Polish clergy of the Warthegau – which pointed to a future intended for Germany itself once the war was over.

How much support did these radical policies, an essential part of Hitler's purpose in launching the war, have among the German people? There is no simple answer. There is no clear dividing line between radical Nazis and the rest. The army as well as the SS were involved in atrocities. Although Brauchitsch as commander-in-chief passed on the protests of some of his senior commanders against the behaviour of the SS, he was not prepared to make an issue of the matter with Hitler.[27] Army commanders were given to understand that they had to accept the actions of the SS as part of a necessary ethnic programme authorized by the führer. It has been argued that in any case regular troops shared Nazi attitudes to a great extent. And with the rapid expansion of the army, to some four million soldiers in 1940, it is claimed that they were also representative of civilian society in Germany of which they had until recently been a part.[28] What was happening in Poland was hardly a secret from anyone who wanted to know, given the scale of the operations and the number of Germans involved, quite apart from the evidence closer to home of the conditions of forced Polish labour in German factories and farms.[29] Were the occupation policies then supported by a general German consensus rather than by only an extreme minority?

There is a strong argument to be made along these lines.[30] What happened in Poland was made possible by thousands of petty officials, ordinary police, railway staff and others as well as the party elites. It can be explained in terms of an attitude of superiority towards the East in general, Poles and later Serbs and the peoples of the Soviet Union, Jews and especially the unassimilated Jewish populations of eastern Europe who retained their traditional dress and religious customs. Ingrained attitudes towards these groups merged all too easily with Nazi racial imperialism.[31] The American correspondent, William Shirer, recorded the lack of enthusiasm among Berliners when the war broke out but two weeks later he noted, 'I have still to find a German, even among those who don't like the regime, who sees anything wrong in the German destruction of Poland.'[32] That referred simply to the conquest of Poland. But the violence of the German occupation may also be linked to previous experience – the First World War and German atrocities in the First World War – and the cult of violence by extremist groups in the Weimar Republic.[33] Violence against its enemies had continued throughout the Third Reich in prisons, concentration camps and the pogrom of 1938 to name only the most obvious examples. And during the war the campaign against 'enemies at home' as well as abroad became more intense and it was easy for public opinion to develop in the same way.[34]

However, it would be facile to conclude that by 1939 most Germans had become dedicated Nazis, let alone – as has been suggested – that Germans had been 'eliminationist' towards Jews since the nineteenth century.[35] There were people who were shocked by what happened. Ulrich von Hassell, a former ambassador, noted in his diary on 22 October 1939 that among those who knew in Berlin there was a sense of shame at the way the war had been conducted in Poland 'partly through the horrifying bestialities of the SS, above all against Jews'.[36] Hassell was reflecting the views of a well-informed conservative elite, critical of the regime. As he noted, the wider public continued to celebrate the victory over Poland. But even some of those who committed atrocities were not necessarily convinced Nazis. Allowance must be made for the context. The same people could be anxious and depressed at the outbreak of war in 1939 and become brutal conquerors in 1940. An army of occupation is always in danger of committing atrocities against the people over whom it is set. When those atrocities are authorized or even ordered by those in command, it is not surprising that they occur. The apparent indifference of most Germans on the home front may also be explained in other ways apart from enthusiastic Nazism. The call of patriotism, the intoxicating effect of victories and the magnetism of the Hitler cult all encouraged people to overlook the incipient genocide in Poland. It was easy to be swayed by the regime's own propaganda about the atrocities committed by Poles against ethnic Germans and German prisoners of war and also the claim that allegations of German atrocities were a revival of the enemy propaganda of the First World War. In addition, as the war extended in 1940–41, people had other concerns apart from what was happening in their name in Poland, the Balkans or the Soviet Union. Successful opposition in wartime was difficult and dangerous. Known opponents were in danger and the range of offences carrying capital punishment was extended to crush any sign of unrest.[37] The authorities were determined to prevent another collapse of the home front as in 1917–18. Fear of defeat with all its consequences also helped rally support. Individual church leaders managed to mobilize public resistance against the main euthanasia programme and contributed to Hitler's order to halt it in August 1941 but such opportunities were extremely rare.[38]

Nevertheless, it remains the fact that Hitler was able to carry out his occupation policies in Poland and elsewhere without serious challenge. German attitudes ranged from willing participation to general support, tacit acquiescence, indifference, shame and the occasional protest. The occupation of Poland showed the way in which traditional German attitudes towards the east and Nazi racial doctrine could be bridged. That was sufficient for Hitler to move from overthrowing the Versailles Treaty to war for racial empire.

VICTORY IN THE WEST

Before Poland had been defeated, Hitler was already planning to carry the war to the western powers. He knew he would face opposition from his military commanders whom he had led to expect that war in the west would not happen before 1943. They regarded an immediate attack as madness. They doubted the possibility of success against the French fortification of the Maginot line. They also remembered how the violation of Belgian neutrality had been turned into effective propaganda against Germany in the First World War. Above all they understood that war in the west, against France and Britain, would change what was still in terms of actual fighting a local war against Poland into a war for the control of western Europe. And they could see that if even only Britain could hold out, in time a war of attrition could lead to Germany's defeat as in the First World War because of the greater resources of the British empire especially if it was backed by the United States. They wanted Germany to remain on the defensive and look for a diplomatic settlement.[39]

Hitler was prepared to offer Britain and France a peace which left Poland and eastern Europe in the hands of Germany and the Soviet Union. But if that was rejected, he intended to attack in the west as soon as possible. As with other critical decisions, he prepared his arguments with some care but, having made up his mind, he was unwilling to make any concessions and simply ordered his military chiefs to obey. They were therefore faced with the alternatives of submission or rebellion. As in the summer of 1938 there was talk of resistance and a coup but once again the moment passed without action.[40] Hitler's will, supremely confident as he was that he had the support of the people and the ordinary soldier, proved too strong for the generals. Indeed when it came to the point they doubted whether their junior officers would follow them. The victories of April–June 1940, reversing the defeat of 1918, provided in the short term the most spectacular possible confirmation of his judgement.

On 27 September, Hitler started to work on his military chiefs, presenting them with an array of political and technical arguments for an assault on the west ideally in a month's time. His basic message was that the war was likely to continue and that time was working against them. Treaties (in other words the pact with the Soviet Union) would last only so long as they were in line with state's interests; the neutral powers were frightened of Germany but knew that (unlike Germany) Britain did not threaten their existence; the great powers also had no love for Germany as it threatened the European status quo. The present situation was therefore unstable and could be exploited by Britain. In addition, the economic resources of the other side were greater with their international transport links. And militarily, both in psychological and armament terms, time was working against Germany. The prestige of their victory over Poland would soon fade. The French army would improve over the next six months and the British would be able to deploy a considerable number of divisions over the next one to two years. In terms of armaments, although German equipment was incomplete its relative strength would not improve. The other side would use the next few months to improve their anti-tank and anti-aircraft defence which would undermine what had so far proved 'the key to our success'. Worse still was 'the possible alteration in the strategic starting point'. France and Britain were unlikely to attack the 'west wall' on the Franco-German frontier. Instead, they could violate Belgian and Dutch neutrality (or secure the agreement of those states, weakened by the Allied blockade against Germany) and from there attack the Ruhr with long-range artillery. Germany could therefore not afford to wait but, if a peaceful settlement could not be reached, must attack first, the sooner the better. Hitler then launched into a range of detailed arguments about troop strengths and equipment, designed to forestall objections from his service chiefs. The attack he declared would 'not be more difficult than Poland' – the French were not up to the standard of the Poles but the English would be the decisive factor. The war aim would be 'To force Britain to its knees, to destroy France'.[41]

At the same time, Hitler made his offer of peace. To Goebbels, at least, he gave the impression that he hoped it would succeed but, in any case, it would give him an alibi. As he told Goebbels, if the West refused the offer 'then it is absolutely clear where the guilt for the war lies and the conflict begins'.[42] In his speech to the Reichstag on 6 October, Hitler once more presented himself as a man of peace.[43] He started with the victory over Poland (in a war made necessary because the Poles had misinterpreted his reasonable offers as weakness), a victory which had restored the reputation of the German army stolen from it in 1918. He then praised co-operation with the Soviet Union arguing that it showed that the fears that Germany had ambitions for 'world dominion', for the Urals, the Ukraine or Romania were simply 'sick fantasies'. He made it clear that Germany and the Soviet Union would not allow Poland to become a source of unrest once more. He poured scorn on the Versailles settlement and the inability of the League of Nations to revise it, and justified his own policy as one of securing the rights of 80 million Germans and therefore bringing stability. He then listed all Germany's neighbours, guaranteeing friendly relations with each and underlining his desire for good relations with France and, above all, with Britain describing it as 'my life's goal' to bring the German and British nations together. 'Why should there be a war in the west now?', he asked. It would solve nothing – even if it achieved a change of regime in Germany, a new Versailles would only store up the same problems for the future. Germany made no demands which threatened the British empire. The return of German colonies was a matter of elementary justice in the share of the earth's raw materials but not something to be decided by force. Finally, he held out the prospect of economic agreements, limitations on armaments and extensions to the Geneva convention restricting the use of certain weapons. If, however, his offer of peace was rejected then destruction would follow, not only on the mainland – 'There are no longer any islands'.

While he waited for reactions to his speech, Hitler continued to plan for war. He composed a memorandum, which he read to Brauchitsch and Halder on 10 October, elaborating the arguments for an early attack in the west.[44] The same day a directive was issued to the armed forces to plan an offensive through Luxembourg, Belgium and Holland 'at the earliest possible moment and in greatest possible strength'.[45] The purpose was to defeat the enemy forces and occupy as much territory as possible in Holland, Belgium and northern France to serve as a base for the air and sea war against Britain and the protection of the Ruhr. Having heard of the British rejection of his peace offer, Hitler moved to set the date for the attack and on 22 October he settled on 12 November.[46]

There was no escape for his service chiefs. Opposition was not to be expected from Raeder or Göring, though the latter continued to encourage peace feelers with Britain and was pessimistic about the outcome of the war.[47] The responsibility therefore fell on the army command. Here there was a sense of desperation. On 14 October, Halder discussed in detail with Brauchitsch what he (Halder) saw as the three alternatives: 'attack, wait, fundamental changes'. Brauchtisch said that none of these offered definite prospects of success, least of all the last as it was 'basically negative and would create weak points'. It was their duty, he added, to 'explain the military prospects soberly and to advocate every possibility of peace'.[48] This bare summary was the only note of a discussion between the two most senior army officers of whether they should carry out Hitler's orders to attack, wait for the other side to attack, or overthrow Hitler. It was clear that Brauchitsch saw little hope in any of them, particularly the last since it would create instability which might be exploited by Britain and France. Nevertheless, as Kershaw points out, it was an 'extraordinary fact that in the early stages of a major war the two highest representatives of the army were airing the possibility of a form of *coup d'état* involving the removal of Hitler as head of state'.[49]

Brauchitsch was not prepared to organize a coup. Instead he tried to persuade Hitler, and to get other senior commanders to persuade Hitler, that the army was not ready. Hitler dismissed these arguments with contempt telling Goebbels that 'an army will never be ready' but what mattered was 'whether we are more ready than the others. And that is certain'.[50] After a furious confrontation with Hitler on 5 November, Brauchitsch was reduced to a nervous wreck though he is reported to have told Halder that, if others took action, he would not resist.[51] Unlike Brauchitsch, Halder did think seriously of taking the awesome responsibility for a coup, if all other methods failed.[52] He sounded out sympathetic army commanders and by the end of October contact had also been established with the group of younger officers in the military intelligence department under Canaris, who had been active in a similar way in September 1938. Halder was also in touch with Weizsäcker at the Foreign Ministry who was himself part of a circle of like-minded civilians including Goerdeler, the Prussian Finance Minister Johannes Popitz, Ulrich von Hassell, and Schacht.

These were significant people, representative of those conservative elites who had become disillusioned and saw Hitler as leading Germany on 'an unstoppable journey into the abyss'.[53] Their moral integrity and repugnance towards the regime is not in doubt. Their ideas for a coup, however, suffered from all sorts of difficulties. First, they depended on the army to carry it out. That meant Halder and, in the absence of an order from Brauchitsch, Halder as chief of the general staff could act only through the army commanders. Those consulted reported that they could not be sure of their officers let alone the troops. The rapid expansion of the officer corps from 3800 professional officers in 1935 to 22 000 in 1938 had diluted its solidarity and traditional values. The doubts of the army commanders killed the possibility of a coup and by the middle of November Halder gave up the idea.

Even had the army been willing to act, there would still have been major obstacles, indeed the situation was now less favourable than it had been in September 1938. Hitler was more popular after his blood-less triumph over Czechoslovakia and easy victory in Poland. The fear of what would follow his removal was correspondingly greater as was shown by the popular reaction in November to his narrow escape from a bomb planted by George Elser, a workman acting on his own, which exploded in the Bürgerbräukeller in Munich soon after Hitler had left the annual meeting commemorating the 1923 putsch.[54] Despite the hardships of war, many people felt that they were all now in the same boat and domestic upheaval would benefit only the enemy.[55] That chimed with a tendency to blame Britain for continuing the war by refusing to accept that Poland was none of its business. In these circumstances, Goebbels' propaganda accusing the British secret service of planting the bomb in Munich had some success. For the civilian opposition there was also the problem of what kind of altern-ative they could offer to the Third Reich – they stood for the rule of law but they were not democrats and in any case a return to the Weimar Republic would not have been a winning platform.[56] For a time the idea of recruiting Göring for a transitional role was even considered.[57] There was also the awkward problem of what peace terms they could expect. They wanted to preserve the fruits of some of Hitler's victories, Austria, the Sudetenland and the frontiers of 1914 in Poland.[58] If their coup happened before the attack in the West, then it would lack a popular base at home. If, on the other hand, they waited for the attack and the expected subsequent military reverses or defeat, then they could hardly expect favourable peace terms.[59] In these circumstances it is not surprising that little emerged from the opposition, 'the other Germany', as Hassell called it.[60] There were individual actions, for instance enquiries through the good offices of the Vatican of what peace terms might be available to a post-Hitler Germany and warnings given by Canaris's assistant, Hans Oster, to his friend the Dutch military attaché, of the dates of Hitler's planned invasion.[61] In the main, however, there was only conversation among the group, though that was important in itself to maintain hope in the possibility of a better future.

Hitler did not suspect a conspiracy though he lashed out at 'the spirit of Zossen', where the army headquarters were located, south of Berlin.[62] To strengthen the will of the military, he addressed a group of some 200 generals and representatives of the other services on 23 November, showing complete confidence in his own judgement and his ability to win them over.[63] His general theme was that each of his decisions had been difficult (and frequently opposed) and each had proved right. He would be accused, he said, of wanting to 'Fight and fight again' but 'In fighting I see the fate of all creatures. Nobody can avoid fighting if he does not want to go under'. There followed the usual theme of expanding living space for the needs of the population rather than contracting population to the available living space. 'No calculated cleverness is of any help here, solution only with the sword.... Struggles are different from those 100 years ago. Today we can speak of a racial struggle. Today we fight for oil fields, rubber, mineral wealth etc.' Britain had opposed Germany since 1870, he declared.[64] Both Bismarck and Moltke [the Prussian chief of the general staff in the wars of unification] had thought there would have to be another war but, at that time, there was the danger that it would be a two-front war. Now 'for the first time in history', Germany would have to fight only on one front but 'no one can know how long that will remain so'. Russia would keep to the pact only as long as it was to her benefit. Other factors were still in Germany's favour – Italy so long as Mussolini was there, Yugoslavia's fear of Italy, Romania's fear of Russia, the neutrality laws in the United States, but in six months things could be different. Having referred to the recent assassination attempt, Hitler added 'in all modesty' that he was irreplaceable – 'Neither a military man nor a civilian could replace me.' That statement was not mere arrogance – it was also a shrewd reminder to his audience that, however much they might doubt his judgement, a coup had no prospect of success. Hitler then resumed his main theme, 'Time is working for our adversaries'. He illustrated that in relation to British and French rearmament. He also praised the achievements of all three services in Poland, while delivering a thinly veiled rebuke to Brauchitsch for having tried to persuade him that the conduct of the troops in Poland showed they were not ready for war in the west. He repeated his earlier arguments about the 'Achilles heel' of the exposed position of the Ruhr which made it necessary to violate the neutrality of Belgium and Holland. 'The question is not the fate of a National Socialist Germany, but who is to dominate Europe in the future.' If Germany occupied Belgium and Holland then Britain could be attacked effectively by air and submarines and by laying mines off the coast. Once more appealing to history, he compared his decision to those of Frederick the Great, also taken in the teeth of opposition from his advisers, and Bismarck. He would attack France and Britain through Belgium and Holland 'at the most favourable and earliest moment'. Whether it would be successful depended 'upon a kind of Providence' but the prerequisite was that 'the leadership must give... an example of fanatical unity'. He threatened to 'annihilate everyone who is opposed to me'. He added almost as an afterthought, 'behind me stands the German people, whose morale can only grow worse.' He would 'stand or fall in this struggle'. There would be 'no capitulation to the outside, no revolution from within'.

It was in its own terms an effective performance, designed to show that there was no alternative to what he proposed and that his decision was both in accord with the modern imperatives of race and the long struggle of Prussia and Germany to overcome the problem of its security as a power in the centre of Europe with potential enemies on both sides. The reaction of his audience appears to have been mixed. Hassell heard from Goerdeler that the more innocent among them had been impressed but the cleverer ones thought he sounded like 'a frenzied Genghis Khan'.[65] Some of the generals were indignant at the implied criticism of the army. Brauchitsch offered to resign but Hitler brusquely dismissed the idea, telling him to do his duty. Halder tried once more to persuade Brauchitsch to act but he was not to be moved saying that they could not create 'rule by force of the bayonet'.[66] Doubts and resentment among the generals persisted but they were now resigned to following Hitler's orders.

Hitler was lucky as well as shrewd. He had been lucky that the French had not attacked during the Polish campaign when they could have mobilized forces superior to the German defence in the west.[67] He was also lucky that his plan to attack in November had been repeatedly postponed by bad weather, which would have impeded the Luftwaffe, by worries about the transport situation and perhaps also because of residual uncertainty in his own mind despite his firm front to the generals.[68] The delay, which led to the final postponement of the invasion in January until the following spring, was vital in allowing German forces time to re-equip the substantial losses – up to 50 per cent in some armoured divisions – sustained in the campaign against Poland.[69]

The delay was also vital in allowing the development of the plan that was to lead to victory.[70] When on 10 October Hitler ordered the army to produce a plan for an offensive, they responded five days later with a proposal to attack through Belgium, Holland and Luxembourg, engaging the enemy at as many points as possible and occupying the coast to enable the war to be continued against Britain. This initial response was little more than a hasty improvisation at a time when Brauchitsch and Halder were still hoping to persuade Hitler that the risks were too great. Hitler was not impressed and nor was General Keitel in the Armed Forces High Command. On 25 October, Hitler suggested that the main attack should be launched south of Liège, subsequently turning to the north-west to cut off the enemy forces which would have moved into Belgium. This manoeuvre, which Churchill later likened to the curved cut of a sickle, was a much bolder strategy. The same idea had occurred independently to General von Manstein, Chief of Staff of one of the army groups who then consulted the expert in tank warfare, General Guderian. They concluded that it would be possible for tanks to attack successfully through the wooded Ardennes, where they would have the advantage of surprise, before turning north to cut off the allied armies in Belgium. At first the army high command refused to discuss Manstein's proposals and, when he persisted, he was transferred to a command in the east. But further studies led to a softening of the opposition. Manstein also managed to present his ideas to Hitler on 17 February, thanks to the intervention of the army's representative on Hitler's personal staff, Colonel Schmundt. Hitler was favourably impressed and the new plan, incorporating Manstein's ideas, was adopted on 24 February.

While planning the western offensive, Hitler was also concerned to anticipate possible moves by Britain in Scandinavia and the Baltic.[71] Germany was dependent on imports of Swedish iron ore, which supplied almost half its total requirement. Those imports depended in winter on transport from the north Norwegian port of Narvik. In addition the main route for German submarines lay between Norway and the Shetland islands since the British had mined the English channel. Raeder had pointed out to Hitler in October 1939 the value of bases on the Norwegian coast for the submarine war. When the Soviet Union attacked Finland on 30 November, Raeder became concerned that Britain might use the excuse of sending help to Finland to occupy part of Norway. He introduced Vidkun Quisling, a former Norwegian minister of war and leader of an extreme nationalist party, to Hitler and Hitler then authorized the Armed Forces High Command to make preparations for a possible occupation of Norway which would also include Denmark. These preparations were accelerated after a British destroyer attacked a German supply ship, the *Altmark*, freeing the British prisoners of war on board, in Norwegian waters on 16 February. On 1 March Hitler issued a directive for the occupation of Denmark and Norway to be prepared – the so-called 'Weser exercise' – to anticipate British action, to secure the iron ore supplies and to provide the navy and Luftwaffe with expanded bases for operations against Britain. The action was to have 'the character of a *peaceful* occupation', designed to protect the neutrality of the two countries.[72] When peace was concluded between the Soviet Union and Finland on 12 March, Hitler looked for a new justification to act and with Raeder pressing him that the operation would have to be carried out sooner or later, it was finally set for 9 April. Britain had also decided to act and on 8 April mined Norwegian waters off Narvik, confirming Hitler's judgement that Germany had to forestall Britain and also providing him with a welcome excuse. He told Goebbels that by laying mines Britain had 'positively provided us with the springboard'.[73]

The occupation of Denmark was completed without difficulty.[74] The Danish government accepted the German ultimatum and ordered a ceasefire, hoping thereby to hold Germany to its promise to allow Denmark control of its internal affairs. Initially German influence was exercised through the German Foreign Ministry and attempts by the German minister in Copenhagen to replace the Danish coalition with more compliant ministers were resisted. The occupation of Norway was less smooth.[75] The Norwegian government rejected the German ultimatum and, with the king, was able to escape from Oslo before the Germans took over. British and French support was slow in coming but although by the end of April southern Norway was under German control, the Royal Navy cleared Narvik of German warships and on 28 May the port was recaptured by French and Norwegian troops. However, the success of the intervening German offensive in France led to an Allied decision to evacuate Norway at the beginning of June and the Norwegian king and his government went into exile in Britain. The German campaign had revealed weaknesses in co-ordinating an operation of all three armed services, a problem compounded by Hitler's constant interference in the running of the campaign and his loss of nerve when things went badly.[76]

The final outcome was satisfactory for the Germans but their naval losses were heavy in relation to the size of their fleet and the occupation of Norway required some 300 000 troops as a garrison. Politically too the situation was complicated. Given the resistance of the Norwegian government, Hitler appointed a Nazi Reich Commissioner, Josef Terboven on 24 April. Quisling who had attempted to stage a coup on 9 April was supported by Raeder and Rosenberg but he had negligible support in Norway itself where he was seen as a traitor. Terboven negotiated with Norwegian leaders for a new government which would replace the government in exile and avoid German direct rule. To achieve that he was prepared to exclude Quisling. However Hitler backed Quisling with the result that Terboven's negotiations failed and on 25 September he appointed a government with a majority from Quisling's party. That provoked the resignation of the Norwegian judiciary and other forms of passive resistance. Hitler intended the occupation of Denmark and Norway to be permanent forming 'a north Germanic confederation', defended by German troops and uniting their foreign, economic and tariff policies with those of Germany.[77] The Scandinavians were to be treated as racial allies, unlike the Czechs and Poles. In fact Germany was never accepted in either country, except by a small minority, as anything other than a conqueror with whom a *modus vivendi* had to be reached so long as the occupation continued.

Hitler had intended the attack in the west to follow the invasion of Denmark and Norway in the middle of April. It was delayed by the difficulties in Norway and then bad weather but eventually launched on 10 May. It was an immediate and astonishing success, despite the rough equivalence of the forces on each side, with the 'sickle cut' plan achieving surprise against a relatively weakly defended part of the front. Holland surrendered on 15 May and British, French and Belgian forces were trapped between two German armies and forced to retreat to the coast. From the area around Dunkirk 338 000 men were miraculously evacuated with the help of a flotilla of small boats. They were also helped by Hitler's decision taken together with the commander of the army group concerned, General von Rundstedt, but against the wishes of Brauchitsch and Halder, to hold up the advance of German tanks on Dunkirk for two days. The decision was taken then for military reasons not from any desire, as was later alleged, to spare Britain humiliation.[78] Hitler wanted to preserve the tanks for the rest of the French campaign and in any case he expected the Luftwaffe to be able to finish off the forces caught on the Dunkirk beaches. Despite the setback at Dunkirk, the rest of the German campaign went according to plan. Belgium surrendered on 28 May and France on 22 June. Holland was occupied and given a German civilian administration. Belgium was occupied under German military government. Britain remained undefeated but, unlike the First World War, Germany controlled the continent.[79]

With his sense for theatre and the symbolism of national rebirth, Hitler studied the ceremonies of the armistice and the Versailles treaty of 1918–19.[80] The French were made to sign in the same railway carriage and in the same place as the Germans had in 1918. Hitler was present initially but said nothing. Goebbels recorded on hearing Hitler's account of the event: 'The disgrace is now wiped out. It feels as though one has been reborn.'[81] With the success of the western offensive, Hitler reached the height of his popularity. One official reported that for the first time there was 'real enthusiasm for the war'.[82] Hitler received an ecstatic reception in Berlin on 6 July.[83] Brauchitsch in an order of the day to the troops on 25 June praised his 'unique greatness' and Keitel referred to him as 'the greatest warlord of all time'.[84] Even some members of the opposition were moved. Weizsäcker, despite his reservations, remembered how it had felt in 1918 for those who had lost relatives and had to ask themselves whether it had all been in vain. He wished his father had been alive to see the day.[85]

With most of the continent under its control, or at least under its influence, Germans could dream of a new world. Officials planned for an economic 'New Order' in Europe which would be self-sufficient and, with a population of 200 million, on the scale of the United

States or the British empire.[86] In the meantime, Germany's needs were met by confiscation of military equipment and raw materials, by running up huge debts with foreign banks which were made to pay for their nationals' exports to Germany and by charging the defeated inflated 'occupation costs'. At the same time, German firms were able to acquire stakes in their European competitors and benefit from the confiscation of Jewish property as well as the supply of foreign labour – by 1941 there were 3 million of them including over a million prisoners of war.[87]

THE BRITISH ENIGMA

In June 1940 Hitler basked in his victory and the adulation it brought – tears in his eyes at the reception in Berlin.[88] But so long as Britain was neither defeated nor willing to make peace, he knew his victory was incomplete. He was acute enough now to subordinate all other considerations to getting Britain out of the war. The armistice terms with France were framed to serve that aim. He did not want France to continue the war from its North African colonies. Nor did he want the French navy to defect to Britain. He therefore proposed terms which the French could accept. They gave Germany control of north and west France – and most of its industry – as a base against Britain. But they left much of the rest of France and its empire under the control of the new government based in Vichy under Marshal Pétain, a hero from the First World War. Technically Vichy also controlled the German occupied north and west but it was subject there to the German authorities in Paris. In addition, Germany re-annexed Alsace and Lorraine and imposed a German administration on Luxembourg. Italy which had joined the war at the last minute, on 11 June, concluded a separate armistice establishing its own occupation zone in the south-east. Mussolini had more far-reaching ambitions for territorial gain on the mainland and in the French empire but he was too weak to pursue them against Hitler who insisted on the priority of war with Britain. Britain, Hitler warned, hoped that if she could hold out for just one year then 'the war would be lost to Germany for within that time she could count on the active cooperation of America'.[89]

Hitler hesitated about the tactics to pursue against Britain. His objective had been to deliver a 'knockout blow' to force Britain to accept its exclusion from the continent.[90] He still hoped that his victory in the west might be enough to bring that about. He had no desire to see the break-up of the British empire which, he thought, would benefit mainly other powers – Japan, the United States and the Soviet Union.[91] But Churchill, who had become Prime Minister on 10 May 1940, was determined to continue the war. To make the point, the Royal Air Force launched bombing raids on west German cities and the Royal Navy bombarded part of the French fleet in the Algerian port of Mers-el-Kébir to prevent it falling into German hands.

Hitler faced a dilemma of his own making. He did not have the naval force for a successful invasion of Britain, at least not until he had control of the air. He therefore considered every possible option for bringing Britain to accept peace. After mulling it over in his alpine retreat for a week, he made one last appeal to Britain to see reason in his victory speech to the Reichstag on 19 July.[92] He tried to dispel any hope that Britain might still have of victory – the area under German control, he pointed out, stretched from the north of Norway to the Spanish frontier; German stocks of weapons, munitions, raw materials and food, he claimed, were better than before the western offensive and would be sufficient for a war of any length; German morale was firm without 'hurrah patriotism' but 'with the fanatical determination of a race, which knows the fate awaiting it should it suffer defeat'; the German relationship with Russia was firmly established on a clear division of interests. Despite the negative reaction from Britain, he continued to hope for several days that the speech would bring about a change of attitude. Only on 23 July after a broadcast by the Foreign Secretary, Lord Halifax, did he accept that the British rejection was final.[93]

He now cast around for alternative ways of forcing Britain to submit. Already on 16 July he had issued a directive for preparations to be made for a cross-Channel invasion by the middle of August but with the qualification that it would be carried out 'if necessary' and on condition that the British air force had first been neutralized.[94] But he remained doubtful about a landing and was soon persuaded by the naval chiefs that the earliest date possible would be mid-September. He started to consider other ideas, including taking Gibraltar in co-operation with Franco in Spain to close the western entrance of the Mediterranean to the British navy. However, he was also attracted by a very different plan. Puzzling over why Britain would not make peace even though its position was, in his view, 'militarily hopeless', he had already suggested to Halder on 13 July, that 'Britain still has hopes of Russia'.[95] Stalin had reacted to the German victory in the west by consolidating the Soviet hold over the Baltic states and also forcing Romania to cede the province of Bessarabia and the northern part of the province of Bukovina. These were defensive moves but they were seen by Germany as potentially threatening, especially given its dependence on Romanian oil. Halder agreed with Hitler and had already started to think about how to counter the Russian danger. In a meeting with the commanders-in-chief on 21 July Hitler referred to the difficulty of an invasion of Britain and British hopes of Russia, and the army command started to address the specific objectives of a possible campaign against the Soviet Union.[96]

As it became clear that the navy would not be ready for an invasion of Britain before the spring of 1941, Brauchitsch and Halder drew back from the idea of attacking the Soviet Union which would bring Germany into the dreaded situation of a two-front war. They preferred to maintain good relations with Russia and harass Britain by attacking Gibraltar, supporting the Italians in North Africa against the British stronghold in Egypt, attacking Haifa where the British oil pipeline from Iraq reached the Mediterranean, attacking the Suez canal and encouraging the Soviet Union to expand into the Persian gulf. Taken together, they argued, these operations would deliver a decisive blow to the British in the Mediterranean, drive them out of Asia, build up the Italian empire in the Mediterranean and enable Germany with Soviet help to extend its empire in western and northern Europe. Then, they concluded, Germany 'could face a war with Britain lasting for years with equanimity'.[97] Hitler, however, had come to the opposite conclusion. On 31 July he again met his military and naval chiefs. They agreed to start air attacks on Britain and decide within 8–10 days whether the effect had been sufficient for a landing to be risked; if not the operation would be put off until the spring. After Raeder had left the meeting, Hitler expressed scepticism about a landing, and added that although air and submarine attacks on Britain could be decisive they would take one to two years.[98] He then launched into what he saw as the crucial issue, as recorded in Halder's notes:

England's hope is Russia and America. If the hope in Russia is removed then America is also out of the picture because the removal of Russia means an enormous increase in the power of Japan in East Asia.

Russia is the East Asian sword of England and America against Japan....

If... Russia is smashed, then England's last hope is extinguished. Germany is then the master of Europe and the Balkans.
Decision: *In the course of this conflict Russia must be destroyed. Spring 1941.*[99]

In a typically bold stroke, Hitler intended to raise the stakes. By eliminating the Soviet Union he thought he would increase the Japanese threat to the United States in the Pacific, as well as to the British empire in Asia. That would deter the United States from entering the European war, force Britain to make peace and leave Germany in control of the whole continent giving it the resources for world war in the future.

Hitler was, as always, determined to seize the initiative.[100] He was uncomfortable with a situation of stalemate in the war with Britain, with the probability of increasing American support to the British, and with Soviet unease at the sudden growth in German power. He wanted to turn the tables by a dramatic move. His argument about the way in which Japan would be able to neutralize America and therefore also Britain was highly speculative. Rather more realistic was the calculation that he needed the whole continent under his control in order to face the wars with Britain and the United States that would follow. Eliminating the Soviet Union would remove the danger of an attack in the rear as Germany became drawn into war with Britain and the United States. It would also give Germany direct control of vital raw materials where in 1940 it still depended on trade agreements with its Soviet partner.[101] In addition a land war with the Soviet Union was the only war which Germany was equipped to fight, as was shown by its inability to launch an invasion of Britain. At the same time Hitler and his military chiefs underestimated the Red Army, a common mistake after Stalin's purges and its poor performance against Finland in 1939–40. All these factors are sufficient to explain Hitler's instinct that war with the Soviet Union was the logical next step and he presented it to his military chiefs in these terms. Yet it was also the realization of what had been his ultimate aim since the 1920s, the war for living space in the Soviet Union against 'Jewish Bolshevism'. That was to give it a new character as a racial war, more explicit and systematic and no less terrible than the occupation of Poland. Hitler's language in discussing the attack on the Soviet Union betrays the excitement he felt at the prospect. Alternative proposals never had the same attraction. He was seized by the idea as the fulfilment of his destiny, even if it was no longer to be the final stage of German expansion but only a step on the way to global war.

Hitler had decided to pin his faith on invasion of the Soviet Union. Yet it presented certain difficulties which he discussed with his military chiefs at their meeting on 31 July.[102] Victory, he said, depended not simply on occupying territory but crushing the state 'in one stroke'. It would also be problematic to have to halt the operations over the winter. That meant it could not start before May 1941 as, he calculated, it would take five months to complete and it was therefore too late for a campaign in 1940. It would also be necessary to increase the German army from 120 divisions which would be needed for the campaign in the east to a total of 180 divisions. German rearmament over the next eight months was devoted to producing the equipment, especially the tanks, for the invasion force and at the same time investing in aircraft and fuel for the war with Britain and America which was expected to follow.[103]

The delay until the spring of 1941 meant that there was time to consider other possible operations against Britain first. They might, as Hitler suggested at the meeting on 31 July, provide camouflage for the preparations against the Soviet Union. He may also have reflected that, if successful, they would secure Germany's rear for the Soviet offensive and prepare the way for a future global war. Various schemes were canvassed by the Armed Forces High Command and the navy – Gibraltar, North Africa, Suez – and during the autumn of 1940 Hitler took them seriously. There is no indication, however, that he regarded them as a substitute for the attack on the Soviet Union but rather as a useful addition, unlike the naval chiefs who wanted a more prominent role and dreamt of an overseas empire.

Ribbentrop too still hoped to make the British empire rather than the Soviet Union the prime target for Germany. He negotiated a Tripartite Pact with Japan and Italy which was signed on 27 September 1940 and was fully in accord with Hitler's thinking. Under its terms Japan recognized German and Italian leadership in the 'New Order' in Europe and Germany and Italy did the same for Japan in 'Greater East Asia' (recognizing implicitly that French Indo-China and the Dutch East Indies were in its sphere) and all three promised to assist one another by all means if any of them was attacked by a power not so far involved in the war, i.e. the United States.[104] Ribbentrop continued to hope that the Soviet Union could also be persuaded to align its interests with the pact powers against Britain and look to expansion in the

Persian gulf and India rather than eastern Europe. Hitler was unconvinced. Germany took measures to protect its supply of nickel from Finland, in September negotiating the right to send troops to Norway via Finland. At the end of August Germany also imposed (with Italy) a new territorial settlement on Romania, forcing it to cede territory to Hungary and Bulgaria, in return for a German guarantee and, in October, German troops were sent to provide protection against the Soviet Union.[105] Since the Soviet Union was not consulted and regarded both Finland and Romania as within its sphere of interest, these measures did not bode well for Ribbentrop's grand strategy.

The idea of a cross-Channel invasion was finally abandoned on 17 September after the Luftwaffe's failure to gain control of the air in what Churchill called the 'Battle of Britain'. Ideas for a 'peripheral' strategy in the Mediterranean against Britain now engaged Hitler's interest.[106] In August he approved plans to take Gibraltar by early 1941 and support an Italian advance from its colony in Libya through Egypt to the Suez canal. The fear that the United States might enter the war sooner rather than later gave an additional impetus – on 6 September, Roosevelt agreed to provide Britain with 50 destroyers in exchange for the right to bases in the West Indies. A further motive was to prevent the French colonies in North Africa being taken from the control of the Vichy government – there was an abortive attack by British and Free French (Gaullist) forces on Dakar in French West Africa on 23 September. Hitler had already given orders for preparations to be made to occupy the Azores, the Canaries and the Cape Verde islands to prevent the British or Americans establishing bases off the coast in the Atlantic. Admiral Raeder pressed the urgency of a Mediterranean strategy in a private briefing of Hitler on 26 September, stressing that the British had always regarded the Mediterranean as 'the pivot of their world empire' and suggesting that, apart from Gibraltar and Suez, there should be an advance from Suez through Palestine and Syria which would neutralize Turkey and perhaps also increase Russian fear of Germany, making an invasion of Russia from the north unnecessary.[107] He also urged the need to co-operate with the French government to prevent the British and Americans establishing bases in North West Africa. Hitler agreed with 'the general trend' but indicated that problems would arise in reconciling the wishes of Italy, France and Spain as would first be necessary. There was also the problem, recognized by Raeder, that the fleet was too small for the possible commitments of the Mediterranean strategy, especially if the

United States became involved. The programme of January 1939 for a fleet of battleships had been cancelled on the outbreak of war and the resources transferred to submarines instead as the more effective weapon against Britain.

Hitler and Ribbentrop tried to find a formula that would bring Spain and Vichy France into the war without alienating Mussolini. But Hitler himself referred to this as being 'possible only through a grandiose fraud'.[108] Italy still had claims on the French mainland, Corsica, Tunis and French Somaliland. Spain wanted Gibraltar, French Morocco and part of Algeria. Germany intended to redraw the frontier to annex not only Alsace and Lorraine but also the iron ore mines of Longwy and Briey and other 'corrections'. Hitler could not expect Pétain to join forces with Germany and at the same time undermine him by imposing humiliating terms – in addition there was the fear that, if its status was questioned, French Morocco would simply defect from Vichy control. Hitler's attempts to find a mutually acceptable solution in meetings with Mussolini, Franco and Pétain in October were a failure.[109] He did not want to alienate Mussolini; he was not prepared to concede anything beyond Gibraltar to Franco; and he had nothing to offer Pétain other than the hope of African colonies once Britain had been defeated.[110] His efforts to persuade Franco and Pétain that Britain was already effectively defeated and it was just a question of how to bring the war to an end more quickly were obviously unconvincing. Neither was willing to take the risk of joining Germany, a lack of confidence which conveyed a clear message to Hitler. To make matters worse, Mussolini, annoyed at not having been informed about the decision to send German troops to Romania, decided on a *fait accompli* of his own and invaded Greece on 28 October, an action which Hitler considered foolish.[111]

The effort to get the Soviet Union to fall in with German plans was equally unsuccessful. Molotov was invited to Berlin for discussions in November where Hitler tried to persuade him that they should take a long view of the future and not allow themselves to be distracted by differences which had arisen from the necessities of war.[112] Molotov, however, refused to be distracted by future prospects of what Ribbentrop called 'the great liquidation of the British Empire' and made clear Soviet discontent over German actions in Finland and Romania. He also expressed interest in Bulgaria and in acquiring 'real guarantees' from Turkey to allow passage of Soviet ships through the Black Sea straits into the Mediterranean. None of this gave comfort to Hitler who was drawn into a prolonged verbal duel by Molotov and refused to attend the subsequent dinner in the Soviet embassy. Because of the danger of a British air raid, Ribbentrop and Molotov then had to continue their conversation in the Foreign Ministry's shelter which somewhat took away from Ribbentrop's grand vision. Asked for an answer as to whether the Soviet Union would like an outlet to the Indian ocean, Molotov pointed out that 'the Germans were assuming that the war against England had actually been won.'

FROM BARBAROSSA TO WORLD WAR

The Molotov visit convinced Hitler that the Soviet Union would not join – as Ribbentrop hoped – a global alliance with Italy and Japan against Britain. There was now no alternative in his mind to destroying the Soviet Union to achieve mastery of the continent and force Britain to admit defeat. On 5 December he discussed the situation with Halder and Brauchitsch.[113] He told them to go ahead with plans for the seizure of Gibraltar, at the latest in January, and to make preparations to support the Italians against Greece in March. On the other hand, they could forget about an invasion of Britain and also an operation in Libya. Preparations for the Soviet war, however, were to proceed 'in full gear' to be ready to start at the end of May. Halder outlined the plans of the general staff for operations north and south of the natural barrier of the Pripet marshes. Hitler agreed, adding that it was essential to prevent the Russian armies withdrawing ahead of the German attack. They had to be encircled and destroyed, so that they could not regroup. Hitler sounded confident – the Russian armies were poorly equipped, the Russians themselves of 'inferior quality' and their armies 'leaderless'. On 18 December, Hitler issued the directive to the armed forces to prepare by 15 May for what he now called 'Operation Barbarossa', with the objective 'to crush Soviet Russia in a rapid campaign' which was to be achieved by destroying the Russian army in western Russia by daring tank operations and preventing the Russians retreating 'into the depths of Russia'.[114]

Hitler again discussed the general situation with military chiefs on 9 January.[115] By then the idea of seizing Gibraltar had been effectively abandoned because Franco refused his support. On the other hand, Hitler was concerned at the way in which Italian forces were being driven back by the British in Libya and by the Greeks in Albania.

The first, he considered not of much strategic importance but he thought it could have a damaging psychological effect. He therefore decided to send a tank force to block the British advance, a decision confirmed in February when Rommel was despatched to lead what became the Afrika Korps.[116] The second was more of a problem. Hitler wanted the Balkans secured before the attack on the Soviet Union and feared British intervention in Greece from which it could threaten Italy and the Romanian oil fields from the air, and also open a route to assist Soviet forces. The armed forces had already been instructed in December to plan for the occupation of the north coast of the Aegean Sea and, if necessary, the whole of Greece 'probably in March'. Another concern was that France's North African colonies might, under General Weygand, stage a revolt and to meet that contingency a plan was drawn up in December to occupy the whole of France and seize the French fleet.

The main discussion on 9 January was, however, again about the invasion of the Soviet Union. Hitler advanced some new arguments. Stalin was clever. He would not act openly against Germany but he would exploit any difficult situation that might arise. Should the British hold out and be supported by the Americans and the Russians then the situation for Germany would be 'very difficult'. So far, Hitler said, he had always destroyed the most important positions of the enemy – that was why Russia must now be eliminated. The objective was to annihilate the Russian army and to occupy or destroy its most important industrial centres. That would bring enormous relief to Germany which would then be able to concentrate its resources on building up the Luftwaffe and the navy. In addition, 'the giant space of Russia holds immeasurable riches'. If Germany controlled them it would be in an impregnable situation and able 'to conduct in future even a war against continents'.

The decision to invade the Soviet Union was Hitler's.[117] The military leadership did not challenge him though doubts remained.[118] They could not afford a repetition of their opposition to the western offensive in 1939 followed by Hitler's triumph in 1940. In any case, they shared Hitler's poor opinion of the Soviet forces. However, had Hitler decided to act defensively and organize his existing empire after the victory over France, they would have accepted that too. The navy would have preferred such a strategy and priority could have been given to naval and air rearmament rather than the additional burden of increasing the army, and doubling the number of tank divisions, in preparation for Barbarossa. Despite Stalin's claims on Finland, part of Romania, Bulgaria and the Dardanelles, there is no likelihood that he would have taken the offensive against Germany as Hitler, indeed, recognized. And simply by waiting, Germany's strategic position would have improved as Japanese expansion in Asia made conflict with the United States and Britain more likely.

But this hypothetical alternative was not likely to appeal to Hitler. He was never content to leave the initiative to others. He had to be in control. He also had another agenda apart from, as he saw it, the need to break the strategic impasse. The war against the Soviet Union was to be a different kind of war. It would provide the space for a German racial empire at the expense of the local population and above all the Jews. It would become, as he put it later, 'our India'.[119] That had always been his ultimate purpose. Indeed, he admitted that one problem with the alternative strategy would be that if it succeeded against Britain, 'he would no longer be able to arouse the German people against Russia; so Russia must be finished off first.'[120]

Hitler made no secret of what was required. Following his usual practice, he explained the purpose of the operation to some 100 of the senior commanders involved on 30 March, speaking for almost two and a half hours.[121] In addition to his usual argument about Russia being key to the defeat of Britain and some comments on the need to concentrate the attack on vital points because of the vastness of the country, he was explicit about the special nature of the war as 'a conflict of two ideologies'. Bolshevism was 'antisocial criminality' and 'a huge danger for the future'. They must not allow the concept of comradeship between soldiers to influence them: 'The Communist is no comrade either before the battle or after the battle. We are dealing with a war of annihilation.' Otherwise, he warned, they would find themselves again facing a Communist enemy in 30 years time. He then became more specific: their task was 'annihilation of Bolshevik commissars and the communist intelligentsia'. Anticipating that some of the army commanders might protest, as they had in Poland, he added that such measures were not for military courts, the commanders themselves must give the lead and deal with communist officials as the criminals they were. The war, he added would be 'very different from the war in the west. Harshness in the east would mean lenience in the future'. The army commanders would have to make the sacrifice of overcoming their objections.

In fact, unlike the initial situation in Poland, the military leadership was willing to co-operate. It shared Hitler's hatred of the Bolsheviks and, especially the Communist party commissars in the Red Army who were widely regarded as 'Jewish Bolsheviks'.[122] It also shared, in large measure, wider racist attitudes with the army's own propaganda for the troops referring in 1941 to the Soviet Union as a 'multitude of Slav, Caucasian and Asiatic peoples' (soldiers were warned particularly against the last), all held together by the 'might of the Bolshevik rulers' and with 'Jewry strongly represented'.[123] Military leaders may also have been influenced by fear for their own standing with Hitler – in competition with the SS – if they offered resistance and the feeling, after the Polish experience, that resistance was in any case futile.[124] The result was that the army itself drew up decrees to give effect to Hitler's instructions and agreed with the SS on the division of responsibilities between them. A directive was issued on 19 May for the conduct of the campaign which urged 'ruthless and energetic action against Bolshevik agitators, guerillas, saboteurs, and Jews, and the total elimination of all active or passive resistance' and on 6 June a further decree stated that political commissars were not to be taken prisoner but taken aside and 'finished off'.[125] These decrees were not simply the work of Keitel and Jodl in the Armed Forces High Command. Halder was also deeply involved and Brauchitsch accepted the result though he added amendments to the commissar decree to make it appear justifiable. This compliance showed the extent to which the army command now endorsed Nazi ideology, though there were some examples of senior officers who refused to implement the measures.[126]

In a parallel movement to accommodate itself to the führer's will, General Thomas of the military's economic staff accepted the proposal of the senior official of the Agriculture Ministry Herbert Backe, which had Hitler's support, that the Ukraine should provide the solution to Germany's food needs. On 2 May 1941 Thomas and the ministries involved agreed that the German army should be fed from Russia and that, in addition supplies should be taken for German needs even though as a result 'many millions of people will die of starvation'.[127] Once again this showed just how far military leaders had come in accepting the logic of fighting a racial war.

Before Barbarossa could be launched, Hitler had to deal with the threatening situation in the Balkans. His original plan had been to invade Greece through Romania and Bulgaria. Bulgaria was persuaded to join the Tripartite Pact (of Germany, Italy and Japan) on 1 March and to allow German troops into its territory. With Romania, Hungary and Slovakia already members of the Pact, this left only Yugoslavia. It agreed to join the Pact in return for a guarantee of its territorial integrity on 25 March but two days later its government was overthrown by Serb officers. Hitler would not tolerate such defiance and immediately ordered that Yugoslavia be destroyed as quickly as possible.[128] The invasion of Yugoslavia and Greece were now launched together on 6 April. The Serb element of Yugoslavia was punished for its show of independence, as Poland had been. The undefended city of Belgrade was bombarded in the first stage of the war; Yugoslavia was broken up with Germany, Italy, Hungary and Bulgaria all acquiring territory and the Croats being allowed to establish a state of their own which proceeded to terrorize its Serb minority. Serb resistance was met with great brutality – 100 executions for every German soldier killed.[129] The whole Balkan operation was conducted with great efficiency by the German forces: Yugoslavia surrendered on 17 April and Greece on 21 April. British units were evacuated to Crete but at the end of May the Germans took Crete (though sustaining heavy losses) and drove the British back to Egypt. A failed attempt to support a revolt against British influence in Iraq, at the same time, hardly detracted from the overall success of the campaign.

Hitler now set the date for the invasion of the Soviet Union as 22 June. Although he later blamed the Balkans operation for the loss of a vital month from the original date envisaged, in fact weather conditions would have forced a delay in any case. The German forces numbered over 3 million men with 3600 tanks and 2700 aircraft – the largest invasion force in European history. The Soviet forces facing them had only slightly fewer men (2.9 million) and outnumbered them in tanks (14 000–15 000) and aircraft (8000–9000). But despite numerous warnings, Stalin refused to accept that a German attack was imminent and, more importantly Soviet planning was for only limited German incursions on the front initially, allowing Soviet forces to group and mount a counter-offensive. They did not foresee that the Germans would launch an all out strategic offensive from the first day.[130] As a result, half the Soviet air force was destroyed on the ground and the three German army groups – in the North pushing through the Baltic states towards Leningrad, in the Centre towards Smolensk and in the South into the Ukraine – made rapid progress. On 3 July Halder noted that the objective of destroying the bulk of the Russian army had been achieved and that 'the Russian campaign has been won in the space of two weeks', though he added that it would be many more weeks before it was over because of 'the vastness of the country and the stubbornness of the resistance which is carried on by every means'.[131]

Anticipating victory, Hitler's mind turned to the exploitation of the new empire. Although the concept of 'living space' in the east had been his stated objective since the 1920s, he still thought of it only in the most crude and general terms. Detailed planning was for others to work out and compete over in the usual way – the military's economic staff, Göring's Four Year Plan organization, Himmler for nationality and resettlement questions, Rosenberg's new Ministry for the Occupied Eastern Territories and the Reich Commissars who were now appointed to rule the Baltic and Belorussia (named Ostland) and the Ukraine. Hitler set the scene, describing the task as 'cutting up the giant cake according to our needs, in order to be able: first, to dominate it; second, to administer it; and third, to exploit it.'[132] The Crimea was to be evacuated and resettled only with Germans. The partisan war, which had been ordered by Stalin, would have the advantage of allowing the German forces 'to exterminate everyone who opposes us'. German rule would extend over time at least to the Urals and only the Germans would be allowed to carry arms. The eastern territories were to become 'a Garden of Eden' – they were vital whereas colonies were of only secondary importance. British rule in India was to be the model. In his rambling talk at nights in his headquarters in East Prussia, Hitler filled out the picture of a racial empire that would provide food and raw materials to the conquerors and be ruled by German settlers who would form a 'living wall' against the east, while the great Russian cities of Leningrad and Moscow would disappear from the face of the earth.[133]

Hitler's imagination was running far ahead of reality. The Russian armies had not been destroyed and their ability to put new forces into the field confounded German predictions. On 11 August Halder noted 'The whole situation makes it increasingly clear that we have underestimated the Russian colossus... At the outset of the war we reckoned with about 200 enemy divisions. Now we have already counted 360.'[134] Differences between Hitler and the army command, which had been glossed over in the original planning, now surfaced. Hitler thought that the main objectives should be Leningrad in the north and the Ukraine in the south; he considered Moscow less important. Halder wanted to concentrate on Moscow. Hitler, already anticipating that the campaign would last into a second year, insisted that the Soviet army around

Kiev should be destroyed, allowing the occupation of the Ukraine with its grain and opening the way to the Donets industrial basin and the Crimea. Once that had been achieved, however, in another stunning victory at the end of September, Hitler agreed to a move against Moscow despite the fact that winter was approaching. By the end of November with their tanks within 18 miles of the city, the German offensive ground to a halt. On 5 December, Soviet forces launched a counter-attack and by the end of the month the Germans had been driven back some 175 miles. Hitler's insistence that the front be held may have avoided a rout. He feared that a retreat from Moscow would invite the fate of Napoleon, as his enemies hoped.[135] Although the German armies were still far from defeated, that could not hide the fact that Barbarossa had failed and Germany was committed to an extended war in the east without an alternative strategy. Hitler's replacement of Brauchitsch with himself as commander-in-chief of the army on 19 December 1941 did nothing to hide this failure.

Rather than a Garden of Eden, the German invasion created conditions closer to Dante's inferno. By the end of January 1942, German losses of wounded, captured, missing or dead numbered over 900 000. Soviet losses were much higher, including some 3 300 000 prisoners of war of whom 2 million were dead by January 1942.[136] This statistic itself shows the way the campaign was conducted. Some 600 000 had been shot in accordance with the decrees against commissars and others considered dangerous. The rest died mainly as a result of supplying prisoners with starvation rations so that the German army could be fed from the land. Similarly the population of Leningrad was deliberately reduced to famine after the city had been cut off in October 1941. In addition, the SS and police *Einsatzgruppen* were active in the rear. It has been estimated that they murdered over 700 000 Jews between June 1941 and April 1942.[137] These horrors would be dwarfed by plans which were taking shape from the summer of 1941 under the aegis of Himmler, Göring, and Heydrich and with the active encouragement of Hitler, for a 'final solution' to remove Jews from all the areas under German control (which was to lead to a programme of systematic extermination in 1942).[138] Hitler had threatened in his speech to the Reichstag on 30 January 1939 that if 'international finance Jewry' succeeded in plunging the world once more into war then the result would be 'the annihilation of the Jewish race in Europe' and he recalled and renewed the threat in a speech in Berlin on 30 January 1941.[139] For Hitler and other leading Nazis like Goebbels, the Jew was the universal enemy uniting the forces of British (and American) capitalism or 'plutocracy' with the Bolshevik menace. The war would never be won until this racial enemy had been eliminated.[140] At the same time plans were also taking shape for a vast resettlement scheme for Germans in the east, requiring the evacuation of an estimated 31–46 million or even 51 million people from Poland, the Ukraine and Byelorussia over 30 years.[141]

What light do these facts shed on the German willingness to sustain Hitler's war for racial empire? As we have seen, the armed forces had become a full partner in carrying out Hitler's plans, where in Poland they had still been a more or less reluctant accomplice. For this development there are many possible reasons. In addition to shared racist and ideological attitudes towards Slavs, Jews and Communists, there were the imperatives of war. The huge scale of the campaign with its vast distances, problems of supply, of timing, of climate, the apparently inexhaustible Russian reserves of men and equipment not to mention attacks by partisans, and increasingly the sense that the outcome would be decisive for the whole war contributed to a psychology of allowing any measure, however extreme, to be used.[142] Stalin too employed brutal methods towards his own side and German prisoners of war were also mistreated. There are still unanswered questions. Estimates of the number of German soldiers directly involved in atrocities vary from 5 per cent to 60–80 per cent. But in any case such figures may be misleading. The worst atrocities occurred in the rear areas, while most of the troops were at the front. But, whatever weight should be given to the imperatives of war as an explanation, the war in the east – so different to the war in the west – cannot be understood without the overt racism of German attitudes. So far as organized genocide against the Jews was concerned, the German army was not the instigator of the process – that was Hitler and the SS – but army commanders did nothing to prevent it happening.[143] And the turning point in morale came not from repulsion at Nazi methods but with the experience of retreat and the dawning realization that the war might be lost. Even then fear of what defeat would bring proved a powerful motive to keep fighting.

Evidence of public opinion at home suggests a similarly stark conclusion. So long as Hitler was successful, support was maintained. The high point had been the victory over France in June 1940. Thereafter, as the war extended and final victory proved elusive, opinion became more volatile. With each new campaign Hitler presented himself as the injured peace maker who had been forced by the machinations of international Jewry into a new operation though, of course, one for which Germany was well prepared.[144] The run of successes up to the autumn of 1941 seemed to confirm his judgement. But as it became clear that Soviet strength had been underestimated, the public's confidence, as registered by the secret police intelligence service, was shaken.[145] Goebbels monitored the mood swings between what he saw as over-optimism and undue pessimism, a sign, he thought, that the German people were 'not yet a world nation'.[146] A dramatic statement by Hitler's press secretary, Otto Dietrich, on 9 October that the war in the east was 'decided' led to temporary elation but was followed by a predictable reaction as the war continued.[147] With Hitler's support, Goebbels shifted the tone of propaganda from the military bulletins proclaiming new victories, which were no longer credible, to an emphasis on the need to stand firm and accept sacrifices in support of the heroic armies which were fighting to save Europe from Bolshevism. In a keynote article in November he argued that it was not when the war ended that mattered but in what way.[148] Thereafter, he registered with satisfaction that this approach helped to steady opinion despite the reverses of the winter on the eastern front and in North Africa.[149] Nevertheless the mood remained mixed as the third winter of the war took hold, letters from the front revealed a grim picture, the regime was forced on 20 December into a belated appeal for winter clothing for the troops and Brauchitsch and other senior commanders were replaced.[150]

Hitler's war for racial empire became by the winter of 1941 a desperate struggle for survival against an equally ruthless enemy. But, if Barbarossa had been successful, would the German people have been content to colonize and defend the vast 'living space' up to the Urals as Hitler intended? Were they now so thoroughly nazified that no distinction could be made between Hitler's war and their war? As the occupation regimes in Poland and the Soviet Union showed, there was no shortage of suitable talent to carry out his wishes. The brutality of Reichskommissar Erich Koch in the Ukraine was considered excessive even by Goebbels.[151] But that represented one extreme in the spectrum of opinion. As Goebbels recognized, National Socialism had a long way to go before it had prevailed 'not only as power but also as ideology'.[152] The Christian churches still represented an alternative focus of loyalty with which, so long as the war continued, Hitler preferred to avoid open conflict.[153] In public speeches he had frequently referred to the

vast extent of the British empire and of the United States compared
to German territory and he had made veiled allusions to 'a new
ordering of ethnographic relationships' and the spread to other nations
of Germany's 'racial awareness' about the Jews.[154] The programme of
genocide against the Jews, however, remained an official secret – even
Himmler acknowledged that it was too terrible to be made public.
That created divisions within the German population between those
who knew and took pride in carrying out an unpleasant but in their
eyes heroic task, those who knew and had doubts but suppressed them
and those who were more or less aware of terrible things happening
but could ignore them. The secrecy created different kinds of living
a lie, each of which helped the programme to proceed unhindered.[155]
The vast resettlement plan and talk of a new India was also reserved
for insiders. In public Hitler blamed the war on the Jews, Churchill,
Stalin and Roosevelt. And to maintain support from the autumn of
1941, Germans were told that they were fighting for survival against
Bolshevism.[156] The distinction between Hitler's war and Germany's
war had to be blurred.

Even had Barbarossa been successful, there would have been no
peace. Hitler hoped in August and September 1941 that Stalin might
capitulate and he was prepared to allow a Soviet regime to continue
beyond the Urals and develop as an Asian power.[157] In December
he spoke vaguely of a possible 'half peace' where after the defeat of
the Soviet Union, Germany would be impregnable on the European
continent.[158] But this was a dreamworld. In practice Hitler's empire
would have required constant war against enemies beyond its frontiers
and the suppression of resistance, which was already making itself felt,
in occupied countries. Hitler said he would like a war every 15 or 20
years to maintain the military spirit of the German people.[159] That was
not what the overwhelming majority of the German public wanted.
Despite the points of convergence, as he knew, Hitler's vision of the
future was not shared by most Germans.

The escalation from the European war to world war had already
taken place, following the Japanese attack on the American fleet in
Pearl Harbor on Hawaii on 7 December 1941. Hitler immediately
decided to declare war on the United States.[160] Roosevelt's increasing
support for Britain in 1941 – through the Lend-Lease programme
and allowing American naval vessels to escort British convoys – had
convinced Hitler that it was only a matter of time before the United
States came into the war against Germany. An American declaration

of war would have been a further blow to morale, recalling the turning point in the First World War in 1917. Yet, as he told the Gauleiter, the public would have found it hard to accept a German declaration of war on the United States without the Japanese action in East Asia.[161] He had also apparently been warned at the end of November by his most trusted economic expert, Fritz Todt, that once America entered the war, it could no longer be won.[162] Since the summer of 1940 he had hoped that the threat of Japan would focus American attention on the Pacific. In the spring of 1941 he (and Ribbentrop) had tried unsuccessfully to persuade the Japanese Foreign Minister, Yosuke Matsuoka, to attack Singapore to weaken Britain and deter the United States from entering the European war.[163] He now saw in the Japanese attack on Pearl Harbor the fulfilment of his hopes, reducing America's capacity to help Britain and freeing Germany for all-out submarine war in the Atlantic. Although not committed to declaring war by the Tripartite Pact he did not hesitate, summoning the Reichstag for 11 December to announce the decision.[164] Public opinion was unenthusiastic about the further extension of the war but the initial Japanese success and its invasion of the Philippines and advance through Malaya, threatening Singapore, helped to lift the mood, providing a contrast to the reverses on the eastern front and also the feeble record of Germany's other main ally, Italy.[165] Goebbels saw the Japanese victories as a godsend.[166] In fact, the German people were now committed to a war they could not win.

Conclusion

> You British had the whole of India. All we wanted was a piece of Poland.[1]

An account of Germany and the origins of the Second World War must include not simply Hitler and the Nazis but their ability to carry the German public with them. As the above quotation shows, that story began in the 1890s with German aspirations to be a world power on the model of the British empire. The experience of the First World War with its unparalleled losses ending in defeat led to intense soul-searching about what had gone wrong.[2] Among a section, mainly of the Protestant middle class, that resulted in a renewed and more fanatical nationalism against those who were perceived to be enemies at home and abroad. The depression seemed to confirm the radical nationalist view that the ideology of the Paris peace – democracy, the League of Nations and international trade – did not correspond to reality. The only security seemed to them to lie in acquiring and exploiting empire or 'living space' in a Darwinian struggle for survival between different nations or races. That brought Hitler and the Nazis to power, as some 37 per cent of German voters turned to them. In power, Hitler managed German public opinion deftly, presenting himself as a man of peace concerned only to claim the same rights for Germany as other nations already enjoyed. That stance, buttressed by rearmament, gained overwhelming support and helped to popularize the Nazis with the half of the nation, mainly Catholic and Socialist, who were not natural supporters. It also helped to undermine the will of the democracies, in any case never strong, to maintain the peace settlement.

The virtuous circle – from Hitler's point of view – of domestic support for foreign policy translating into success in removing the sanctions of the Versailles Treaty, itself feeding back into greater popularity at home reached its culmination in the reoccupation of the

Rhineland in 1936. Thereafter there was a counter-current in German opinion, essentially one of fear that Hitler's policies would lead to a new European war. That reached significant proportions at the time of the crisis over Czechoslovakia in September 1938, as was evidenced by the SPD reports and recognized by Goebbels and military intelligence and not hidden from Hitler himself. Partly as a result, he allowed himself to be persuaded into the Munich agreement.

Thereafter he responded to the challenges at home and abroad by pre-emptive escalation. Whatever the case in other policy areas, the decisions over war and peace were his. He calculated the prospects of victory in each situation and imposed his views on the military commanders. In 1939 he took the risk of European war over Poland, though he still hoped – particularly after the Nazi–Soviet pact – that the democracies would not fight (and in terms of the military response he was right). To the German public, he continued to present himself as a man of peace but in Poland he found a popular enemy. The victories that followed in 1939–40 raised public support to new levels, as they healed the trauma of 1918, created a German dominated western Europe, and appeared to open the way to victory over Britain.

Those victories also led to the creation in Poland of the first Nazi racial empire. That aim, unlike the revision of Versailles and the assertion of equal rights, had never been clearly stated though it was hinted at. Goebbels on one occasion claimed that this was a deliberate tactic. In a speech to press representatives on 5 April 1940 he said:

> National Socialism...never had a doctrine in the sense that it discussed specific points or problems. It wanted to get to power. Only after that could a programme be achieved or constructed. If someone asked us how we thought of the solution to this or that problem we answered, we don't know yet. We had our goals already, but we did not present them for public criticism.... Today we say 'living space'. Everyone can understand under that what he wants. What we want we will know at the right time...[3]

Although the tactic may well not have been as deliberate as Goebbels claimed, the comment about not exposing further aims for public criticism rings true and shows the regime's uncertainty about how far its more ambitious goals would command public support.

The extent of support for racial empire is debatable. It is undeniable, however, that it was sufficient for Hitler to do what he wanted in Poland and that shows the degree to which Nazism was able to build on older feelings of superiority towards the peoples of eastern Europe and anti-Semitism. Hitler expected the further escalation in June 1941 against the Soviet Union to be decisive both in winning the war and extending the racial empire to the Urals. Again he was able to impose his will with no significant opposition and the occupied Soviet territories were subjected to the full force of Nazi ideology. But by December it was clear that the campaign had failed in its purpose, to defeat Russia in a single summer. Public support now had to be maintained by different means, increasingly the fear of what would follow defeat. The final escalation, the declaration of war against the United States, had nothing behind it other than the hope that Japanese victories would change the course of the conflict. Germany was already committed to what Hassell had described in 1939 as 'an unstoppable journey into the abyss' from which, paradoxically, only defeat would rescue it.[4]

Notes

INTRODUCTION

1. An authoritative account is Gerhard L. Weinberg, *The Foreign Policy of Hitler's Germany*, vol. i, *Diplomatic Revolution in Europe 1933–1936*; vol. ii, *Starting World War II, 1937–1939* (Chicago, London: 1970, 1980).

2. Hannah Arendt, *The Origins of Totalitarianism* 3rd edn (London: 1967); Michael Burleigh, *The Third Reich. A New History* (London: 2000); Ian Kershaw, *The Nazi Dictatorship. Problems and Perspectives of Interpretation* 4th edn (London: 2000) and the same author's monumental biographical study, *Hitler: 1889–1936 Hubris* (London: 1998), *1936–1945 Nemesis* (London: 2000). Another history of the Third Reich on the grand scale is Richard Evans' three-volume work of which two have been published at the time of writing: *The Coming of the Third Reich, The Third Reich in Power* (London: 2003, 2005). There is an excellent selection of documents in English: J. Noakes, G. Pridham (eds), *Nazism 1919–1945*, 3 vols. (Exeter: 1983, 1984, 1997) and Jeremy Noakes (ed.), *Nazism 1919–1945*, vol. 4 (1998). On the history of the concept of totalitarianism, Markus Huttner, *Totalitarismus und Säkulare Religionen* (Bonn: 1999).

1. DEBATES AND THEMES

1. Thomas Nipperdey, *Germany from Napoleon to Bismarck 1800–1866* (English edn, Dublin: 1996), 1.

2. For instance, Christian Leitz, 'Germany' in Robert Boyce and Joseph A. Maiolo (eds), *The Origins of World War Two. The Debate Continues* (Basingstoke: 2003), 11–31.

3. A. J. P. Taylor, *The Origins of the Second World War* (London: 1961; revised edn 1963, Harmondsworth: 1964); E. M. Robertson (ed.), *The Origins of the Second World War: Historical Interpretations* (London: 1971); Gordon Martel (ed.), *The Origins of the Second World War Reconsidered. The A. J. P. Taylor Debate After Twenty-Five Years* (2nd edn, London: 1999); Robert Boyce and Esmonde M. Robertson, *Paths to War. New Essays on the Origins of the Second World War* (London: 1989).

4. Alan Bullock, 'Hitler and the Origins of the Second World War' in Robertson (ed.), *Origins*, 189–224; H. R. Trevor-Roper, 'Hitler's War Aims' in H. W. Koch (ed.), *Aspects of the Third Reich* (Basingstoke: 1985), 235–50; Klaus Hildebrand, *The Foreign Policy of the Third Reich* (English edn, London: 1973); Andreas Hillgruber, *Hitlers Strategie. Politik und Kriegsführung 1940–1941* (Frankfurt am Main: 1965).

5. Kershaw, *Nazi Dictatorship*, p. 70 and his excellent summary of the debate ibid.; especially Chapters 4 and 6. Hans Mommsen, 'Hitler's position in the Nazi system' in id., *From Weimar to Auschwitz* (Oxford: 1991), 163–88.

6. Tim Mason, 'Intention and Explanation: a Current Controversy about the Interpretation of National Socialism' in Gerhard Hirschfeld and Lothar Kettenacker (eds), *Der Führerstaat; Mythos und Realität* (Stuttgart: 1981), 23–40.

7. R. J. Overy, *War and Economy in the Third Reich* (Oxford: 1994), 205–32.

8. Wilhelm Deist et al. (eds), *Germany and the Second World War*, vol. 1, *The Build-up of German Aggression* (English edn, Oxford: 1990); Wilhelm Deist, *The Wehrmacht and*

German Rearmament (London: 1981); R. J. Overy, *Goering. The 'Iron Man'* (London: 1984); Alfred Kube, *Pour le mérite und Hakenkreuz.* *Hermann Göring im Dritten Reich* (Munich: 1986); Adam Tooze, *The Wages of Destruction. The Making and Breaking of the Nazi Economy* (London: 2006).

9. The pioneering work here was Hans-Adolf Jacobsen, *Nationalsozialistische Aussenpolitik 1933–1938* (Frankfurt am Main: 1968). See in brief id., 'The Structure of Nazi Foreign Policy 1933–1945' in Christian Leitz (ed.), *The Third Reich* (Oxford: 1999), 51–93.

10. Ian Kershaw, ' "Working Towards the Führer". Reflections on the Nature of the Hitler Dictatorship' in Leitz (ed.), *Third Reich*, 229–52; also Kershaw, *Hitler*, i, xix–xxx, 527–91.

11. A recent model of judicious balance is Evans, *The Third Reich in Power*.

12. Ian Kershaw, *The 'Hitler Myth'. Image and Reality in the Third Reich* (Oxford: 1987, 2001).

13. The rest of this chapter sets out themes which are argued in more detail below. References to the sources are given there.

14. For a fine survey see Jörg Echternkamp, 'Im Kampf an der inneren und äußeren Front. Grundzüge der deutschen Gesellschaft im Zweiten Weltkrieg' in id. (ed.), *Das Deutsche Reich und der Zweite Weltkrieg*, vol. 9, part 1, 1–92.

2. HITLER'S WORLD

1. Kershaw, *Hubris*, 27–69; Brigitte Hamann, *Hitler's Vienna: A Dictator's Apprenticeship* (English edn, Oxford: 1999) and id., 'Hitler and Vienna: The Truth About His Formative Years' in Hans Mommsen (ed.), *The Third Reich Between Vision and Reality. New Perspectives on German History 1918–1945* (Oxford: 2001), 23–37.

2. Adolf Hitler, *Mein Kampf* (English edn, London: 1969), 90–3.

3. *Mein Kampf*, 145, 148, 185–6; Kershaw, *Hubris*, 70–105.

4. *Mein Kampf*, 158–60, 187.

5. On the association of Hitler's mentality with his wartime experience and the views of a wider public, see Neil Gregor, *How to Read Hitler* (London: 2005) and id., 'Hitler' in Steven Casey and Jonathan Wright (eds), *Mental Maps of the Era of Two World Wars* (forthcoming, Basingstoke: 2007).

6. For an illuminating analysis of these influences see Geoffrey Stoakes, *Hitler and the Quest for World Dominion* (Leamington Spa: 1986).

7. *Mein Kampf*, 598. The 1969 English edition has 'folkish theory' but this is an inadequate translation of 'völkischen Rassentheorie'.

8. Stoakes, *Hitler*, 90–110. *Mein Kampf*, 128–30, 558–75, 607–8.

9. Kershaw, *Hitler*, 169–219; Albrecht Tyrell, *Vom 'Trommler' zum 'Führer'* (Munich: 1975).

10. *Mein Kampf*, 116–19, 133–43.

11. Ibid; 263–4.

12. Ibid; 119–27.

13. Ibid; 597.

14. Gerhard L. Weinberg (ed.), *Hitler's Second Book* (English edn, New York: 2003), 80.

15. Weinberg, *Hitler's Second Book*, 30, 53.

16. *Mein Kampf*, 125–33.

17. Ibid; 571–5. See also Gerhard L. Weinberg, 'The World Through Hitler's Eyes' in idem, *Germany, Hitler and World War II* (Cambridge: 1995), 46–7.

18. Stoakes, *Hitler*, 174–91; *Mein Kampf*, vol. 2, Chapter 14.

19. *Mein Kampf*, 559–61; Stoakes, *Hitler*, 197–200.

20. Weinberg, *Hitler's Second Book*, 164–74, and *Mein Kampf*, 581–2; Stoakes, *Hitler*, 199.

21. See the summary in Kershaw, *Nazi Dictatorship*, 154–9.

22. Weinberg, *Hitler's Second Book*, 227, and on the movement for European union 113–18.

23. *Mein Kampf*, 578–81.

24. Weinberg, *Hitler's Second Book*, 155–6.

25. Ibid., 157–9, 173.

26. *Mein Kampf*, 565, 569–70; Weinberg, *Hitler's Second Book*, 136–44.

27. Weinberg, *Hitler's Second Book*, 173–4.

28. Ibid., 136.

29. Götz Aly, Susanne Heim, *Architects of Annihilation* (English edn, London: 2002); Ulrich Herbert, *Best. Biographische Studien über Radikalismus, Weltanschauung und Vernunft, 1903–1989* (3rd edn, Bonn: 1996) and id., 'Ideological Legitimization and Political Practice of the Leadership of the National Socialist Secret Police' in Mommsen (ed.), *The Third Reich*, 95–108.

3. FROM THE MARGIN TO THE MAINSTREAM

1. 'Protestant' is used here as a denominational label. The total nominal membership of the Protestant church during the Weimar Republic was almost 40 million – over 60 per cent of the German population. However, this included many members, especially of the working class, who did not go to church although they did not formally leave it. That left about 20 million members of the Protestant middle classes (about a third of the total population) of whom 11 million attended church regularly. See J. R. C. Wright, *'Above Parties'. The Political Attitudes of the German Protestant Church Leadership 1918–1933* (Oxford: 1974), vi.

I refer to 'middle classes' plural because the German term *Mittelstand* covers many different kinds of occupation – the 'old' middle class of craftsmen, small shop-keepers, farmers, rentiers and pensioners, the 'new' middle class of clerical workers, and a whole range of other groups – businessmen, civil servants and professional people. For a discussion of the impact of the depression and guide to further reading, see Evans, *The Coming of the Third Reich*, 232–65.

2. Hans Mommsen, *The Rise and Fall of Weimar Democracy* (English edn, Chapel Hill and London: 1996), 269–544.

3. Jonathan Wright, *Gustav Stresemann. Weimar's Greatest Statesman* (Oxford: 2002).

4. Peter Krüger, *Die Aussenpolitik der Republik on Weimar* (Darmstadt: 1985), 529.

5. Evans, *The Coming of the Third Reich*, 309–461.

6. For Nazi policies towards different social groups, Noakes, Pridham (eds), *Nazism. 2: State, Economy and Society 1933–1939* (Exeter: 1984).

7. W. G. Sebald, *On the Natural History of Destruction* (English edn, London: 2003), 101.

4. DISMANTLING VERSAILLES, 1933–36

1. The group also included senior naval staff. Germany as yet had no air force.

2. Andreas Wirsching, '"Man kann nur Boden germanisieren." Eine neue Quelle zu Hitlers Rede vor dem Spitzen der Reichswehr am 3. Februar 1933', *Vierteljahrshefte für Zeitgeschichte*, Jg. 49 (2001), 517–50. For General Liebmann's account, see J. Noakes, G. Pridham (eds), *Nazism 1919–1945*, vol. 3, *Foreign Policy, War and Racial Extermination* (Exeter: 1988), 20–21.

3. Hitler's reference was to the expulsion from Poland in the 1920s of a few thousand members of the German minority who did not take Polish nationality. Although the legal basis of the expulsions was contested, and the German minority undoubtedly suffered various forms of discrimination by the Polish authorities, there was a legal framework under the Versailles Treaty for what happened and the minority was able to appeal to the League of Nations for redress, although in practice the League's efforts to

help tended to be too little too late. Compared with what happened in German occupied territory in the East after 1939, this was child's play. Christian Raitz von Frentz, *A Lesson Forgotten. Minority Protection Under the League of Nations. The Case of the German Minority in Poland, 1920–1934* (New York: 1999), 145–50.

4. Liebmann's notes refer to 'eastern satellites', i.e. Poland and Czechoslovakia, rather than Russia; Noakes, Pridham (eds), *Nazism*, vol. 3, 21.

5. The phrase occurs in General Liebmann's notes, Noakes, Pridham (eds), *Nazism*, vol. 3, 21.

6. Wirsching, 'Man kann nur Boden germanisieren', 543–4.

7. Klaus-Jürgen Müller, *The Army, Politics and Society in Germany, 1933–45* (Manchester: 1987), 30. This volume of essays gives a brilliant perspective on the military leaders' attitudes. See, further, the recent volume by Jürgen Förster, *Die Wehrmacht im N-S Staat. Eine strukturgeschichtliche Analyse* (Munich: 2007) and on the different meanings of 'total war' and their application to Germany, id., 'From "Blitzkrieg" to "Total War". Germany's War in Europe' in Roger Chickering, Stig Förster and Bernd Greiner (eds), *A World at Total War. Global Conflict and the Politics of Destruction, 1937–1945* (Cambridge: 2005), 89–107.

8. Noakes, Pridham (eds), *Nazism*, vol. 3, 18.

9. John L. Heineman, *Hitler's First Foreign Minister. Constantin Freiherr von Neurath, Diplomat and Statesman* (Berkeley: 1979), 25–7.

10. Peter Krüger, Erich J. C. Hahn, 'Der Loyalitätskonflikt des Staatssekretärs Bernhard Wilhelm von Bülow im Frühjahr 1933', *Vierteljahrshefte für Zeitgeschichte*, Jg. 20 (1972), 376–410.

11. Tooze, *Wages of Destruction*, 49–53, 86–7.

12. Noakes, Pridham (eds), *Nazism*, vol. 2, 266–76.

13. For an account of the twists and turns of Schacht's career, see Christopher Kopper, *Hjalmar Schacht. Aufstieg und Fall von Hitlers mächtigstem Bankier* (Munich: 2006).

14. See above, pp. 1–3.

15. Kershaw, *Nazi Dictatorship*, Chapter 4.

16. Jacobsen, *Nationalsozialistische Aussenpolitik*.

17. Institut für Zeitgeschichte, Munich, ZS 874. Records of the interrogation of Dietrich by Allied officers, 18 Feb., 1 May, 7 Oct. 1947.

18. Edward W. Bennett, *German Rearmament and the West, 1932–1933* (Princeton: 1979).

19. Neurath to the head of the German delegation at the conference, Rudolf Nadolny, 15 Feb. 1933; *Documents on German Foreign Policy* (hereafter DGFP), series C, vol. I, doc. 20; Rainer F. Schmidt, *Die Aussenpolitik des Dritten Reiches 1933–1939* (Stuttgart: 2002), 142–55.

20. Nadolny to the Foreign Ministry, 17 March 1933; DGFP, C I, doc. 94.

21. Neurath to Nadolny, 22 March 1933; ibid., doc. 106.

22. Ibid., doc. 226.

23. Max Domarus, *Hitler. Speeches and Proclamations 1932–1945*, vol. 1, *The Years 1932 to 1934* (English edn, London: 1990), 324–34; Wolfram Wette, 'Ideology, Propaganda, and Internal Politics as Preconditions of the War Policy of the Third Reich' in Deist et al. (eds), *Germany and the Second World War*, vol. 1, 96–104.

24. Ivone Kirkpatrick, a member of the British embassy staff in Berlin from 1933–39, wrote later; 'Hitler was a wonderful actor. At times when he was beating his breast and assuring his visitor of his own devotion to peace, I was almost overwhelmed by the performance; and I was tempted to believe that my judgement must have gone to pieces in ever doubting the man's sincerity.' Ivone Kirkpatrick, *The Inner Circle* (London: 1959), 69.

25. Robert J. Young, *France and the Origins of the Second World War* (London: 1996). For a defence of French policy at the disarmament conference see Thomas R. Davies,

'France and The World Disarmament Conference of 1932–34', *Diplomacy and Statecraft*, vol. 15 (2004), 765–80.

26. Meeting on 13 Oct. 1933; DGFP, C I, doc. 499.

27. As, for instance, in Hitler's broadcast on 14 Oct. 1933, which was billed as a 'declaration of peace and honour'; Domarus, *Hitler Speeches*, 1, 367–74.

28. Martin Chalmers (ed.), *I shall bear witness. The diaries of Victor Klemperer 1933–41* (English edn, London: 1999), 49–50.

29. Weinberg, *Foreign Policy*, i, 57–74.

30. DGFP, C I, doc. 142.

31. Cabinet meeting, 14 July 1933; DGFP, C I, doc. 362.

32. Hermann Rauschning, *Hitler Speaks* (London: 1939), 114. Doubts have been expressed about whether Rauschning would really have had the conversations with Hitler which he later claimed but there is independent evidence that, as a leading representative of the Nazi party in Danzig, he did see Hitler to discuss Poland. It is also noticeable that he quoted the same remarks in a book published the previous year, before Hitler demonstrated his contempt for the Polish agreement and concluded the Nazi-Soviet pact. Hermann Rauschning, *Germany's Revolution of Destruction* (English edn, London: 1939; German edn, Zurich: 1938), 251. For the literature on the question of authenticity, see Kershaw, *Nazi Dictatorship*, 136.

33. Address to SA and military chiefs, 28 Feb. 1934; Robert J. O'Neill, *The German Army and the Nazi Party, 1933–1939* (2nd edn, London: 1968), 40–1.

34. Entry for 19 August 1935; Elke Fröhlich (ed.) for the Institut für Zeitgeschichte, *Die Tagebücher von Joseph Goebbels*, I, vol. 3/I, 279. Goebbels wrote up his diary one or sometimes more days after the events he recorded. My references are always to the date at which he made the diary entry.

35. Christian Leitz, *Nazi Foreign Policy, 1933–1941* (London: 2004), 68. On the Polish side, see Anita J. Prażmowska, *Eastern Europe and the Origins of the Second World War* (Basingstoke: 2000), 141–3.

36. Goebbels diary entry for 2 December 1936; Fröhlich (ed.), *Tagebücher*, I, vol. 3/II, 273.

37. Klaus Hildebrand, *Das vergangene Reich. Deutsche Außenpolitik von Bismarck bis Hitler* (Stuttgart: 1995), 587.

38. Otto Meissner, *Staatssekretär unter Ebert, Hindenburg, Hitler* (3rd edn, Hamburg: 1950), 344–5.

39. Wacław Jędrzejewicz (ed.), *Diplomat in Berlin 1933–1939* (New York: 1968), 127.

40. Ibid., 113.

41. Diary entry, 27 Jan. 1934; Chalmers (ed.), *I shall bear witness*, 62.

42. Dieter Ross, *Hitler und Dollfuss* (Hamburg: 1966).

43. In his Reichstag speech on 30 Jan. 1934; Domarus, *Hitler Speeches*, 1, 425. One success of this kind was achieved in the Free City of Danzig where in elections on 28 May 1933 the Nazis won over 50 per cent of the vote.

44. Cabinet meeting, 26 May 1933; DGFP, C I, doc. 262.

45. In his speech to the Reichstag on 30 January 1934 he moved straight from a defence of the agreement with Poland to a polemical attack on the Austrian government for suppressing the Nazi party. Domarus, *Hitler Speeches*, 1, 424–5.

46. Weinberg, *Foreign Policy*, i, 87–107.

47. Memorandum by Bülow of a meeting between Hitler, Neurath, Blomberg, von Hassell (German ambassador to Italy) and himself, 10 April 1934. DGFP, C II, doc. 393.

48. DGFP, C II, doc. 329.

49. Kershaw, *Hitler*, i, 523.

50. Manfred Funke, *Sanktionen und Kanonen. Hitler, Mussolini und der internationale Abessinienkonflikt* (Düsseldorf: 1970), 28–9.

51. Jens Petersen, *Hitler–Mussolini. Die Entstehung der Achse Berlin–Rom 1933–1936* (Tübingen: 1973), 361–6, 370.

52. It may also have been a relief to Papen. After he had made a critical speech about aspects of the Nazi revolution on 17 June, two of his staff were murdered during the Röhm purge and he was put under house arrest.

53. Klaus-Jürgen Müller, *General Ludwig Beck* (Boppard: 1980), 358.

54. Kershaw, *Hitler*, i, 519–21.

55. Klaus-Jürgen Müller, *Das Heer und Hitler* (Stuttgart: 1969), 139–41.

56. *Deutschland Berichte der Sozialdemokratischen Partei Deutschlands, 1934–1940* (Frankfurt am Main: 1980), *1934*, 301. The reports were compiled monthly from information supplied by party members within Germany. The purpose was to create an alternative source of information from that of Nazi propaganda, both for circulation within Germany and to influence foreign opinion. On the quality of the reports and, in particular, their desire to give an accurate and unbiased picture, see Bernd Stöver, 'Loyalität statt Widerstand. Die sozialistischen Exilberichte und ihr Bild vom Dritten Reich', *Vierteljahrshefte für Zeitgeschichte*, Jg. 43 (1995), 437–71.

57. Schmidt, *Aussenpolitik*, 58.

58. Domarus, *Hitler Speeches*, vol. 2, *The Years 1935 to 1938*, 790 (In this instance and in some of the other quotations below I have preferred my translation from the German text.) Kershaw, *Hitler*, i, 529–91.

59. Wilhelm Deist, 'Rearmament of the Wehrmacht' in Deist et al. (eds), *Germany and the Second World War*, vol. 1, 413–15.

60. Geoffrey Roberts, *The Soviet Union and the Origins of the Second World War* (London: 1995), 9–20; Young, *France*, 21–5.

61. The one exception was trade since Germany needed raw materials from the Soviet Union for rearmament. Even here, however, the results were disappointing until the Nazi-Soviet pact of 1939 led to an enormous expansion in economic relations. Leitz, *Nazi Foreign Policy*, 81–3; Roberts, *Soviet Union*, 21–48.

62. Rolf Ahmann. '"Localization of Conflicts" or "Indivisibility of Peace": The German and the Soviet Approaches towards Collective Security and East Central Europe 1925–1939' in idem, Adolf M. Birke and Michael Howard (eds), *The Quest for Stability. Problems of West European Security 1918–1957* (Oxford: 1993), 201–29.

63. Goebbels diary entry for 2 January 1934; Fröhlich (ed.), *Tagebücher*, I, vol. 2/III, 350.

64. Schmidt, *Aussenpolitik*, 166–8; Kershaw, *Hitler*, i, 546–7. Evans suggests that the special features of the Saar make it doubtful how far such a vote was representative of attitudes within Germany; id., *The Third Reich in Power*, 623–6.

65. Wilhelm Deist, 'Rearmament of the Wehrmacht', 491.

66. Ibid., 421–2.

67. Friedrich Hossbach, *Zwischen Wehrmacht und Hitler* (Wolfenbüttel: 1949), 94–6; Müller, *Heer*, 208–9.

68. Heineman, *Hitler's First Foreign Minister*, 91–2.

69. Paul Schmidt, *Statist auf diplomatischer Bühne 1923–45* (Bonn: 1953), 300; Kershaw, *Hitler*, i, 552–5.

70. The Earl of Avon, *The Eden Memoirs. Facing the Dictators* (London: 1962), 133.

71. Schmidt's record of the discussions; DGFP, C III, doc. 555.

72. Schmidt, *Statist*, 307.

73. *Deutschland Berichte, 1935*, 275–82.

74. For a perceptive warning by an émigré Catholic journalist, Waldemar Gurian, of the way in which Hitler's demand for equality, as well as his unilateral actions and the pressures of rearmament, would lead to war, see his newsletter, *Deutsche Briefe*, which was smuggled into Germany – here the issue for 22 March 1935. Heinz Hürten (ed.), *Deutsche Briefe 1934–1938*, Bd. 1 (Mainz: 1969), 267–71.

75. Diary entry for 23 March 1935; Chalmers (ed.), *I Shall Bear Witness*, 142.

76. Hans-Günther Seraphim (ed.), *Das politische Tagebuch Alfred Rosenbergs* (Munich: 1964), 76–7.

77. Müller, *Heer und Hitler*, 208; Petersen, *Hitler–Mussolini*, 395–403.

78. Fröhlich (ed.), *Tagebücher*, I, vol. 3/I, 204, 218–20.

79. Goebbels is clearly here reflecting Hitler's view that by 1936 Germany would be safe from attack. On 12 March 1935, Hitler also told Rosenberg: 'In one year's time no-one will dare to attack us any longer'. Seraphim, *Tagebuch*, 75.

80. Manfred Messerschmidt, 'Foreign Policy and Preparation for War' in Deist et al. (eds), *Germany and the Second World War*, vol. 1, 605–14; N. H. Gibbs, *Grand Strategy*, vol. 1, *Rearmament Policy* (London: 1976), 144–55.

81. Domarus, *Hitler Speeches*, 2, 667–79. See also a semi-official volume, with a preface by Ribbentrop, produced to justify the reoccupation of the Rhineland to an English audience: F. J. Berger (ed.), *Locarno. A Collection of Documents* (London: 1936), 119–57.

82. Michael Bloch, *Ribbentrop* (2nd edn, London: 2003), 82.

83. Heineman, *Hitler's First Foreign Minister*, 132. The Foreign Ministry was not even kept informed of the progress of the negotiations; Jost Dülffer, 'Zum "decision-making process" in der deutschen Außenpolitik 1933–1939' in Manfred Funke (ed.), *Hitler, Deutschland und die Mächte* (Düsseldorf: 1976), 192.

84. On Rosenberg and other early Nazi contenders for Hitler's favour in foreign policy, see Wolfgang Michalka, *Ribbentrop und die deutsche Weltpolitik 1933–1940* (Munich: 1980), 40–9.

85. Bloch, *Ribbentrop*, 1–36.

86. Ibid., 37–75.

87. There is a graphic description of the *Büro Ribbentrop* seething with youth, energy and brutality (and with bright yellow curtains) compared to the old world dignity of the Foreign Ministry which was already described to the author by one of its elderly officials in 1938 as 'a kind of international museum' in E. Amy Buller, *Darkness over Germany* (London: 1943), 55–79 (quotation p. 63).

88. Heineman, *Hitler's First Foreign Minister*, 130.

89. Gibbs, *Grand Strategy*, vol. 1, 155–70.

90. Appointed ambassador in London in 1936 Ribbentrop soon acquired the epithet 'Brickendrop'. Among jokes at his expense it was said that Germany could not be short of raw material if it exported Ribbentrop. This kind of humour, prompted by his gauche behaviour, showed up the social division between the diplomatic elite and someone of Ribbentrop's background, a kind of snobbery to which the Nazis were acutely sensitive. Bloch, *Ribbentrop*, 120–45; Buller, *Darkness*, 62.

91. Schmidt, *Statist*, 317–18.

92. Dülffer, 'Zum "decision-making process" ', 191–2.

93. Bloch, *Ribbentrop*, 82–3.

94. Berger (ed.), *Locarno*, 154; Domarus, *Hitler Speeches*, 2, 677; Kershaw, *Hitler*, i, 556.

95. Deist, 'Rearmament of the Wehrmacht', 430–1.

96. Heineman, *Hitler's First Foreign Minister*, 112–16.

97. Berger (ed.), *Locarno*, 149; Domarus, *Hitler Speeches*, 2, 674.

98. Ibid., 113–16, 157–67. Hitler and Neurath also made it clear to the British ambassador in Berlin, Sir Eric Phipps, on 14 Dec. 1935 that the Franco-Soviet pact might lead Germany to put an end to the demilitarized zone; DGFP, C IV, doc. 462.

99. Memorandum by Hassell, of a meeting with Hitler on 14 Feb. 1936; DGFP, C IV, doc. 564.

100. Goebbels diary entry for 19 Aug. 1935; Fröhlich (ed.), *Tagebücher*, I, vol. 3/I, 279.

101. Goebbels diary entries for 13, 17, 19 Oct. and 23 Nov. 1935; Fröhlich (ed.), *Tagebücher*, I, vol. 3/I, 309, 312–14, 333. Funke, *Sanktionen und Kanonen*, 43–5, 59–72.

102. DGFP, C IV, doc. 485. E. M. Robertson, *Hitler's Pre-War Policy and Military Plans 1933–1939* (London: 1963), 66–9. For Italian policy, see Robert Mallett, *Mussolini and the Origins of the Second World War, 1933–1940* (Basingstoke: 2003), 48–82.

103. Memorandum by Hassell, dated 20 Jan. 1936, of a meeting with Hitler on 17 Jan.; DGFP, C IV, doc. 506.

104. Diary entry for 21 Jan. 1936; Fröhlich (ed.), *Tagebücher*, I, vol. 3/I, 366.

105. Hossbach, *Zwischen Wehrmacht und Hitler*, 97.

106. Jędrzejewicz (ed.), *Diplomat in Berlin*, 252.

107. For an interesting argument that Neurath kept the information he had about France from Hitler, in order to increase his own reputation with Hitler for standing firm, see Zachary Shore, *What Hitler Knew* (Oxford: 2003), 48–67.

108. Memorandum by Hassell, 14 Feb. 1936; DGFP, C IV, doc. 564.

109. Ibid., 22 Feb. 1936; doc. 579.

110. Robertson, *Hitler's Pre-War Policy*, 75–6.

111. Entry for 29 Feb. 1936; Fröhlich (ed.), *Tagebücher*, I, vol. 3/I, 387–9. Entries for 1 and 2 March 1936; ibid., vol. 3/II, 29–30.

112. Weinberg, *Foreign Policy*, i, 250–1.

113. Goebbels' diary entry for 4 March 1936; Fröhlich (ed.), *Tagebücher*, I, vol. 3/II, 31–2.

114. Ibid., entry for 6 March 1936; Fröhlich (ed.), *Tagebücher*, I, vol. 3/II, 33–4.

115. Hossbach, *Zwischen Wehrmacht und Hitler*, 98.

116. Schmidt, *Statist*, 325.

117. Deist, 'Rearmament of the Wehrmacht', 430–1; Schmidt, *Statist*, 325.

118. Hossbach, *Zwischen Wehrmacht und Hitler*, 98; Müller, *Heer und Hitler*, 214–15.

119. Diary entry for 8 March 1936; Fröhlich (ed.), *Tagebücher*, I, vol. 3/II, 36.

120. Kershaw, *Hitler*, i, 574–80.

121. Esmonde Robertson, 'Zur Wiederbesetzung des Rheinlandes 1936' in *Vierteljahrshefte für Zeitgeschichte*, Jg. 10 (1962), 202–5.

122. For von Hassell see Gregor Schöllgen, *A Conservative against Hitler* (London: 1991), 58–9.

123. Domarus, *Hitler Speeches*, 2, 762–79.

124. Entry for 8 March 1936; Fröhlich (ed.), *Tagebücher*, I, vol. 3/II, 35.

125. Ibid., 36.

126. Kershaw, '*Hitler Myth*', 126–9.

127. Hürten (ed.), *Deutsche Briefe*, i, 110–11.

128. Domarus, *Hitler Speeches*, 2, 790, 797; Kershaw, *Hitler*, i, 591.

129. Entry for 31 March 1936; Fröhlich (ed.), *Tagebücher*, I, vol. 3/II, 52–3.

130. Domarus, *Hitler Speeches*, 2, 803.

131. *Deutschland Berichte, 1936*, 300–20, 460–78.

5. PREPARING FOR WAR: FROM RHINELAND OCCUPATION TO *ANSCHLUSS*

1. Noakes, Pridham (eds), *Nazism*, vol. 3, 67; Michalka, *Ribbentrop*, 216–7.

2. Bloch, *Ribbentrop*, 119.

3. Michalka, *Ribbentrop*, 122–38.

4. Hitler periodically revived Germany's demand for colonies, for instance in his speech to the Reichstag on 30 January 1937 but without ever following it up seriously. Domarus, *Hitler Speeches*, 2, 871; Hildebrand, *Das vergangene Reich*, 634–5; id. *Vom Reich zum Weltreich. Hitler, NSDAP und koloniale Frage 1919–1945* (Munich: 1969), 441–624.

5. Entry for 9 June 1936; Fröhlich (ed.), *Tagebücher*, I, vol. 3/II, 102.

6. Entry for 21 Oct. 1936; ibid., 219. The pact was signed on 25 November. The Italian annexation of Abyssinia was recognized on 24 October and the Spanish National

Government on 18 November but Manchukuo, after resistance from the Foreign Ministry, not until 12 May 1938 when Ribbentrop had become Foreign Minister.

7. Ibid., 249.

8. Entry for 13 July 1937; ibid., I, vol. 4, 217.

9. Entry for 28 Jan. 1937; ibid., vol. 3/II, 349. Blomberg's presentation resulted from the preparation of a new directive for the armed forces which was finalized in June 1937 and preceded by a war game during the winter of 1936-7. I am grateful to Professor Klaus-Jürgen Müller for this information. On German military planning, see Deist, 'Rearmament of the Wehrmacht', 526-37.

10. Entry for 23 Feb. 1937; Fröhlich (ed.), Tagebücher, I, vol. 3/II, 389. The Peace of Westphalia in 1648 established the European state system in its modern form, based on acceptance of the principle of state sovereignty and ending 30 years of religious wars. Hitler was predicting the overthrow of this state system and its replacement by a German continental empire.

11. Entry for 15 March 1937; ibid., vol. 4, 52.

12. Entry for 3 August 1937; ibid., 247.

13. On the development of Hitler's views towards Britain, see Axel Kuhn, Hitlers aussenpolitisches Programm. Entstehung und Entwicklung 1919-1939 (Stuttgart: 1970) and Josef Henke, England in Hitlers politischem Kalkül 1933-1939 (Boppard am Rhein: 1973).

14. On the rearmament dates see Deist, 'Rearmament of the Wehrmacht', 453.

15. Taylor, Origins, 98.

16. Hans Mommsen, 'Reflections on the Position of Hitler and Göring in the Third Reich' in Thomas Childers, Jane Caplan (eds), Reevaluating the Third Reich (New York, 1993), 86-97; Hans Mommsen, 'Hitler's Position in the Nazi System', 163-88.

17. Kershaw, Hitler, ii, 13-17.

18. Report from the German embassy in Spain, 23 July 1936; DGFP, D III, doc. 4.

19. Joachim von Ribbentrop, Zwischen London und Moskau (Leoni am Starnberger See: 1953), 88-90; Michalka, Ribbentrop, 115-16.

20. Stefan Martens, Hermann Göring (Paderborn: 1985), 65-7; Christian Leitz, Economic Relations Between Nazi Germany and Franco's Spain 1936-1945 (Oxford: 1996), 15-17. There is an argument, however, that Göring made the economic motive important from the start; Kube, Göring (Munich: 1986), 163-6.

21. Martens, Göring, 66.

22. Entry dated 27 July 1936; Fröhlich (ed.), Tagebücher, I, vol. 3/II, 140.

23. Leitz, Economic Relations, 20-52.

24. Weinberg, Foreign Policy, i, 296-9.

25. Hassell pointed out the advantage of the war for German-Italian relations, and of a Nationalist Spain as a check on Britain and France, in a memorandum dated 18 December 1936, which was passed to Hitler; DGFP, D III, doc. 157; also Weinberg, Foreign Policy, i, 298.

26. Weinberg, Foreign Policy, i, 299.

27. Noakes, Pridham (eds), Nazism, vol. 2, 277-80; Tooze, Wages of Destruction, 71-98.

28. Kube, Göring, 138-50; Overy, Goering, 36-47.

29. Kube, Göring, ibid.

30. Noakes, Pridham (eds), Nazism, vol. 2, 281-7; Tooze, Wages of Destruction, 203-43.

31. Kube, Göring, 151-6.

32. Ibid., 156-63, 185-94.

33. Hans-Erich Volkmann, 'The National Socialist Economy in Preparation for War' in Deist et al. Germany and the Second World War, vol. 1, 278-80.

34. This section is indebted to Deist, 'Rearmament of the Wehrmacht', 421-504. There is a useful summary in Deist, Wehrmacht and German Rearmament, 36-85. See also Edward L. Homze, Arming the Luftwaffe. The Reich Air Ministry and the German Aircraft Industry

1919–39 (Lincoln: 1976) and Jost Dülffer, *Weimar, Hitler und die Marine* (Düsseldorf: 1973).

35. This was, however, also simply a revival of the strategy of the Prussian and Germany army during the nineteenth century which had always considered a combination of defence and counter-attack as necessary given Germany's central European position; Matthias Strohn, 'The German Army and the Conduct of the Defensive Battle 1918–1938' (D.Phil. thesis, Oxford: 2007).

36. Fromm was head of the department charged with organizing rearmament and clashed with Beck who represented operational needs. Fromm was concerned both about the foreign policy consequences of headlong rearmament and the weaknesses in terms of training of officers, inadequate motor transport for infantry (because of the concentration on tanks) and the economic strains which would result. He favoured instead a slower pace to produce over a longer period rearmament 'in depth', which would be better able to sustain a long war. His views were rejected by Blomberg and Fritsch who accepted Hitler's orders to prepare for war as soon as possible. Bernhard R. Kroener, *'Der starke Mann im Heimatkriegsgebiet.' Generaloberst Friedrich Fromm. Eine Biographie* (Paderborn: 2005), 232–61.

37. Deist, 'Rearmament of the Wehrmacht', 528–30; Müller, *Beck*, 243–7.

38. Noakes, Pridham (eds), *Nazism*, vol. 2, 287–9; Kube, *Göring*, 156–7.

39. Noakes, Pridham (eds), *Nazism*, vol. 2, 289–91; Kube, *Göring*, 147, 160.

40. Overy, *Goering*, 64–5; also R. J. Overy, *War and Economy in the Third Reich* (Oxford: 1994), 93–118.

41. Tooze, *Wages of Destruction*, 99–134; Evans, *Third Reich in Power*, 370–7, 392–400. Important case studies of individual firms include Peter Hayes, *Industry and Ideology. I G Farben in the Nazi Era* (New edn, Cambridge: 2001); Neil Gregor, *Daimler-Benz in the Third Reich* (New Haven: 1998).

42. Overy, *War and Economy*, 116, 118, and, on Gustav Krupp, ibid., 119–43.

43. Tooze, *Wages of Destruction*, 126.

44. Overy, *War and Economy*, 110, 131–2.

45. For further reading and a lucid analysis of the whole area of resistance, opposition, dissent and consent in the Third Reich, see Kershaw, *Nazi Dictatorship*, pp. 183–217. On Goerdeler, see the edition by Sabine Gillmann and Hans Mommsen (eds), *Politische Schriften und Briefe Carl Friedrich Goerdelers*, 2 vols. (Munich: 2003).

46. Noakes, Pridham (eds), *Nazism*, vol. 2, 228–32; Jane Caplan, *Government Without Administration* (Oxford: 1988), 321–38.

47. Hermann Graml, 'Resistance Thinking on Foreign Policy' and Hans Mommsen, 'Social Views and Constitutional Plans of the Resistance' in Hermann Graml, Hans Mommsen, Hans-Joachim Reichhardt and Ernst Wolf, *The German Resistance to Hitler* (London: 1970).

48. On the churches see, in brief, Kershaw, *Nazi Dictatorship*, 210–12. Also still useful is J. S. Conway, *The Nazi Persecution of the Churches 1933–45* (London: 1968). On the grand scale but unfortunately uncompleted and covering only the period 1918 to 1937 is Klaus Scholder, *Die Kirchen und das Dritte Reich* 3 vols., with vol. 3 by Gerhard Besier (Frankfurt am Main, vol. 1, 2nd edn and vol. 2, 3rd edn, 2000–1). The first two volumes are also available in English, *The Churches and the Third Reich* (London: 1987–8). Also in English is a volume of his essays: Klaus Scholder, *A Requiem for Hitler and Other New Perspectives on the German Church Struggle* (London: 1989). On the Catholic Church, see Heinz Hürten, *Deutsche Katholiken 1918–1945* (Paderborn: 1992) and id., *Katholiken, Kirche und Staat* (Paderborn: 1994). On the reactions of the officer corps, see Müller, *Heer und Hitler*, 195–204.

49. Noakes, Pridham (eds), *Nazism*, vol. 2, 499–520.

50. There is a large literature on working-class attitudes. Still worth reading as a model of historical writing is Tim Mason, 'The containment of the working class in Nazi

Germany' in Jane Caplan (ed.), *Nazism, Fascism and the Working Class* (Cambridge: 1995), 231–73. For a summary of recent criticisms, see Kershaw, *Nazi Dictatorship*, 200–2. For a balanced and sympathetic view of the position of labour, see Evans, *Third Reich in Power*, 455–503.

51. *Deutschland Berichte, 1936*, 963–72, 1091–111, 1377–92, 1543–60.

52. For instance, *Deutschland Berichte, 1936*, 963, 1548.

53. Ibid., 968.

54. Ibid., *1937*, 12.

55. Ibid., 143–8 and for the following months of 1937, ibid., 303–14, 463–72 (on middle-class attitudes), 611–21, 763–70, 1085–94, 1231–4, 1365–9, 1523–32, 1655–67.

56. Ibid., 1366.

57. Ibid., 1661.

58. Ibid., *1938*, 9–22, quote on p. 15.

59. Ibid., 256–70, 276–84.

60. Ibid., 267.

61. Stöver in arguing that the reports do not suggest any popular support for over-throwing the regime – and hence give a more objective picture than one might have expected from the SPD – downplays the substantial evidence they also contain of fear of war; 'Loyalität statt Widerstand', 456–61. See also id., *Volksgemeinschaft im Dritten Reich. Die Konsensbereitschaft der Deutschen aus der Sicht sozialistischer Exilberichte* (Düsseldorf: 1993).

62. Noakes, Pridham (eds), *Nazism*, vol. 3, 71.

63. Kube, *Göring*, 192–3. For a different interpretation that Schacht did not expect Hitler to yield, Kopper, *Schacht*, 316–18.

64. Heineman, *Neurath*, 156–66; on Weizsäcker, Rainer A. Blasius, *Für Großdeutschland – gegen den großen Krieg* (Cologne: 1981), 43; Müller, *Beck*, 256–9; Kube, *Göring*, 206–9. For a more detailed discussion of Hitler's views in the context of those of his professional advisers see Jonathan Wright and Paul Stafford, 'Hitler, Britain and the Hoßbach Memorandum', *Militärgeschichtliche Mitteilungen*, Jg. 42 (1987), 95–106.

65. Noakes, Pridham (eds), *Nazism*, vol. 3, 59–67; Wright, Stafford, 'Hitler, Britain and the Hoßbach memorandum', 91–5.

66. Kershaw, *Hitler*, ii, 36–7.

67. DGFP, Series D vol. I, doc. 19; Noakes, Pridham (eds), *Nazism*, vol. 3, 72–9.

68. Hossbach, *Zwischen Wehrmacht und Hitler*, 217–20.

69. On the Mussolini visit, see Weinberg, *Foreign Policy*, ii, 279–83. Hossbach suggests that Mussolini impressed Hitler both in his capacity as Italy's Minister of War and by showing expert knowledge which Hitler did not possess; Hossbach, *Zwischen Wehrmacht und Hitler*, 187.

70. Weinberg, *Foreign Policy*, ii, 35–51.

71. Noakes, Pridham (eds), *Nazism*, vol. 3, 83–4; Müller, *Beck*, 261–5.

72. National Archives, WO 208 (Director of Military Intelligence) 3779. On the history of the document see Wright, Stafford, 'Hitler, Britain and the Hoßbach memorandum', 78–82 and Bradley F. Smith, 'Die Überlieferung der Hossbach-Niederschrift im Licht neuer Quellen', *Vierteljahrshefte für Zeitgeschichte*, Jg. 38 (1990), 329–36.

73. The fact that there were two copies requires revision of Wright, Stafford, *op. cit*, 78–9.

74. Dülffer, *Weimar, Hitler und die Marine*, 450–1.

75. *Trial of the Major War Criminals Before the International Military Tribunal* (Nuremberg: 1947), vol. IX, p. 307; Kube, *Göring*, 195.

76. Hossbach, *Zwischen Wehrmacht und Hitler*, 218–19.

77. Taylor, *Origins*, 170.

78. H. W. Koch, 'Hitler and the Origins of the Second World War: Second Thoughts on the Status of Some of the Documents' in Robertson (ed.), *Origins of the Second*

World War, 168; also H. W. Koch, 'Hitler's Programme and the Genesis of Operation "Barbarossa" ' in id. (ed.), *Aspects of the Third Reich*, 285–322.

79. Karl-Heinz Janßen, Fritz Tobias, *Der Sturz der Generäle. Hitler und die Blomberg-Fritsch-Krise 1938* (Munich: 1994).

80. Entries for 26, 27, 28, 30 Jan., 1, 2, 4 Feb., Fröhlich (ed.), *Tagebücher*, I, vol. 5, 115–31.

81. Entry for 1 Feb., ibid., 127–8.

82. Wright, Stafford, 'Hitler, Britain and the Hoßbach memorandum', 103–6.

83. DGFP, D I, doc. no. 93, p. 168.

84. Kershaw, *Hitler*, ii, 65–86 gives a vivid account of these events.

85. Memorandum by Keppler (whom Hitler had appointed to coordinate the different factions of the Nazi party in Austria in June 1937) of a discussion with Hitler on 28 Feb. 1938; DGFP, D I, doc. 328.

86. Müller, *Beck*, 255–6. Beck's critique is further evidence of the authenticity of the Hossbach memorandum though Beck did not comment on everything Hitler said. For Beck's views, see below pp. 108–9.

87. Hitler complained to Goebbels, for instance, of the Foreign Ministry's 'lack of any clear plan'; diary entry for 15 Jan. 1937; Fröhlich (ed.), *Tagebücher*, I, vol. 3/II, 329.

88. Kube, *Göring*, 215–49.

89. Hossbach, *Zwischen Wehrmacht und Hitler*, 219.

6. TO WAR IN EUROPE: FROM *ANSCHLUSS* TO THE INVASION OF POLAND

1. Diary entry for 20 March 1938; Fröhlich (ed.), *Tagebücher*, I, vol. 5, 221–2.

2. Hitler's address, 5 November 1937; DGFP, D I, doc. 19, p. 35; Hitler's speech to representatives of the German press, 10 November 1938; Noakes, Pridham (eds), *Nazism*, vol. 3, 114.

3. DGFP, D II, doc. 133. Walter Görlitz (ed.), *Generalfeldmarschall Keitel. Verbrecher oder Offizier? Erinnerungen, Briefe, Dokumente des Chefs OKW* (Göttingen: 1961), 182–3.

4. DGFP, D II, doc. 132; Weinberg, *Foreign Policy*, ii, 339–40.

5. Leonidas E. Hill (ed.), *Die Weizsäcker-Papiere 1933–1950* (Frankfurt am Main: 1974), 128.

6. DGFP, D II, doc. 175.

7. Weinberg, *Foreign Policy*, ii, 364–73.

8. Directive dated 30 May 1938; DGFP, D II, doc. 221.

9. Messerschmidt, 'Foreign Policy and Preparation for War', 657.

10. Müller, *Beck*, 281–7, 502–12; Weinberg, *Foreign Policy*, ii, 365–6.

11. For British policy, see R. A. C. Parker, *Chamberlain and Appeasement. British Policy and the Coming of the Second World War* (Basingstoke: 1993), 140–48.

12. Kershaw, *Hitler*, ii, 99–100.

13. DGFP, D II, docs. 184, 186.

14. Beck was present and his notes provide the best source for what Hitler said. Müller, *Beck*, 512–20.

15. The timing is mentioned in another source for the meeting, the account by Fritz Wiedemann, who had been Hitler's commanding officer during the war and was present as one of Hitler's personal adjutants. Müller, *Beck*, 513.

16. Henke, *England in Hitlers politischem Kalkül*, 150–62.

17. DGFP, D II, doc. 221.

18. Müller, *Beck*, 527. Hitler put his favourite engineer, Fritz Todt, in charge of the 'west wall', a clear sign of the importance he attached to it. Todt had previously made his name in organizing the building of the new autobahns; Franz Wilhelm Seidler, *Fritz Todt. Baumeister des Dritten Reiches* (Munich: 1986).

19. Müller, *Beck*, 293. A. J. P. Taylor later revived the argument that Hitler 'played a game of bluff with everyone – with the Western Powers, with the generals, even with himself'; Taylor,*Origins*, 208.

20. Beck's memorandum, dated 12 November 1937; Müller, *Beck*, 498–501.

21. Ibid.

22. Ibid., 521–8.

23. Memorandum dated 15 July 1938; Müller, *Beck*, 538.

24. For the military aspects, see in particular the memorandum dated 3 June 1938; Müller, *Beck*, 528–37.

25. Müller, *Beck*, 580.

26. Nicholas Reynolds, *Treason Was No Crime. Ludwig Beck Chief of the German General Staff* (London: 1976).

27. A useful summary of Beck's views may be found in Müller, *The Army, Politics and Society*, 54–99. For full references, see Müller, *Beck*, 127–41, 272–311 and also Müller, *Heer und Hitler*, 300–44. I am grateful to Professor Müller for allowing me also to see passages from his forthcoming biography of Beck.

28. Müller, *Beck*, 298–301.

29. Memorandum dated 29 May 1938; Müller, *Beck*, 527.

30. Memorandum and note for an oral presentation to von Brauchitsch, dated 16 July 1938; Müller, *Beck*, 542–54.

31. Hoffmann argues that Beck intended to overthrow the regime and that his language here was a 'fiction' to win over Brauchitsch, despite the military oath of loyalty to Hitler. I follow Müller in thinking that Beck meant what he said, though his views soon developed further and, had his proposal been carried out in the autumn of 1938, the regime could hardly have been stabilized under Hitler in the way Beck suggested. Peter Hoffmann, *The History of the German Resistance 1933–1945* (London: 1977), 76; Müller, *Heer und Hitler*, 326–32.

32. Notes dated 19 July and 29 July 1938; Müller, *Beck*, 554–60.

33. Rainer A. Blasius, *Für Großdeutschland*, 29–72.

34. See, with varying interpretations, Hoffmann, *The History of the German Resistance*, 81–96; Klemens von Klemperer, *German Resistance Against Hitler. The Search for Allies Abroad, 1938–1945* (Oxford: 1992), 105–110; Müller, *Heer und Hitler*, 345–77; Christian Hartmann, *Halder. Generalstabschef Hitlers 1938–1942* (Paderborn: 1991), 99–116; Susanne Meinl, *Nationalsozialisten gegen Hitler. Die nationalrevolutionäre Opposition um Friedrich Wilhelm Heinz* (Berlin: 2000), 268–98.

35. The so-called free corps were volunteer paramilitary forces which had been used to suppress left-wing movements in Bavaria, Berlin and the Ruhr after the war and also to resist incursion by Polish troops in the East. On this group within the opposition, see Meinl, *Nationalsozialisten gegen Hitler*.

36. Ibid., 294.

37. The surviving contemporary source material is patchy as much was either never written down or subsequently destroyed and post-war evidence by those who survived is inevitably coloured by the desire to justify their actions. This adds to the difficulty of reaching a judgement about how seriously the conspirators intended to carry out a coup.

38. *Deutschland Berichte, 1938*, 379–90, 684–91, 913–47, 970–79.

39. Ibid., 381, 384–5, 563.

40. Ibid., 689, 927.

41. Ibid., 384–9, 562.

42. Ibid., 916–17.

43. Ibid., 916, 924–6.

44. Ibid., 918.

45. Ibid., 915–16.

46. Ibid., 928.

47. Ibid., 930.

48. Wette, 'Ideology, Propaganda and Internal Politics', 121.

49. On Bavaria, for instance, where the sources are well-preserved, see Kershaw, 'Hitler Myth', 133–6.

50. Heinz Boberach (ed.), *Berichte des SD und der Gestapo über Kirchen und Kirchenvolk in Deutschland 1934–1944* (Mainz: 1971), 298.

51. Entries for 28, 31 August and 1 September 1938; Fröhlich (ed.), *Tagebücher*, I, vol. 6, 61, 65, 68.

52. Schmidt, *Statist*, 417.

53. Kershaw, *Hitler*, ii, 101–07.

54. DGFP, D VII, appendix iii, doc. 5.

55. Goebbels diary, entry for 27 September 1938; Fröhlich (ed.), *Tagebücher*, I, vol. 6, 116.

56. Kershaw, *Hitler*, ii, 129–53; Evans, *Third Reich in Power*, 574–92.

57. Kershaw, *Hitler*, ii, 108–09; Weinberg, *Foreign Policy*, ii 408–09.

58. Domarus, *Hitler Speeches*, 2, 1150–61.

59. Entry for 18 September 1938; Fröhlich (ed.), *Tagebücher*, I, vol. 6, 96.

60. Entries for 19–22 September 1938; ibid., 99–106.

61. Schmidt, *Statist*, 417.

62. Goebbels' diary entry for 27 September 1938; Fröhlich (ed.), *Tagebücher*, I, vol. 6, 115.

63. 27 September 1938; Domarus, *Hitler Speeches*, 2, 1183–93.

64. Goebbels' diary entry for 26 September 1938; Fröhlich (ed.), *Tagebücher*, I, vol. 6, 113. Goebbels wrote: 'If we attack the Czechs from our frontier, then the Führer thinks it will last two to three weeks; if we attack them after our entry, then he believes it will be settled in eight days. The radical solution is still the best. Otherwise we will never be rid of the affair.' Kershaw suggests that this entry appears to show a change of intention to a two-stage invasion through the Sudetenland, rather than the original military plan, if – as Hitler believed – Beneš refused to surrender. It can, however, also be read as a reiteration of Hitler's preference for a war to destroy the whole of Czechoslovakia – the radical solution – even if victory took longer than if Germany were first in possession of the Sudetenland. Kershaw, *Hitler*, ii, 115–16.

65. Entry for 28 September 1938; Fröhlich (ed.), *Tagebücher*, I, vol. 6, 117–18.

66. DGFP, D II, doc. 635; Erich Kordt, *Nicht aus den Akten* (Stuttgart: 1950), 264–6; Helmuth Groscurth, *Tagebuch eines Abwehroffiziers 1938–1940* (Stuttgart: 1970), 125.

67. Hill (ed.), *Die Weizsäcker-Papiere*, 170.

68. Groscurth, *Tagebuch*, 128.

69. For the atmosphere in the Reich Chancellery, see Schmidt, *Statist*, 418–21.

70. Goebbels' diary entries for 29 September and 1 October 1938; Fröhlich (ed.), *Tagebücher*, I, vol. 6, 119, 124–5. Kube, *Göring*, 273–6.

71. Blasius, *Für Großdeutschland*, 68–9.

72. *Deutschland Berichte, 1938*, 946, 944.

73. Ibid., 942, 944

74. Ibid., 939–40.

75. Thomas Mann, *Dieser Friede* (Stockholm: 1938), 17–18.

76. Hans Bernd Gisevius, *To the Bitter End* (English edn, London: 1948), 327.

77. Entry for 2 October 1938; Fröhlich (ed.), *Tagebücher*, I, vol. 6, 124–5.

78. In a speech to representatives of the German press, 10 November 1938; Noakes, Pridham (eds), *Nazism*, vol. 3, 114.

79. Michalka, *Ribbentrop*, 240.

80. Kube, *Göring*, 276–8.

81. Schmidt, *Statist*, 425–7.

82. Noakes, Pridham (eds), *Nazism*, vol. 3, 113–16.

83. For instance in his secret speech to senior officers on 10 February 1939; Noakes, Pridham (eds), *Nazism*, vol. 3, 117.

84. Diary entry for 10 October 1938; and again during the crisis leading to the occupation of Prague, entries for 14–15 March 1939; Fröhlich (ed.), *Tagebücher*, I, vol. 6, 139, 285–6.

85. Entry for 18 September 1938; ibid., 98.

86. Hitler's prediction about British rearmament came in his address on 28 May 1938, where he added that French rearmament would also take 'many years'; Müller, *Beck*, 516.

87. See above, p. 93.

88. Note for *Wehrmacht* discussions with Italy, 26 November 1938; DGFP, D IV, doc. 411.

89. Diary entry for 24 October 1938; Fröhlich (ed.), *Tagebücher*, I, vol. 6, 158.

90. Donald Cameron Watt, *How War Came. The immediate origins of the Second World War, 1938–1939* (London: 1989), 40–45.

91. Ribbentrop's memorandum for the Führer, 2 January 1938; DGFP, D I, doc. 93. Bloch, *Ribbentrop*, 158–61; Michalka, *Ribbentrop*, 247–97.

92. Goebbels' diary entry for 13 March 1939; Fröhlich (ed.), *Tagebücher*, I, vol. 6, 283–4.

93. Bloch, *Ribbentrop*, 218–20, 229–31, 240–46; Watt, *How War Came*, 46–57.

94. DGFP, D IV, docs. 81, 152.

95. Memorandum of the discussion on 14 October 1938; DGFP, D IV, doc. 61.

96. Weinberg, *Foreign Policy*, ii, 465–79.

97. Goebbels' diary entry for 10 October 1938; Fröhlich (ed.), *Tagebücher*, I, vol. 6, 139.

98. Meeting of Ribbentrop with the Polish ambassador Lipski, 24 October 1938; DGFP, D V, doc. 81.

99. Weinberg, *Foreign Policy*, ii, 479–90, 498–504.

100. Entries for 1 and 3 February 1938; Fröhlich (ed.), *Tagebücher*, I, vol. 6, 246–7.

101. Kershaw, *Hitler*, ii, 163–8; Watt, *How War Came*, 30–45.

102. Weinberg, *Foreign Policy*, ii, 476–8.

103. Ibid., 484–6.

104. Tooze, *Wages of Destruction*, 300–01.

105. Kershaw, *Hitler*, ii, 161.

106. Kube, *Göring*, 286.

107. Hjalmar Schacht, *My First Seventy-Six Years* (London: 1955), 392–4; Kopper, *Schacht*, 322–9; Tooze, *Wages of Destruction*, 285–300.

108. Kube, *Göring*, 278–99.

109. Kershaw, *Hitler*, ii, 164–5.

110. DGFP, D V, doc. 272.

111. DGFP, D IV, doc. 158.

112. Watt, *How War Came*, 144–56.

113. Goebbels' diary entry for 11 March 1939; Fröhlich (ed.), *Tagebücher*, I, vol. 6, 279–80.

114. Entries for 12–13 March 1939; ibid., 282–3.

115. Memorandum of the conversation between Ribbentrop and the Lithuanian foreign minister, 20 March 1939; DGFP, D V, doc. 400.

116. *Deutschland Berichte, 1939*, 278–86.

117. Wette, 'Ideology, Propaganda and Internal Politics', 117.

118. Goebbels' diary entries for 21 and 23 March 1939; Fröhlich (ed.), *Tagebücher*, I, vol. 6, 294, 296.

119. Kershaw, *Hitler*, ii, 176.

120. Goebbels' diary entry for 25 March 1939; Fröhlich (ed.), *Tagebücher*, I, vol. 6, 300.

121. For instance, his speeches of 30 January and 1 April 1939; Domarus, *Hitler Speeches*, vol. 3, *The Years 1939 to 1940*, 1437–59, 1524–34.

122. DGFP, D VI, doc. 99.

123. DGFP, D VI, docs. 149, 185.

124. Domarus, *Hitler Speeches*, vol. 3, 1561–95.

125. Müller, *Heer und Hitler*, 390–92; Kershaw, *Hitler*, ii, 178–80, 190.

126. DGFP, D VI, doc. 433.

127. Carl J. Burckhardt, *Meine Danziger Mission 1937–1939* (Munich: 1960), 339–46.

128. Roberts, *The Soviet Union*, 62–91.

129. Michalka, *Ribbentrop*, 278–94.

130. DGFP, D VII, docs. 192–3; Kershaw, *Hitler*, ii, 206–9. On the various versions of the text of this address, Winfried Baumgart, 'Zur Ansprache Hitlers vor den Führern der Wehrmacht am 22. August 1939', *Vierteljahrshefte für Zeitgeschichte*, Jg. 16 (1968), 120–49 and ibid., Jg. 19 (1971), 294–304.

131. Entry for 24 August 1939; Fröhlich (ed.), *Tagebücher*, I, vol. 7, 74.

132. Goebbels' diary entry for 25 August 1939; ibid., 76.

133. Kershaw, *Hitler*, ii, 214 and for a detailed account of the whole crisis to which this section is indebted; ibid., 211–23.

134. DGFP, D VII, doc. 271.

135. Entry for 26 August 1939; Fröhlich (ed.), *Tagebücher*, I, vol. 7, 78.

136. Diary entry for 28 August 1939; ibid., 81 and for the further development of the idea, entry for 31 August 1939, ibid., 86.

137. Entry for 29 August 1939; ibid., 82–3.

138. Entry for 30 August 1939; ibid., 84.

139. Kershaw, *Hitler*, ii, 215, 220.

140. Ibid., 230.

141. Chalmers (ed.), *I Shall Bear Witness*, 372.

142. Bloch, *Ribbentrop*, 272–84.

143. Kube, *Göring*, 312–23.

144. Rosenberg's diary entry for 25 August 1939; Seraphim, *Tagebuch*, 92–3.

145. Müller, *Heer und Hitler*, 416–19.

146. Klemperer, *German Resistance*, 112–34.

147. Blasius, *Für Großsdeutschland*, 117–40.

148. *Deutschland Berichte, 1939*, 965.

149. Wette, 'Ideology, Propaganda and Internal Politics', 122–4; Marlis G. Steinert, *Hitler's Krieg und die Deutschen* (Düsseldorf: 1970), 83–7, 91–4.

150. *Deutschland Berichte, 1939*, 975–83.

151. Jochen Klepper, *Unter dem Schatten deiner Flügel. Aus den Tagebüchern 1932–1942* (Munich: 1976), 799.

7. TO WORLD WAR: SEPTEMBER 1939–DECEMBER 1941

1. Klepper, *Unter dem Schatten deiner Flügel*, 798. Klepper's wife, Johanna, was of Jewish descent.

2. Kershaw, *'Hitler Myth'*, 151–68.

3. Echternkamp, 'Im Kampf an der inneren und äußeren Front' in id. (ed.), *Das Deutsche Reich und der Zweite Weltkrieg*, vol. 9, part 1, 10–11. Public opinion before the First World War was also more divided than is often suggested; Mark Hewitson, *Germany and the Causes of the First World War* (Oxford: 2004), 61–84.

4. Jürgen Förster, 'Geistige Kriegführung in Deutschland' in Echternkamp (ed.), *Das Deutsche Reich und der Zweite Weltkrieg*, vol. 9, part 1, 506.

5. Hitler's speech to some 200 officers of the armed forces, 25 January 1939; Andreas Hillgruber, *Hitlers Strategie*, 14; Kershaw, *Hitler*, ii, 167–8.

6. See for example Aly and Heim, *Architects of Annihilation*; Michael Burleigh, *Germany turns Eastwards* (Cambridge: 1988; London: 2002); Winfried Schulze and Otto Gerhard Oexle (eds), *Deutsche Historiker im Nationalsozialismus* (Frankfurt am Main: 2000).

7. Detlev J. K. Peukert, *The Weimar Republic* (English edn, London: 1993), 134–40, 280. Also id., *Inside Nazi Germany. Conformity, Opposition and Racism in Everyday Life* (English edn, London: 1987), 248–9.

8. See, for instance, Burleigh, *The Third Reich*, 407–81.

9. See the important revision in Tooze, *The Wages of Destruction*, 326–67.

10. To the Japanese ambassador, Oshima, on 3 January 1942; Noakes, Pridham (eds), *Nazism*, vol. 3, 228–9.

11. There is an excellent commentary and collection of documents on the occupation of Poland in Noakes, Pridham (eds), *Nazism*, vol. 3, 314–88. See also Martin Broszat, *Nationalsozialistische Polenpolitik 1939–1945* (Stuttgart: 1961); Czesław Madajczyk, *Die Okkupationspolitik Nazideutschlands in Polen 1939–1945* (Cologne: 1988).

12. The conflicts of Nazi policy are discussed in detail in Sonja Schwaneberg, 'The Economic Exploitation of the Generalgouvernement in Poland by the Third Reich 1939 to 1945' (D.Phil. thesis, Oxford: 2006).

13. On policy towards the Jews, see Noakes, Pridham (eds), *Nazism*, vol. 3, 441–77; Peter Longerich, *Politik der Vernichtung. Eine Gesamtdarstellung der nationalsozialistischen Judenverfolgung* (Munich, 1998), 251–92; id., *Holocaust. The Nazi Persecution and Murder of the Jews* (forthcoming, Oxford: 2008); Christopher R. Browning, *The Origins of the Final Solution. The Evolution of Nazi Jewish Policy, September 1939–March 1942* (London: 2004).

14. See above, p. 134.

15. Rosenberg's diary entry for 29 September 1939; Seraphim, *Tagebuch*, 98; Noakes, Pridham (eds), *Nazism*, vol. 3, 319.

16. Diary entries for 10 and 14 October 1939; Fröhlich (ed.), *Tagebücher*, I, vol. 7, 147, 153; Kershaw, *Hitler*, ii, 245, 247.

17. Kershaw, *Hitler*, ii, 245–6; Noakes, Pridham (eds), *Nazism*, vol. 3, 320.

18. Domarus, *Hitler Speeches*, 3, 1836–7.

19. Heydrich as reported by General Wagner; Browning, *Origins*, 3. For the training of the SS as ideological warriors, see Bernd Wegner, *The Waffen SS* (English edn, Oxford: 1990), 133–220.

20. Kershaw, *Hitler*, ii, 246–7.

21. Noakes, Pridham (eds), *Nazism*, vol. 3, 330–33.

22. On Greiser, see Kershaw, *Hitler*, ii, 250–1; on Frank, Martyn Housden, *Hans Frank, Lebensraum, and the Holocaust* (Basingstoke: 2003).

23. Aly, Heim, *Architects of Annihilation*.

24. Noakes, Pridham (eds), *Nazism*, vol. 3, 356–7.

25. Ibid., 545–56; Longerich, *Politik der Vernichtung*, 441–58; Browning, *Origins*, 352–73.

26. On the euthanasia programmes, Noakes, Pridham, ibid., 389–440; Michael Burleigh, *Death and Deliverance. Euthanasia in Germany 1900–1945* (London: 2002).

27. Kershaw, *Hitler*, ii, 247–8.

28. Omer Bartov, 'Soldiers, Nazis and War in the Third Reich' in Leitz (ed.), *The Third Reich*, 131–50. For different perspectives see Christian Hartmann, Johannes Hürter, Ulrike Jureit (eds), *Verbrechen der Wehrmacht. Bilanz einer Debatte* (Munich: 2005).

29. On German attitudes to Polish workers and the way in which attitudes hardened during the war as the regime treated them as racial enemies, see Ulrich Herbert, *Hitler's Foreign Workers. Enforced Labor in Germany Under the Third Reich* (English edn, Cambridge: 1997), 61–94, 106–36.

30. On the question of the degree of consensus for Nazi policies, see Robert Gellately, *Backing Hitler. Consent and Coercion in Nazi Germany* (Oxford: 2001) and Neil Gregor, 'Nazism – A Political Religion? Rethinking the Voluntarist Turn' in id. (ed.), *Nazism, War and Genocide. Essays in Honour of Jeremy Noakes* (Exeter: 2005), 1–21.

31. Klaus–Jürgen Müller, 'The Brutalisation of Warfare, Nazi Crimes and the *Wehrmacht*' in John Erickson and David Dilks (eds), *Barbarossa. The Axis and the Allies* (Edinburgh: 1994), 233–5.

32. Diary entries for 3 September and 20 September; William L. Shirer, *Berlin Diary. The Journal of a Foreign Correspondent 1934–1941* (London: 1941), 162, 175. See also Ian Kershaw, 'Der Überfall auf Polen und die öffentliche Meinung in Deutschland' in Ernst Willi Hansen, Gerhard Schreiber and Bernd Wegner (eds), *Politischer Wandel, organisierte Gewalt und nationale Sicherheit* (Munich: 1995), 237–50.

33. On the subject of German atrocities in the First World War, see John Horne and Alan Kramer, *German Atrocities, 1914. A History of Denial* (New Haven and London: 2001).

34. Echternkamp, 'Im Kampf an der inneren und äußeren Front. Grundzüge der deutschen Gesellschaft im Zweiten Weltkrieg' in id. (ed.), *Das Deutsche Reich und der Zweite Weltkrieg*, vol. 9, part 1, 15–16.

35. For the 'eliminationist' thesis, see Daniel Jonah Goldhagen, *Hitler's Willing Executioners. Ordinary Germans and the Holocaust* (London: 1997).

36. Ulrich von Hassell, *Die Hassell – Tagebücher 1938–1944*; Friedrich Freiherr Hiller von Gaertringen (ed.) (Berlin: 1989), 130.

37. Gellately, *Backing Hitler*, 70–89; Nikolaus Wachsmann, '"Soldiers of the Home Front": Jurists and Legal Terror during the Second World War' in Gregor (ed.), *Nazism, War and Genocide*, 75–93.

38. Noakes, Pridham (eds), *Nazism*, vol. 3, 423–33.

39. Müller, *Heer und Hitler*, 471–4.

40. Ibid., 474–573; Harold C. Deutsch, *The Conspiracy Against Hitler in the Twilight War* (London: 1968).

41. General Halder's notes; Hans-Adolf Jacobsen (ed.), *Generaloberst Halder. Kriegstagebuch*, vol. 1 (Stuttgart: 1962), 86–90. Kershaw, *Hitler*, ii, 264–5.

42. Diary entry for 30 September 1939; Fröhlich (ed.), *Tagebücher*, I, vol. 7, 130–1. On 3 October, Hitler said he believed peace would be restored; entry for 4 October; ibid., 136.

43. Domarus, *Hitler Speeches*, 3, 1830–48.

44. Noakes, Pridham (eds), *Nazism*, vol. 3, 152–4.

45. H. R. Trevor-Roper (ed.), *Hitler's War Directives 1939–1945* (London: 1966), 50–1.

46. Kershaw, *Hitler*, ii, 266.

47. Ibid., 267; Kube, *Göring*, 324–7.

48. Halder, *Kriegstagebuch*, vol. 1, 105; Müller, *Heer und Hitler*, 479–80.

49. Kershaw, *Hitler*, ii, 268.

50. Diary entry for 7 November 1939; Fröhlich (ed.), *Tagebücher*, I, vol. 7, 184.

51. Müller, *Heer und Hitler*, 525.

52. Ibid., 480–546; Hartmann, *Halder*, 162–72. Betraying his conflicting emotions, Halder told Groscurth on 1 November with tears in his eyes that 'for weeks he had gone to Emil [Hitler] with a pistol in his pocket so as, in the event, to shoot him down'. Groscurth, *Tagebücher*, 223.

53. Hassell's diary entry for 22 October 1939; *Hassell – Tagebücher*, 130.

54. Kershaw, *Hitler*, ii, 271–5.

55. *Deutschland Berichte*, *1939*, 1023–30; Kershaw, 'Hitler Myth', 146.

56. Mommsen, 'Social Views and Constitutional Plans of the Resistance' in Graml et al. (eds), *German Resistance*, 55–147.

57. *Hassell – Tagebücher*, 128.

58. Graml, 'Resistance thinking on foreign policy' in idem et al. (eds), *German Resistance*, 4–29.

59. *Hassell – Tagebücher*, 135.

60. Ibid., 20.

61. Klemperer, *German Resistance*, 171–80, 192–8.

62. Kershaw, *Hitler*, ii, 270; Halder, *Kriegstagebuch*, vol. 1, 132.

63. DGFP, D VIII, doc. 384, p. 441; Kershaw, *Hitler*, ii, 275–8.

64. Incidentally revising the views he had expressed in the 1920s in the *Second Book*; see above, p. 15.

65. *Hassell – Tagebücher*, 145.

66. Müller, *Heer und Hitler*, 550.

67. Hans Umbreit, 'The battle for Hegemony in Western Europe' in Klaus A. Maier et al. (eds), *Germany and the Second World War*, vol. 2 (English edn, Oxford: 1991), 229–31.

68. Ibid., 241–2.

69. Ibid., 233.

70. Ibid., 238–53; Kershaw, *Hitler*, ii, 289–91.

71. Klaus A. Maier, Bernd Stegemann, 'Securing the Northern Flank of Europe' in Klaus A. Maier et al. (eds), *Germany and the Second World War*, vol. 2, 181–96.

72. Trevor-Roper (ed.), *Hitler's War Directives*, 61–4.

73. Goebbels' diary entry for 9 April 1940; Fröhlich (ed.), *Tagebücher*, I, vol. 8, 41–2.

74. Maier, Stegemann, 'Securing the Northern Flank of Europe', 211–12, 223–5.

75. Ibid., 204–23.

76. Kershaw, *Hitler*, ii, 289.

77. Goebbels' diary entry for 11 April 1940; Fröhlich (ed.), *Tagebücher*, I, vol. 8, 47.

78. Kershaw, *Hitler*, ii, 295–6.

79. The sudden victory was often attributed to 'blitzkrieg' tactics. This word, however, can be understood in different ways. Hitler certainly wanted an all-out campaign to achieve swift victory, since he calculated that Germany would lose a long war. However, military planners did not expect France to be defeated in a single campaign – they prepared for further stages including trench warfare as in the First World War. It was only after the fall of France that a coordinated 'blitzkrieg' strategy was developed against the Soviet Union with the objective of destroying Soviet forces in a single campaign, while at the same time preparing for war against Britain and the United States. Karl-Heinz Frieser, *Blitzkrieg-Legende. Der Westfeldzug 1940* (2nd edn, Munich: 1996); Tooze, *Wages of Destruction*, 333–8, 430–1.

80. Goebbels' diary entry for 16 June 1940; Fröhlich (ed.), *Tagebücher*, I, vol. 8, 176.

81. Entry for 22 June 1940; ibid., 186; Kershaw, *Hitler*, ii, 299.

82. Steinert, *Hitlers Krieg*, 129; Kershaw, *'Hitler Myth'*, 155–6.

83. Kershaw, *Hitler*, ii, 300.

84. Manfred Messerschmidt, *Die Wehrmacht im NS-Staat* (Hamburg: 1969), 25; Kershaw, *Hitler*, ii, 300.

85. Hill (ed.), *Die Weizsäcker Papiere*, 207.

86. Noakes, Pridham (eds), *Nazism*, vol. 3, 276–303; Tooze, *Wages of Destruction*, 380–93.

87. Herbert, *Hitler's Foreign Workers*, 111–16, 133–36.

88. Goebbels' diary entry for 7 July 1940; Fröhlich (ed.), *Tagebücher*, I, vol. 8, 209.

89. Memorandum of the meeting between Hitler and Mussolini, 18 June 1940; DGFP, D 9, doc. 479.

90. Goebbels' diary entries for 21 and 25 April 1940; Fröhlich (ed.), *Tagebücher*, I, vol. 8, 66, 73. Kershaw, *Hitler*, ii, 293.

91. Goebbels' diary entry for 3 July 1940; Fröhlich, ibid., 202; report of a briefing by the Propaganda Ministry, 15 July 1940; Noakes, Pridham (eds), *Nazism*, vol. 3, 172; Kershaw, *Hitler*, ii, 298, 302.

92. Domarus, *Hitler Speeches*, 3, 2042–63.

93. Goebbels' diary entries for 21–24 July 1940; Fröhlich (ed.), *Tagebücher*, I, vol. 8, 230–34; Kershaw, *Hitler*, ii, 304, 306.

94. Trevor-Roper (ed.), *Hitler's War Directives*, 74–9.

95. Ibid., 74; Halder, *Kriegstagebuch*, vol. 2, 21.

96. Halder, *Kriegstagebuch*, vol. 2, 30–3.

97. Halder's diary entry for 30 July 1940; ibid., 45–6.

98. The German navy inflicted heavy losses but lacked sufficient submarines to bring about a decisive result. From June 1941 as a result of the 'Ultra' decoding system, the British could also read the German naval signals. Noakes, Pridham (eds), *Nazism*, vol. 3, 240–47; Tooze, *Wages of Destruction*, 397–400.

99. Halder's diary entry for 31 July 1940; Halder, *Kriegstagebuch*, vol. 2, 49.

100. The authoritative study of Hitler's decision making in 1940–41 remains Hillgruber, *Hitlers Strategie*; Rolf–Dieter Müller, Gerd R. Ueberschär, *Hitler's War in the East 1941–1945. A Critical Assessment* (Revised edn, New York, Oxford: 2002), 32–4.

101. Tooze, *Wages of Destruction*, 396–425.

102. Halder's diary entry for 31 July 1940; Halder, *Kriegstagebuch*, vol. 2, 49–50.

103. Tooze, *Wages of Destruction*, 429–60.

104. Michalka, *Ribbentrop*, 278–94; Bloch, *Ribbentrop*, 327–45.

105. Gerhard L. Weinberg, *A World at Arms. A Global History of World War II* (Cambridge: 1994), 182–6.

106. This section is indebted to Ian Kershaw, 'Did Hitler Miss his Chance in 1940?' in Gregor (ed.), *Nazism, War and Genocide*, 110–30.

107. Noakes, Pridham (eds), *Nazism*, vol. 3, 186–7.

108. Halder's diary entry for 3 October 1940; Halder, *Kriegstagebuch*, vol. 2, 124.

109. Meetings with Mussolini on 4 and 28 October 1940; with Franco on 23 and Pétain on 24 October 1940. Andreas Hillgruber (ed.), *Staatsmänner und Diplomaten bei Hitler* (Frankfurt am Main: 1967), 230–47, 266–94.

110. Hitler's suggestion of colonial gains was made at his meeting with the French Vice-Premier, Pierre Laval, on 22 October 1940, prior to the meeting with Pétain; Hillgruber, *Staatsmänner*, pp. 263–5.

111. Kershaw, *Hitler*, ii, 331.

112. Molotov's discussions with Hitler and Ribbentrop took place on 12–13 November 1940; DGFP D VIII, docs. 325–9.

113. Halder, *Kriegstagebuch*, vol. 2, 209–14; Hans-Adolf Jacobsen (ed.), *Kriegstagebuch des Oberkommandos der Wehrmacht*, vol. 1 (Frankfurt: 1965), 203–9. On the development of German plans, see Ernst Klink 'Land Warfare' in Horst Boog et al. (eds), *Germany and the Second World War*, vol. 4 (English edn, Oxford: n.d.), 225–325.

114. Trevor-Roper (ed.), *Hitler's War Directives*, 93–8; Kershaw, *Hitler*, ii, 335.

115. Jacobsen (ed.), *Kriegstagebuch des Oberkommandos der Wehrmacht*, vol. 1, 253–8.

116. Rommel, disobeying orders, took the offensive and drove the British back towards Egypt although by the end of the year he was forced to withdraw again.

117. Kershaw, *Hitler*, ii, 341–4 and id., 'Did Hitler Miss his Chance in 1940?'

118. Halder noted of a conversation with Brauchitsch on 28 January that the purpose of the operation was not clear – it would not hit the British, it would not improve Germany's economic position and, if Italy collapsed, a southern front would be opened while their hands were tied in Russia. Halder, *Kriegstagebuch*, vol. 2, 261.

119. Hitler to the German ambassador in France, Otto Abetz, 16 September 1941; DGFP, D 13, doc. 327; Jürgen Förster, 'Securing "Living Space"' in Boog et al. (eds), *Germany and the Second World War*, vol. 4, 1236.

120. Halder's diary entry for 17 February 1941; Halder, *Kriegstagebuch*, vol. 2, 283; Kershaw, *Hitler*, ii, 336.

121. Halder, *Kriegstagebuch*, vol. 2, 335–8; Johannes Hürter, *Hitlers Heerführer. Die deutschen Oberbefehlshaber im Krieg gegen die Sowjetunion 1941/42* (Munich: 2006), 1–13.

122. Förster, 'Geistige Kriegführung' in Echternkamp (ed.), *Das Deutsche Reich und der Zweite Weltkrieg*, vol. 9, part 1, 519–38.

123. 'Guidelines for the conduct of the troops in Russia', 19 May 1941. Ibid., 522.

124. Hartmann, *Halder*, 241–54.

125. Noakes, Pridham (eds), *Nazism*, vol. 3, 483–7; Jürgen Förster, 'Operation Barbarossa as a War of Conquest and Annihilation' in Boog et al. (eds), *Germany and the Second World War*, vol. 4, 491–513.

126. Kershaw, *Hitler*, ii, 358–9.

127. Tooze, *Wages of Destruction*, 476–80; see also Alex J. Kay, *Exploitation, Resettlement, Mass Murder. Political and Economic Planning for German Occupation Policy in the Soviet Union, 1940–1941* (New York, Oxford: 2006), 123–6.

128. Trevor-Roper (ed.), *Hitler's War Directives*, 108–10.

129. Mark Wheeler, 'Yugoslavia' in I. C. B. Dear, M. R. D. Foot (eds), *The Oxford Companion to the Second World War* (Oxford: 1995), 1298.

130. Geoffrey Roberts, *Stalin's Wars. From World War to Cold War 1939–1953* (New Haven: 2006), 61–81.

131. Halder, *Kriegstagebuch*, vol. 3, 38.

132. Memorandum of a meeting with Rosenberg, Keitel, Göring, Lammers (head of the Reich Chancellery) and Martin Bormann (head of the party chancellery), 16 July 1941; DGFP, D XIII, doc. 114.

133. Werner Jochmann (ed.), *Adolf Hitler. Monologe im Führerhauptquartier 1941–1944* (Hamburg: 1980), 39, 68, 71; English version: H. R. Trevor-Roper (ed.), *Hitler's Table Talk 1941–1944* (London: 1953), 5, 40, 44; Kershaw, *Hitler*, ii, 400–5.

134. Halder, *Kriegstagebuch*, vol. 3, 170.

135. Kershaw, *Hitler*, ii, 453, 455; Goebbels' diary entry for 21 August 1941; Fröhlich (ed.), *Tagebücher*, II, vol. 1, 281.

136. Christian Streit, *Keine Kameraden. Die Wehrmacht und die sowjetischen Kriegsgefangenen 1941–1945* (Bonn: 1991).

137. Noakes, Pridham (eds), *Nazism*, vol. 3, 501.

138. Ibid., 501–9; Browning, *Origins*, 309–423.

139. Domarus, *Hitler Speeches*, 3, 1149, *Hitler Reden*, 2, 1663. In the second speech Hitler interestingly misdated his original threat to his speech to the Reichstag on the outbreak of war on 1 September 1939, underlining the way in which in his mind Jews and their destruction were linked to the war.

140. Tobias Jersak argues that until August 1941 Hitler's policy was to postpone the elimination of the Jews to the end of the war. The Jewish populations of eastern Europe were regarded as a hostage to deter American intervention, while various schemes were aired for removing those of western Europe – to Madagascar, Palestine or even the United States. However the Atlantic Charter signed by Churchill and Roosevelt in August 1941 convinced Hitler that 'international Jewry' had brought Britain and the United States into a common front and his policy then changed to the immediate genocide of all European Jews as the means to victory. Tobias Jersak, 'A Matter of Foreign Policy: "Final Solution" and "Final Victory" in Nazi Germany', *German History*, vol. 21 (2003), 369–91; id., 'Entscheidungen zu Mord und Lüge. Die deutsche Kriegsgesellschaft und der Holocaust' in Echternkamp (ed.), *Das Deutsche Reich und der Zweite Weltkrieg*, vol. 9, part 1, 275–318.

141. Czesław Madajczyk (ed.), *Vom Generalplan Ost zum Generalsiedlungsplan* (Munich: 1994); Tooze, *Wages of Destruction*, 466–76.

142. Christian Hartmann, 'Wie verbrecherisch war die Wehrmacht? Zur Beteiligung von Wehrmachtsangehörigen an Kriegs- und NS- Verbrechen' in id. et al. (eds), *Verbrechen der Wehrmacht*, 69–79; Hürter, *Hitlers Heerführer*. See also the review article by Norman M. Naimark, 'War and Genocide on the Eastern Front, 1941-1945', *Contemporary European History*, vol. 16 (2007), 259–74.

143. Hürter, *Hitlers Heerführer*, 596–9.

144. For instance his Reichstag speech on 4 May 1941 (the Balkan campaign), his proclamation to the German people on 22 June and speech on 3 October (Barbarossa) and, finally, his Reichstag speech on 11 December (declaration of war on the United States); Domarus, *Hitler Reden*, 2, 1697–709, 1725–32, 1758–67, 1793–811.

145. Goebbels' diary entries for 19 August and 24 September 1941; Fröhlich (ed.), *Tagebücher*, II, vol. 1, 259, 484. Kershaw, *'Hitler Myth'*, 169–76; Kershaw, *Hitler*, ii, 421–4.

146. Entry for 27 September 1941; Fröhlich (ed.), *Tagebücher*, II, vol. 1, 505.

147. Jeremy Noakes (ed.), *Nazism 1919–1945*, vol. 4, *The German Home Front in World War II* (Exeter: 1998), 477–9; Goebbels' diary entry for 4 November 1941; Fröhlich (ed.), *Tagebücher*, II, vol. 2, 230.

148. Noakes (ed.), *Nazism*, vol. 4, 481; Goebbels' diary entries for 5, 6 November 1941; Fröhlich (ed.), *Tagebücher*, II, vol. 2, 234, 240.

149. Goebbels' diary entries, 8, 13, 16, 20 November, 4 December; Fröhlich (ed.), *Tagebücher*, II, vol. 2, 253, 279–80, 301–2, 321, 425–6.

150. Noakes (ed.), *Nazism*, vol. 4, 536–9.

151. Goebbels' diary entry for 24 December 1941; Fröhlich (ed.), *Tagebücher*, II, vol. 2, 571–2.

152. Diary entry for 5 December 1941; ibid., 437.

153. Goebbels' diary entries for 30 November and 14 December 1941; ibid., 397–8, 506–9. Kershaw, *Hitler*, ii, 424–30.

154. Speeches of 6 October 1939 and 30 January 1941; see above p.*144 and Domarus, *Hitler Reden*, 2, 1663.

155. See the original argument by Tobias Jersak, 'Entscheidungen zu Mord und Lüge', 319–55.

156. Goebbels' diary entry for 20 November 1941; Fröhlich (ed.), *Tagebücher*, II, vol. 2, 319–21.

157. Goebbels' diary entries for 19 August and 24 September 1941; ibid., vol. 1, 262, 482.

158. Goebbels' account of Hitler's speech to the Gauleiter on 12 December 1941; diary entry for 13 December 1941; ibid., vol. 2, 497. Kershaw, *Hitler*, ii, 448–9.

159. Conversation on the night of 19–20 August 1941; Trevor-Roper (ed.), *Hitler's Table Talk*, 28.

160. Bernd Wegner, 'Hitler's Grand Strategy Between Pearl Harbor and Stalingrad' in Horst Boog et al. (eds) *Germany and the Second World War*, vol. 6 (English edn, Oxford: 2001), 112–16; Kershaw, *Hitler*, ii, 442–9.

161. Goebbels' diary entry, 13 December 1941; Fröhlich (ed.), *Tagebücher*, II, vol. 2, 494.

162. Tooze, *Wages of Destruction*, 507–8, though Seidler points out that there is no contemporary record of this comment; *Todt*, 356–7. Hitler had put Todt in charge of ammunition production in March 1940; ibid., 349–53.

163. DGFP, D XII, docs. 78, 222, 266.

164. Domarus, *Hitler Reden*, ii, 1794–811.

165. Goebbels' diary entries for 9–11, 23 December 1941; Fröhlich (ed.), *Tagebücher*, II, vol. 2, 455, 458, 462, 471, 473, 566.

166. Entry for 18 December 1941; ibid., 535.

CONCLUSION

1. Elderly German to the author, Summer 1963.

2. See the brilliant memoir by Sebastian Haffner, *Defying Hitler* (English edn, London: 2003), 8–24.

3. Hillgruber, *Hitler's Strategie*, 22.

4. See above, p. 152.

Select Bibliography

PRIMARY SOURCES

AVON, The Earl of, *The Eden Memoirs. Facing the Dictators* (London: 1962)

BERGER, F. J. (ed.), *Locarno. A Collection of Documents* (London: 1936)

BOBERACH, HEINZ (ed.), *Berichte des SD und der Gestapo über Kirchen und Kirchenvolk in Deutschland 1934–1944* (Mainz: 1971)

BULLER, E. AMY, *Darkness over Germany* (London: 1943)

BURCKHARDT, CARL J., *Meine Danziger Mission 1937–1939* (Munich: 1960)

CHALMERS, MARTIN (ed.), *I Shall Bear Witness. The Diaries of Victor Klemperer 1933–41* (English edn, London: 1999)

Deutschland Berichte der Sozialdemokratischen Partei Deutschlands, 1934–1940 (Frankfurt am Main: 1980)

Documents on German Foreign Policy, Series C, vols. I–VI (London: 1957–83); Series D, vols. I–XIII (London: 1949–64)

DOMARUS, MAX, *Hitler Reden und Proklamationen 1932–1945*, Bd.1, *Triumph (1932–1938)*, Bd.2 *Untergang* (Würzburg: 1962, 1965). Also available in English as *Hitler. Speeches and Proclamations*, 3 vols., covering the years 1932–1940 (London: 1990–97) with the volume for 1941–45 yet to appear.

FRÖHLICH, ELKE (ed.) for the Institut für Zeitgeschichte, *Die Tagebücher von Joseph Goebbels*, Teil I, *Aufzeichnungen*, vols. 2–9 (2nd edn, Munich: 1998–2006); Teil II *Diktate* vols. 1–2 (Munich: 1996)

GILLMANN, SABINE, MOMMSEN, HANS (eds), *Politische Schriften und Briefe Carl Friedrich Goerdelers*, 2 vols. (Munich: 2003)

GISEVIUS, HANS BERND *To the Bitter End* (English edn, London: 1948)

GÖRLITZ, WALTER (ed.), *Generalfeldmarschall Keitel. Verbrecher oder Offizier? Erinnerungen, Briefe, Dokumente des Chefs OKW* (Göttingen: 1961)

GROSCURTH, HELMUTH, *Tagebuch eines Abwehroffiziers 1938–1940* (Stuttgart: 1970)

HAFFNER, SEBASTIAN, *Defying Hitler* (English edn, London: 2003)

HASSELL, ULRICH VON, *Die Hassell – Tagebücher 1938–1944*, Friedrich Freiherr Hiller von Gaertringen ed. (Berlin: 1989)

HILL, LEONIDAS E. (ed.), *Die Weizsäcker-Papiere 1933–1950* (Frankfurt am Main: 1974)

HILLGRUBER, ANDREAS (ed.), *Staatsmänner und Diplomaten bei Hitler* (Frankfurt am Main: 1967)

HITLER, ADOLF, *Mein Kampf* (English edn, London: 1969)

HOSSBACH, FRIEDRICH, *Zwischen Wehrmacht und Hitler* (Wolfenbüttel: 1949)

HÜRTEN, HEINZ (ed.), *Deutsche Briefe 1934–1938* (Mainz: 1969)

JACOBSEN, HANS-ADOLF (ed.), *Generaloberst Halder. Kriegstagebuch*, vols. 1, 2 (Stuttgart: 1962–3)

_____ (ed.), *Kriegstagebuch des Oberkommandos der Wehrmacht*, vol. 1 (Frankfurt: 1965)

JĘDRZEJEWICZ, WACŁAW (ed.), *Diplomat in Berlin 1933–1939* (New York: 1968)

JOCHMANN, WERNER (ed.), *Adolf Hitler. Monologe im Führerhauptquartier 1941–1944* (Hamburg: 1980)

KIRKPATRICK, IVONE, *The Inner Circle* (London: 1959)

KLEPPER, JOCHEN, *Unter dem Schatten deiner Flügel. Aus den Tagebüchern 1932–1942* (Munich: 1976)

MANN, THOMAS, *Dieser Friede* (Stockholm: 1938)

MEISSNER, OTTO, *Staatssekretär unter Ebert, Hindenburg, Hitler* (3rd edn, Hamburg: 1950)

NOAKES, JEREMY (ed.), *Nazism 1919–1945*, vol. 4 (Exeter: 1998)

NOAKES, J., PRIDHAM, G. (eds) *Nazism 1919–1945*, 3 vols. (Exeter: 1983, 1984, 1997)

RAUSCHNING, HERMANN, *Hitler Speaks* (London: 1939)

_____, *Germany's Revolution of Destruction* (English edn, London: 1939)

RIBBENTROP, JOACHIM VON, *Zwischen London und Moskau* (Leoni am Starnberger See: 1953)

SCHACHT, HJALMAR, *My First Seventy-Six Years* (London: 1955)

SCHMIDT, PAUL, *Statist auf diplomatischer Bühne 1923–45* (Bonn: 1953)

SERAPHIM, HANS-GÜNTHER (ed.), *Das politische Tagebuch Alfred Rosenbergs* (Munich: 1964)

SHIRER, WILLIAM L., *Berlin Diary. The Journal of a Foreign Correspondent 1934–1941* (London: 1941)

TREVOR-ROPER, H. R. (ed.), *Hitler's Table Talk 1941–1944* (London: 1953)

_____ (ed.), *Hitler's War Directives 1939–1945* (London: 1966)

Trial of the Major War Criminals before the International Military Tribunal, vol. IX (Nuremberg: 1947)

WEINBERG, GERHARD L. (ed.), *Hitler's Second Book* (English edn, New York: 2003)

WIRSCHING, ANDREAS, '"Man kann nur Boden germanisieren." Eine neue Quelle zu Hitlers Rede vor dem Spitzen der Reichswehr am 3. Februar 1933', *Vierteljahrshefte für Zeitgeschichte*, Jg. 49 (2001)

SECONDARY SOURCES

AHMANN, ROLF, BIRKE, ADOLF M., and HOWARD, MICHAEL (eds), *The Quest for Stability. Problems of West European Security 1918–1957* (Oxford: 1993)

ALY, GÖTZ, HEIM, SUSANNE, *Architects of Annihilation* (English edn, London: 2002)

ARENDT, HANNAH, *The Origins of Totalitarianism* (3rd edn, London: 1967)

BAUMGART, WINFRIED, 'Zur Ansprache Hitlers vor den Führern der Wehrmacht am 22. August 1939', *Vierteljahrshefte für Zeitgeschichte*, Jg. 16 (1968), 120–49 and ibid., Jg. 19 (1971)

BENNETT, EDWARD W., *German Rearmament and the West, 1932–1933* (Princeton: 1979)

BLASIUS, RAINER A., *Für Großdeutschland – gegen den großen Krieg* (Cologne: 1981)

BLOCH, MICHAEL, *Ribbentrop* (2nd edn, London: 2003)

BOOG, HORST et al. (eds), *Germany and the Second World War*, vols. 4 and 6 (English edn, Oxford: 1996, 2001)

BOYCE, ROBERT, MAIOLO, JOSEPH A. (eds), *The Origins of World War Two. The Debate Continues* (Basingstoke: 2003)

BOYCE, ROBERT, ROBERTSON, ESMONDE M. (eds), *Paths to War. New Essays on the Origins of the Second World War* (London: 1989)

BROSZAT, MARTIN, *Nationalsozialistische Polenpolitik 1939–1945* (Stuttgart: 1961)

BROWNING, CHRISTOPHER R., *The Origins of the Final Solution. The Evolution of Nazi Jewish Policy, September 1939–March 1942* (London: 2004)

BURLEIGH, MICHAEL, *Germany Turns Eastwards* (Cambridge: 1988; London: 2002)

_____, *Death and Deliverance. Euthanasia in Germany 1900–1945* (Cambridge: 1994; London: 2002)

_____, *The Third Reich. A New History* (London: 2000)

CAPLAN, JANE, *Government without Administration* (Oxford: 1988)

_____ (ed.), *Nazism, Fascism and the Working Class* (Cambridge: 1995)

CASEY, STEVEN, WRIGHT, JONATHAN (eds), *Mental Maps of the Era of Two World Wars* (forthcoming, Basingstoke: 2007)

CHICKERING, ROGER, FÖRSTER, STIG, GREINER, BERND (eds), *A World at Total War. Global Conflict and the Politics of Destruction, 1937–1945* (Cambridge: 2005)

CHILDERS, THOMAS, CAPLAN, JANE (eds), *Reevaluating the Third Reich* (New York: 1993)

CONWAY, J. S., *The Nazi Persecution of the Churches 1933–45* (London: 1968)

DAVIES, THOMAS R., 'France and The World Disarmament Conference of 1932–34', *Diplomacy and Statecraft*, No. 15 (2004)

DEAR, I. C. B., FOOT, M. R. D. (eds), *The Oxford Companion to the Second World War* (Oxford: 1995)

DEIST, WILHELM, *The Wehrmacht and German Rearmament* (London: 1981)

_____ et al. (eds), *Germany and the Second World War*, vol. 1, *The Build-Up of German Aggression* (English edn, Oxford: 1990)

DEUTSCH, HAROLD C., *The Conspiracy Against Hitler in the Twilight War* (London: 1968)

DÜLFFER, JOST, *Weimar, Hitler und die Marine* (Düsseldorf: 1973)

ECHTERNKAMP, JÖRG (ed.), *Das Deutsche Reich und der Zweite Weltkrieg*, vol. 9, *Die Deutsche Kriegsgesellschaft 1939 bis 1945* (Munich: 2004)

ERICKSON, JOHN, DILKS, DAVID (eds), *Barbarossa. The Axis and the Allies* (Edinburgh: 1994)

EVANS, RICHARD J., *The Coming of the Third Reich*, *The Third Reich in Power* (London: 2003, 2005)

FÖRSTER, JÜRGEN, *Die Wehrmacht im N-S Staat. Eine strukturgeschichtliche Analyse* (Munich; 2007)

FRIESER, KARL-HEINZ, *Blitzkrieg-Legende. Der Westfeldzug 1940* (2nd edn, Munich: 1996)

FUNKE, MANFRED, *Sanktionen und Kanonen. Hitler, Mussolini und der internationale Abessinienkonflikt* (Düsseldorf: 1970)

_____ (ed.), *Hitler, Deutschland und die Mächte* (Düsseldorf: 1976)

GELLATELY, ROBERT, *Backing Hitler. Consent and Coercion in Nazi Germany* (Oxford: 2001)

GIBBS, N. H., *Grand Strategy*, vol. 1, *Rearmament Policy* (London: 1976)

GOLDHAGEN, DANIEL JONAH, *Hitler's Willing Executioners. Ordinary Germans and the Holocaust* (London: 1997)

GRAML, HERMANN et al. (eds), *The German Resistance to Hitler* (London: 1970)

GREGOR, NEIL, *Daimler–Benz in the Third Reich* (New Haven: 1998)

_____ (ed.), *Nazism, War and Genocide. Essays in Honour of Jeremy Noakes* (Exeter: 2005)

_____, *How to Read Hitler* (London: 2005)

HAMANN, BRIGITTE, *Hitler's Vienna: A Dictator's Apprenticeship* (English edn, Oxford: 1999)

HANSEN, ERNST WILLI et al. (eds), *Politischer Wandel, organisierte Gewalt und nationale Sicherheit* (Munich: 1995)

HARTMANN, CHRISTIAN, *Halder. Generalstabschef Hitlers 1938–1942* (Paderborn: 1991)

_____ et al. (eds), *Verbrechen der Wehrmacht. Bilanz einer Debatte* (Munich: 2005)

HAYES, PETER, *Industry and Ideology. I G Farben in the Nazi Era* (New edn, Cambridge: 2001)

HEINEMAN, JOHN L., *Hitler's First Foreign Minister. Constantin Freiherr vonNeurath, Diplomat and Statesman* (Berkeley: 1979)

HENKE, JOSEF, *England in Hitlers politischem Kalkül 1933–1939* (Boppard am Rhein: 1973)

HERBERT, ULRICH, *Best. Biographische Studien über Radikalismus, Weltanschauung und Vernunft, 1903–1989* (3rd edn, Bonn: 1996)

_____, *Hitler's Foreign Workers. Enforced Labor in Germany Under the Third Reich* (English edn, Cambridge: 1997)

HEWITSON, MARK, *Germany and the Causes of the First World War* (Oxford: 2004)

HILDEBRAND, KLAUS, *The Foreign Policy of the Third Reich* (English edn, London: 1973)

_____, *Das vergangene Reich. Deutsche Außsenpolitik von Bismarck bis Hitler* (Stuttgart: 1995)

_____, *Vom Reich zum Weltreich. Hitler, NSDAP und koloniale Frage 1919–1945* (Munich: 1969)

HILLGRUBER, ANDREAS, *Hitlers Strategie. Politik und Kriegsführung 1940–1941* (Frankfurt am Main: 1965)

HIRSCHFELD, GERHARD, KETTENACKER, LOTHAR (eds), *Der Führerstaat: Mythos und Realität* (Stuttgart: 1981)

HOFFMANN, PETER, *The History of the German Resistance 1933–1945* (London: 1977)

HOMZE, EDWARD L., *Arming the Luftwaffe. The Reich Air Ministry and the German Aircraft Industry 1919–39* (Lincoln: 1976)

HORNE, JOHN, KRAMER, ALAN, *German Atrocities, 1914. A History of Denial* (New Haven and London: 2001)

HOUSDEN, MARTYN, *Hans Frank, Lebensraum, and the Holocaust* (Basingstoke: 2003)

HÜRTEN, HEINZ, *Deutsche Katholiken 1918–1945* (Paderborn: 1992)

_____, *Katholiken, Kirche und Staat* (Paderborn: 1994)

HÜRTER, JOHANNES, *Hitlers Heerführer. Die deutschen Oberbefehlshaber im Krieg gegen die Sowjetunion 1941/42* (Munich: 2006)

HUTTNER, MARKUS, *Totalitarismus und Säkulare Religionen* (Bonn: 1999)

JACOBSEN, HANS-ADOLF, *Nationalsozialistische Aussenpolitik 1933–1938* (Frankfurt am Main: 1968)

JANßEN, KARL-HEINZ, TOBIAS, FRITZ, *Der Sturz der Generäle. Hitler und die Blomberg-Fritsch-Krise 1938* (Munich: 1994)

JERSAK, TOBIAS, 'A Matter of Foreign Policy: "Final Solution" and "Final Victory" in Nazi Germany', *German History*, vol. 21 (2003)

KAY, ALEX J., *Exploitation, Resettlement, Mass Murder. Political and Economic Planning for German Occupation Policy in the Soviet Union, 1940–1941* (New York, Oxford: 2006)

KERSHAW, IAN, *The Nazi Dictatorship. Problems and Perspectives of Interpretation* (4th edn, London: 2000)

_____, *Hitler: 1889–1936 Hubris* (London: 1998), *1936–1945 Nemesis* (London: 2000)

_____, *The 'Hitler Myth'* (Oxford: 1987, 2001)

KLEMPERER, KLEMENS VON, *German Resistance Against Hitler. The Search for Allies Abroad, 1938–1945* (Oxford: 1992)

KOCH, H. W. (ed.), *Aspects of the Third Reich* (Basingstoke: 1985)

KOPPER, CHRISTOPHER, *Hjalmar Schacht. Aufstieg und Fall von Hitlers mächtigstem Bankier* (Munich: 2006)

KROENER, BERNHARD R., *'Der starke Mann im Heimatkriegsgebiet.' Generaloberst Friedrich Fromm. Eine Biographie* (Paderborn: 2005)

KRÜGER, PETER, *Die Aussenpolitik der Republik on Weimar* (Darmstadt: 1985)

KRÜGER, PETER, HAHN, ERICH J. C., 'Der Loyalitätskonflikt des Staatssekretärs Bernhard Wilhelm von Bülow im Frühjahr 1933', *Vierteljahrshefte für Zeitgeschichte*, Jg. 20 (1972)

KUBE, ALFRED, *Pour le mérite und Hakenkreuz. Hermann Göring im Dritten Reich* (Munich: 1986)

KUHN, AXEL, *Hitlers aussenpolitisches Programm. Entstehung und Entwicklung 1919–1939* (Stuttgart: 1970)

LEITZ, CHRISTIAN, *Economic Relations between Nazi Germany and Franco's Spain 1936–1945* (Oxford: 1996)

_____ (ed.), *The Third Reich* (Oxford: 1999)

_____, *Nazi Foreign Policy, 1933–1941* (London: 2004)

LONGERICH, PETER, *Politik der Vernichtung. Eine Gesamtdarstellung der nationalsozialistischen Judenverfolgung* (Munich: 1998)

_____, *Holocaust. The Nazi Persecution and Murder of the Jews* (Oxford: forthcoming, 2008)

MADAJCZYK, CZESŁAW, *Die Okkupationspolitik Nazideutschlands in Polen 1939–1945* (Cologne: 1988)

_____ (ed.), *Vom Generalplan Ost zum Generalsiedlungsplan* (Munich: 1994)

MAIER, KLAUS A. et al. (eds), *Germany and the Second World War*, vol. 2 (English edn, Oxford: 1991)

MALLETT, ROBERT, *Mussolini and the Origins of the Second World War, 1933–1940* (Basingstoke: 2003)

MARTEL, GORDON (ed.), *The Origins of the Second World War Reconsidered. The A. J. P. Taylor Debate After Twenty-Five Years* (2nd edn, London: 1999)

MARTENS, STEFAN, *Hermann Göring* (Paderborn: 1985)

MEINL, SUSANNE, *Nationalsozialisten gegen Hitler. Die nationalrevolutionäre Opposition um Friedrich Wilhelm Heinz* (Berlin: 2000)

MESSERSCHMIDT, MANFRED, *Die Wehrmacht im NS-Staat* (Hamburg: 1969)

MICHALKA, WOLFGANG, *Ribbentrop und die deutsche Weltpolitik 1933–1940* (Munich: 1980)

MOMMSEN, HANS, *From Weimar to Auschwitz* (Oxford: 1991)

_____, *The Rise and Fall of Weimar Democracy* (English edn, Chapel Hill and London: 1996)

_____ (ed.), *The Third Reich Between Vision and Reality. New Perspectives on German History 1918–1945* (Oxford: 2001)

MÜLLER, KLAUS-JÜRGEN, *Das Heer und Hitler* (Stuttgart: 1969)

_____, *General Ludwig Beck* (Boppard: 1980)

_____, *The army, politics and society in Germany, 1933–45* (Manchester: 1987)

MÜLLER, ROLF-DIETER, UEBERSCHÄR, GERD R., *Hilter's War in the East 1941–1945. A Critical Assessment* (Revised edn., New York, Oxford: 2002)

NAIMARK, NORMAN H., 'War and Genocide on the Eastern Front, 1941–1945', *Contemporary European History*, vol. 16 (2007)

NIPPERDEY, THOMAS, *Germany from Napoleon to Bismarck 1800–1866* (English edn, Dublin: 1996)

O'NEILL, ROBERT J., *The German Army and the Nazi Party, 1933–1939* (2nd edn, London: 1968)

OVERY, R. J., *Goering. The 'Iron Man'* (London: 1984)

_____, *War and Economy in the Third Reich* (Oxford: 1994)

PARKER, R. A. C., *Chamberlain and Appeasement. British Policy and the Coming of the Second World War* (Basingstoke: 1993)

PETERSEN, JENS, *Hitler–Mussolini. Die Entstehung der Achse Berlin–Rom 1933–1936* (Tübingen: 1973)

PEUKERT, DETLEV J. K., *The Weimar Republic* (English edn, London: 1993)

_____, *Inside Nazi Germany. Conformity, Opposition and Racism in Everyday Life* (English edn, London: 1987)

PRAŻMOWSKA, ANITA J., *Eastern Europe and the Origins of the Second World War* (Basingstoke: 2000)

RAITZ VON FRENTZ, CHRISTIAN, *A Lesson Forgotten. Minority Protection Under the League of Nations. The Case of the German Minority in Poland, 1920–1934* (New York: 1999)

REYNOLDS, NICHOLAS, *Treason was no Crime. Ludwig Beck Chief of the German General Staff* (London: 1976)

ROBERTS, GEOFFREY, *The Soviet Union and the Origins of the Second World War* (London: 1995)

_____, *Stalin's Wars. From World War to Cold War 1939–1953* (New Haven: 2006)

ROBERTSON, E. M., *Hitler's Pre-War Policy and Military Plans 1933–1939* (London: 1963)

_____, 'Zur Wiederbesetzung des Rheinlandes 1936' in *Vierteljahrshefte für Zeitgeschichte,* Jg. 10 (1962)

_____ (ed.), *The Origins of the Second World War. Historical Interpretations* (London: 1971)

ROSS, DIETER, *Hitler und Dollfuss* (Hamburg: 1966)

SCHMIDT, RAINER F., *Die Aussenpolitik des Dritten Reiches 1933–1939* (Stuttgart: 2002)

SCHOLDER, KLAUS, *Die Kirchen und das Dritte Reich* 3 vols. (vol.3 by Gerhard Besier) (Frankfurt am Main, vol. 1 2nd edn and vol. 2 3rd edn, 2000–1). English edn of vols. 1 and 2, *The Churches and the Third Reich* (London: 1987–8)

_____, *A Requiem for Hitler and Other New Perspectives on the German Church Struggle* (London: 1989)

SCHÖLLGEN, GREGOR, *A Conservative Against Hitler* (London: 1991)

SCHULZE, WINFRIED and OEXLE, OTTO GERHARD (eds), *Deutsche Historiker im Nationalsozialismus* (Frankfurt am Main: 2000)

SCHWANEBERG, SONJA, 'The Economic Exploitation of the Generalgouvernement in Poland by the Third Reich 1939 to 1945' (D.Phil. thesis Oxford: 2006)

SEBALD, W. G., *On the Natural History of Destruction* (English edn, London: 2003)

SEIDLER, FRANZ WILHELM, *Fritz Todt. Baumeister des Dritten Reiches* (Munich: 1986)

SHORE, ZACHARY, *What Hitler Knew* (Oxford: 2003)

SMITH, BRADLEY F., 'Die Überlieferung der Hossbach-Niederschrift im Licht neuer Quellen', *Vierteljahrshefte für Zeitgeschichte*, Jg. 38 (1990)

STEINERT, MARLIS G., *Hitler's Krieg und die Deutschen* (Düsseldorf: 1970)

STOAKES, GEOFFREY, *Hitler and the Quest for World Dominion* (Leamington Spa: 1986)

STÖVER, BERND, *Volksgemeinschaft im Dritten Reich. Die Konsensbereitschaft der Deutschen aus der Sicht sozialistischer Exilberichte* (Düsseldorf: 1993)

———, 'Loyalität statt Widerstand. Die sozialistischen Exilberichte und ihr Bild vom Dritten Reich', *Vierteljahrshefte für Zeitgeschichte*, Jg. 43 (1995)

STREIT, CHRISTIAN, *Keine Kameraden. Die Wehrmacht und die sowjetischen Kriegsgefangenen 1941–1945* (Bonn: 1991)

STROHN, MATTHIAS, 'The German Army and the Conduct of the Defensive Battle 1918–1938' (D.Phil. thesis, Oxford: 2007)

TAYLOR, A. J. P., *The Origins of the Second World War* (revised edn, Harmondsworth: 1964)

TOOZE, ADAM, *The Wages of Destruction. The Making and Breaking of the Nazi Economy* (London: 2006)

TYRELL, ALBRECHT, *Vom 'Trommler' zum 'Führer'* (Munich: 1975)

WATT, DONALD CAMERON, *How War Came. The Immediate Origins of the Second World War, 1938–1939* (London: 1989)

WEGNER, BERND, *The Waffen SS* (English edn, Oxford: 1990)

WEINBERG, GERHARD L., *The Foreign Policy of Hitler's Germany*. vol. i, *Diplomatic Revolution in Europe 1933–1936*; vol. ii, *Starting World War II, 1937–1939* (Chicago, London: 1970, 1980)

———, *Germany, Hitler and World War II* (Cambridge: 1995)

———, *A World at Arms. A Global History of World War II* (Cambridge: 1994)

WRIGHT, J. R. C., *'Above Parties'. The Political Attitudes of the German Protestant Church Leadership 1918–1933* (Oxford: 1974)

WRIGHT, JONATHAN, *Gustav Stresemann. Weimar's Greatest Statesman* (Oxford: 2002)

WRIGHT, JONATHAN, STAFFORD, PAUL, 'Hitler, Britain and the Hoßbach Memorandum', *Militärgeschichtliche Mitteilungen*, Jg. 42 (1987)

YOUNG, ROBERT J., *France and the Origins of the Second World War* (London: 1996)

Index